International Practices to Promote Budget Literacy

WORLD BANK STUDY

International Practices to Promote Budget Literacy

Key Findings and Lessons Learned

Harika Masud, Helene Pfeil, Sanjay Agarwal, and Alfredo Gonzalez Briseno

WORLD BANK GROUP

Contents

Boxes

Figures

Tables

Acknowledgments

This book is a product of the Governance Global Practice of the World Bank. The book's principal author was Harika Masud, with valuable contributions from Helene Pfeil, Alfredo Gonzalez Briseno, and Sanjay Agarwal. Saki Kumagai and Akiko Sowomoto provided helpful inputs at various stages. Sanjay Agarwal coordinated the overall effort; and John Ivor Beazley and Maya Gusarova, task team leaders for the Russian Federation: Budget Literacy Reimbursable Advisory Services, provided strategic guidance.

The team members express their sincere appreciation for the valuable comments and suggestions of peer reviewers Soren Nellemann and Sokbunthoeun So (World Bank) and Professor Peter Davies (University of Birmingham).

This book would not have been possible without contributions from colleagues who provided inputs to identify practices to advance budget literacy and who shared their invaluable knowledge for the documented case studies. In particular, the authors express their gratitude to Dr. Phil Lambert (Australian Curriculum, Assessment, and Reporting Authority); Jill Hazeldine (Department of Education, Northern Territory Government); Don Murray (South Australian Certificate of Education Board of South Australia); Dr. Friederike Sözen (Austrian Economic Chambers); Edward L. V. Borba and Roberta Ribeiro (Brazilian Office of the Comptroller General); Rosana Lordelo de Santana (Ministry of Planning, Budget, and Management, Brazil); Ronaldo Iunes (Public Treasury School of Brazil, Ministry of Treasury); Carole Bilyk (Department of Education and Advanced Learning, Manitoba); Darryl Fillier (Department of Education and Early Childhood Development, Newfoundland and Labrador); Susan Nedelcov-Anderson (Ministry of Education, Saskatchewan); Barbara Hillman (Department of Education and Early Childhood Development, New Brunswick); Paul Anderson (CIVIX); Mario Enrique Alfaro Rodriguez (Ministry of Education, Costa Rica); Kristýna Žůrková (Ministry of Education, Youth and Sports, the Czech Republic); Imbi Henno (Ministry of Education and Research, Estonia); Dr. Margus Tõnissaar (University of Tartu); Valérie Tehio (Agence Française de Développement); Dr. Loerwald (Institut für ökonomische Bildung, Germany); Charlotte Afudego (Integrated Social Development Centre, Ghana); Dr. Grace Chang (Education Bureau, Hong Kong SAR, China); Supriya Sharma (Model Youth Parliament, India); Dr. Ciaran Sugrue (University College Dublin); Aoife Rush (National Council for Curriculum and Assessment, Ireland); Laura Lundy (the Centre for

Children's Rights, Queens University Belfast); Dorit Reppert (Council for the Curriculum, Examinations and Assessment, Northern Ireland); Masao Higuchi and Masahiro Nii (Ministry of Education, Culture, Sports, Science and Technology, Japan); Graham Hopwood (the Institute for Public Policy Research, Namibia); Rebecca Prebble (the New Zealand Treasury); Reynald Trillana (the Philippines Center for Civic Education and Democracy); Olga Kożuchowska (Centre for Education Development, Poland); Ulrika Soneson Cilliers, Pedro Hurtado Vega, and Godwin Kudzotsa (Save the Children); Wai Chin Kam and Say Tin Tan (Ministry of Education, Singapore); Joan Houston (Umalusi, South Africa); Dr. Carina America (Stellenbosch University); Dr. Peter Davies (University of Birmingham); Paul Bower and Ruth Dwight (Citizenship Foundation, United Kingdom); Adrian Lyons (Ofsted, United Kingdom); Maureen Pamplin (HM Revenue & Customs); Dr. Anand Marri, Maureen Shields, and Robert Shand (Teachers College, Columbia University); and Shari Davis and Francesco Tena (Mayors Youth Council, City of Boston).

The team also thanks Joan Houston (Umalusi, South Africa), Edward L. V. Borba (Brazilian Office of the Comptroller General), Maureen Shields and Robert Shand (Teachers College, Columbia University), and Hassan Mahtat (the Aflatoun Secretariat) for their outstanding cooperation and participation in the workshop, "Lessons from International Experiences in Strengthening Budget Literacy: Developing a Budget Literacy Curriculum in Russia," which was organized jointly by the Russian Federation's Ministry of Finance and the World Bank on April 2–3, 2015.

The authors are much obliged to CIVIX, the Canadian Foundation for Economic Education, the Manitoba Department of Education and Advanced Learning, the Council for Economic Education, Teachers College, Columbia University, the Mayors Youth Council, and the city of Boston for their generous hospitality, collaboration, and excellent insights for the study tour on an "Overview of International Practices Regarding Budget Literacy in Canada and the United States" from October 29 to November 8, 2015.

The authors express gratitude to the many practitioners of budget literacy who contributed information, comments, and advice for the preparation of this book. The authors also thank Laura Johnson for excellent editorial support.

Finally, the authors are grateful to the Ministry of Finance of the Russian Federation for actively promoting the budget literacy agenda, and for supporting this research as part of the Russia Budget Literacy Project (P153096).

The findings, interpretations, and conclusions expressed in this book are entirely those of the authors and should not be attributed in any manner to the World Bank, to its affiliated organizations, or to members of its Board of Executive Directors or the countries they represent.

About the Authors

Harika Masud joined the World Bank in 2011. As a social development specialist in the Social, Urban, Rural, and Resilience Global Practice, she specializes in issues related to social inclusion, conflict, fiscal transparency, and literacy and citizen engagement. Before the World Bank, Harika worked with the International Budget Partnership's Open Budget Initiative, where she was responsible for implementing the Open Budget Survey, providing technical assistance to civil society organizations and government counterparts and conducting research on fiscal transparency and its relevance to other open government approaches. She has a master's degree in public policy from the University of Michigan, Ann Arbor, and two bachelor's degrees in economics and social sciences from the Lahore University of Management Sciences in Lahore, Pakistan.

Helene Pfeil is a World Bank consultant who specializes in topics related to civic education, citizen engagement, human rights, and public sector reform. Before joining the World Bank, she worked with Transparency International in Berlin, Germany; an international think tank in London, United Kingdom; and the United Nations Development Program in Bratislava, Slovakia. Fluent in English, French, and German, she holds a master's degree in international relations from the London School of Economics and Political Science and a master's degree in international security from Sciences Po Paris in France.

Sanjay Agarwal is a senior governance specialist with more than 20 years of cumulative cross-sectoral experience spanning 21 countries across five regions. At the World Bank, he has been engaged in the operational mainstreaming of a number of citizen engagement approaches, such as fiscal transparency and grievance redress mechanisms. Before the World Bank, he worked with the Indian Administrative Service, where he was exposed to a variety of social development and public sector management issues such as decentralization and local governance, financial management, citizen engagement, and open government approaches. He has a master's degree in behavioral and social sciences from the Indian Institute of Technology in New Delhi, India; and a master's degree in business administration with a focus on strategy and finance from the University of Maryland, College Park.

Alfredo Gonzalez Briseno is a governance specialist with experience on open government, citizen feedback, digital engagement, anticorruption, and regulatory governance issues. Since 2008, he has worked in international organizations such as the World Bank, the International Finance Corporation, and the Inter-American Development Bank. He currently works in the World Bank's Governance Global Practice, supporting the Good Regulatory Practices program and the Regulatory Policy and Management team. A Mexican national, he holds a master's degree in public policy from Georgetown University in Washington, DC, and a bachelor's degree in industrial engineering from Panamericana University in Mexico City, Mexico.

Abbreviations

DGI	General Tax Directorate, Uruguay
EU	European Union
GCSE	General Certificate of Secondary Education
HMRC	Her Majesty's Revenue and Customs
MY	Model Youth
OCR	Oxford, Cambridge and RSA
OECD	Organization for Economic Co-operation and Development
PCCED	Philippines Center for Civic Education and Democracy
PNEF	Programa Nacional de Educação Fiscal (Brazil's national program for fiscal education)
PSHE	Personal, Social, and Humanities Education
PSHEE	Personal, Social, Health, and Economic Education
SAR	Special Administrative Region
U.K.	United Kingdom
UN	United Nations
UNICEF	United Nations Children's Fund

Overview

Budget literacy, defined as *the ability to read, decipher, and understand public budgets to enable and enhance meaningful citizen participation in the budget process*, involves a technical understanding of public budgets and the ability for youth to engage in the budget process. Budget literacy education can potentially close the budget transparency feedback loop by fostering the evolution of youth into civic-minded adults able to analyze the fiscal policy objectives and measures of their governments, and who have the confidence and sense of social responsibility to participate in the oversight of public resources.

This study presents findings from a review of illustrative examples of initiatives promoting budget literacy among youth in selected countries. It aims to raise the profile of budget literacy in discussions about curricula and fill the existing literature gap by documenting a variety of practices that promote budget literacy in a collection of 35 case studies from 34 countries. It systematically analyzes national context, curricular content, learning outcomes, pedagogical approaches, and materials used for school-based initiatives to promote budget literacy. It also elaborates on pedagogical approaches, results and educative implications of beyond-school budget literacy initiatives that are intended to strengthen oversight of public funds to strengthen public service delivery.

This review confirms that a variety of academic subjects provide useful entry points for exploring public budgets, including *economics, social sciences, mathematics, business*, and *life skills*. Budget literacy content is usually concentrated in a dedicated module or class, but elements can also be found elsewhere in the same or other curricula, and the two approaches combined offer students a somewhat complete picture of public budgets.

The diversity of entry points for introducing elements of budget literacy into curricula is due to the multifaceted nature of public budgets. Curricula for different subjects focus on different aspects, such as civic values around budget issues; an understanding of budgets and their implications from an economic standpoint; appreciation of the legal and political context for budget policy-making; and the need for students to develop the skills needed for daily life, including an understanding of various types of taxes and the ability to analyze government data.

A multitiered strategy is frequently adopted to impart budget-literacy concepts. The building blocks to a solid understanding of public finances, including a basic knowledge of democratic processes and the management of personal finances, tend to be scattered across lower educational levels, contributing to a progressive deepening of students' knowledge of this topic over successively higher grades.

Budget-literacy education learning outcomes include: Enhanced knowledge of public budgets, such as government revenues and expenditures, fiscal policy, practical skills for daily living, economic competence, and civic awareness; improved competency in written, verbal, analytical, and numerical skills, among others; and development of values and attitudes, such as thinking proactively about economic phenomena and participating as informed persons in the discussion of economic issues and decision making.

Learning outcomes and acquired knowledge vary in depth and breadth depending on the subjects through which public budget issues are introduced into curricula. Assessment methods also vary widely, including: (1) multiple choice questions geared toward the verification of factual knowledge; (2) data interpretation questions focused on the ability of students to interpret budget data from graphs, charts, and tables; and (3) medium-length open-ended questions meant to evaluate the ability of students to reflect on policy questions and persuasively argue positions.

Pedagogical approaches to teaching budget literacy tend to combine direct instruction with enquiry-based learning, values clarification exercises, and participatory learning. Active participation among students strongly contributes to their assimilation of newly acquired knowledge of budgets. This is demonstrated by the frequent use of simulations, role-play, scenario analysis, debates, art and cartoon analysis, discussions, and interactions with relevant officials as well as essays and reports. Moreover, the space in which primary- and secondary-school students can get acquainted with public budgets is not confined to the classroom. Ministries of finance, comptroller general's offices, tax authorities, broadcasting associations, academics, educators, think tanks, and nongovernmental organizations have developed numerous rich and innovative pedagogical materials and activities to familiarize young people with budget-literacy issues, including field trips, contests, quizzes, public events, the pedagogical use of comic characters, television shows, videos, and games—both online and in print.

Budget literacy education can be incorporated into existing curricula or introduced as a standalone approach that emphasizes civic competence and technical knowledge while teaching youth about public budgets. Using an interesting range of content to initiate stimulating discussions and posing real-life challenges to students can help overcome the dry nature of the subject.

Diverse approaches and materials should be used to teach budget literacy, drawing on instruction methods that make learning about public budgets relevant and compelling. Examples include participatory budgeting, competitions, interactive games, debates, and classroom discussions. Closing the feedback loop by responding to student suggestions can also serve as an important incentive for youth to learn about public budgets. Lastly, budget-literacy teaching materials should account for and build on the existing knowledge base of secondary-school teachers of subjects other than *economics*, because they may not be familiar with budget literacy in depth.

Building capacity for small- or large-scale efforts to promote budget-literacy education requires collaboration with relevant stakeholders, such as teachers, parents, school administrators, policy makers, and civil society organizations. It is also imperative to explore various means of providing ongoing support to educators, including the development of online and printed learning materials such as lesson plans, activity books, and interactive games; the implementation of training programs for teachers; and the establishment of an online or in-person network of support and guidance on budget-literacy instruction for teachers by their peers.

Some aspects of curriculum-driven budget literacy education overlap with the knowledge imparted through beyond-school budget literacy approaches. For instance, youngsters involved in Ghana's Youth Budget Advocacy Group have been introduced to family budgets, routine budget calculations, and the budget cycle at the local and national levels—all of which are themes that have been incorporated in several curricula. However, in addition to the value of their educative implications, beyond-school child and youth-led budget processes have resulted in a range of behavioral, process and policy outcomes such as better management of public resources and improved service delivery, that bode well for the application of budget literacy education and closing of the budget transparency feedback loop over progressive budget cycles.

CHAPTER 1

Background

A budget is a vital document that lays out a government's economic priorities in terms of policies and programs. Throughout the budget cycle—formulation, approval, execution, and oversight—the government allocates and uses public funds; budgets present these allocations and expenditures. A budget allows citizens to gain an appreciation of the competing fiscal priorities and constraints faced by their government, and the budget cycle gives them an opportunity to provide input on public budget priorities, implementation, and outcomes.

The *budget transparency feedback loop* (figure 1.1) shows the assumptions underlying how governments engage citizens around budgets as well as entry points for citizens to participate in the budget cycle. This feedback loop is based on the presumption that when supply-side actors in the budget process—governments—simplify and disseminate budget information for demand-side actors—citizens—this information will then be used by citizens to provide feedback on the budget. If this is to work effectively, elected representatives and citizens must understand, analyze, and discuss the information and then provide constructive feedback. Ultimately, the government should respond to and/or incorporate citizen feedback in future budget cycles, ensuring the sustainability of the feedback loop.

Despite increasing efforts by governments to disclose, simplify, and disseminate budget information, the budget transparency feedback loop tends to unravel on the demand side, particularly when citizens are not budget-literate and when they lack the capacity to analyze and discuss budgets, which is necessary for them to engage in meaningful dialogues with their governments. Citizens are often insufficiently informed about public budgets to constructively participate in budget processes. One way to empower citizens, build a foundation for good citizenship, and remedy the problem of budget illiteracy is to provide budget-literacy education in schools to youth, helping them evolve into civic-minded adults with the essential knowledge needed for analyzing their government's fiscal policy objectives and measures and the confidence and sense of social responsibility to participate in the oversight of public resources. These youth will soon be adult members of society, and as successive cadres of

Figure 1.1 Budget Transparency Feedback Loop

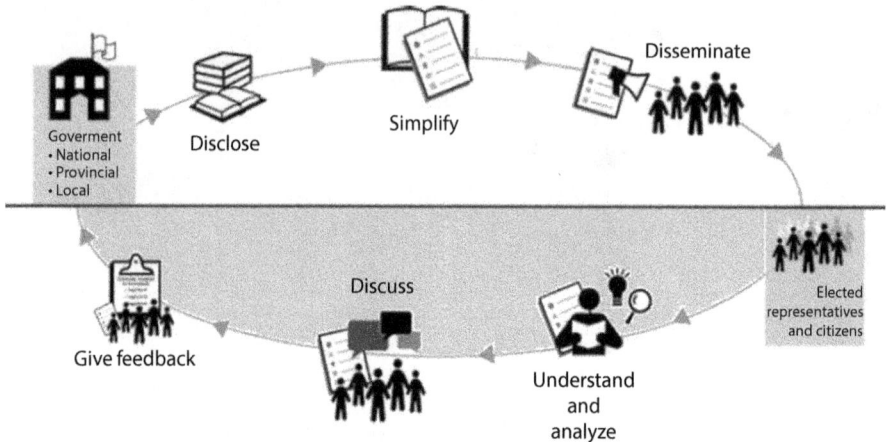

Source: Alton and Agarwal 2013.

budget-literate youth follow them, over the long term, they will be able to close the demand-side gap and thereby improve the quality of governance.

In this study, *budget literacy* is defined as "the ability to read, decipher, and understand public budgets to enable and enhance meaningful citizen participation in the budget process." Budget literacy has two main components: (1) a technical understanding of public budgets, including familiarity with government spending, tax rates, and public debt; and (2) the ability to engage in the budget process, including having practical knowledge of daily issues such as tax filings and access to social benefits as well as an elementary understanding of the economic, social, and political implications of budget policies, the stakeholders involved, and when and how to provide input during the annual budget cycle. See box 1.1 on the importance and relevance of budget literacy.

Rationale and Objectives

The World Bank team's preliminary scrutiny of practices aimed at promoting budget literacy revealed that, unlike financial literacy and citizenship education, concerted approaches to mainstream budget-literacy education at the primary, secondary, and tertiary levels of schooling are limited. Despite the dearth of literature on this topic, there has been no systematic attempt to compile standalone practices for advancing budget literacy that have been adopted by countries. This review seeks to fill this gap by taking stock of illustrative initiatives promoting budget literacy in selected countries.

The presented findings and lessons seek to inform the efforts of practitioners, including policy makers, educational specialists, curriculum experts, fiscal transparency advocates, and civil society organizations interested in improving education or civic engagement and accountability in budget processes.[1] World Bank

Box 1.1 The Importance and Relevance of Budget Literacy

Literature on budget literacy, as defined for this study, is limited, but there is some evidence that evidence confirms its implications for civic competence and improved governance. Davies (2006:20) observes that

"an economically educated citizenry is necessary to reduce the likelihood of the government failing to adhere to the preferences of its electorate… They are also more likely to appreciate longer run implications of economic policy and this may reduce scope for governments to secure short-term support at the expense of long-term disadvantages for citizens."

Miller and VanFossen (2008) argue that an understanding of economic concepts can promote active citizenship and provide an analytical framework that citizens in a democratic society can adopt, and Schug and Wood (2011) assert that low awareness levels around economic issues reduce civic engagement. A national Gallup telephone survey of 1,005 adults (Walstad 1997) found that the most critical factors affecting public opinion on a wide range of economic issues were a general knowledge of economics and an understanding of particular economic issues.

Regarding budget-literacy outcomes among youth, Etizoni (1967) finds that engaging with the federal budget and federal debt enables students to understand the contextual factors that affect economic decisions. Students gain insight into how the federal government's responsibilities and approaches change by examining federal budgets, federal debts, and budget deficits (Mosher 1980). Forsyth's (2006) observation that students without knowledge of budgets and other issues will be unprepared to express views and exert meaningful influence on public policy directions supports these arguments.

Budget literacy is also important for realizing the benefits associated with increased government transparency and accountability. Bellver and Kaufmann (2005) note that transparency is associated with lower levels of corruption, better socioeconomic and human development indicators, and increased economic competitiveness. The World Bank (2011) confirms that budget transparency and monitoring initiatives led by governments and civil society have resulted in improved processes and policy outcomes. Moreover, Melo and Baiocchi's (2006) finding that participatory budgeting is strongly associated with a reduction in extreme poverty, and an increase in access to basic services is supported by Gonçalves (2014) and Touchton and Wampler (2014). However, open and effective governance cannot be realized while a disconnect remains between an extreme focus on the supply-side aspects of government budget information—accessibility, timeliness, and comprehensiveness—and the capacity of citizens to meaningfully analyze their government's budget data and contribute to the budget process. There are ongoing efforts to build the capacity of journalists, civil society, academics, and other stakeholders, but only recently have efforts been made to integrate budget literacy into youth education.

The literature demonstrates a declining emphasis on knowledge of public budgets, compared with the importance of dexterity when managing personal finances and familiarity with the functions of financial institutions. For instance, Schug, Dieterle, and Clark's (2009) analysis of survey responses regarding high school social studies curricula in the United States, found that, when ranked by value of content for economics courses, topics such as *macroeconomics* and critical

box continues next page

thinking about free market institutions lagged far behind *personal finance and consumer educa-tion* (Clark, Schug and Harrison 2009). Similarly, in the United States study based on teacher inter-views and classroom observations, Marri and others (2011) find that the majority of teachers do not use in-depth pedagogy when teaching about the federal budget; instead they devote a disproportionate amount of the time allotted to economic education on *personal finance.*

---

task teams seeking to introduce elements of budget literacy into their programs and projects would also benefit from this review.

Scope

This book, which is meant to be illustrative rather than comprehensive, presents 35 case studies from 34 countries on the basis of a stock-taking exercise of prac-tices promoting budget literacy. A broad range of curricular content, pedagogical approaches, and learning outcomes for budget literacy are documented. Twenty-seven of the case studies focus on school-based initiatives, and eight on beyond-school initiatives.

School-based budget-literacy efforts are aligned with the objectives and design of existing school curricula. Activities are: (1) classroom-based—that is, they are based on existing curricula and mandated and overseen by a ministry of education or another educational authority; or (2) out-of-classroom—that is, they comple-ment the curricula and are led by other entities, such as national tax agencies, aca-demic institutions, or civil society organizations, in collaboration with educational authorities. Because they are based on school curricula, illustrative school-based approaches have been documented for the majority of countries (27).[2] If desk-based research did not uncover any out-of-classroom activities to advance budget literacy in a country, then that section has been omitted in the relevant case study.

Eight case studies of beyond-school budget-literacy initiatives are presented, including examples of youth-led initiatives promoting engagement in the budget process from Ecuador, Ghana, Northern Ireland, Kenya, Nicaragua, South Africa, República Bolivariana de Venezuela, and Zimbabwe. These initiatives are inde-pendent of school learning and are primarily intended to strengthen the oversight of public funds to improve public-service delivery. They have been included in this stock-take because their pedagogical approaches may be relevant to school-based methods for teaching budget literacy.

Method

This stock-take is primarily based on desk and online research as well as inter-views with select practitioners. The key steps taken were: (1) a review of educa-tional policies, standards, and curricula; (2) outreach and compilation of inputs; (3) documentation; and (4) analysis.

1. **Review of educational policies, standards, and curricula.** Countries that are members of the Organization for Economic Co-operation and Development (OECD) were given priority in the research, but non-OECD countries implementing relevant practices to foster budget literacy are also included, allowing us to review a broad variety of topics and pedagogical approaches and materials. The team used online research to examine and compile the educational polices, strategies, and standards of curricula for subjects taught at the primary- and secondary-school levels in 34 countries. Adopting a subject-neutral approach, this process was intended to compile modules or sections of various curricula that included public budget-literacy content, learning outcomes, teaching methods, materials, and—where possible—assessment methods. Illustrative examples of both in- and out-of-classroom school-based initiatives was documented and compiled using available information.

2. **Outreach and compilation of inputs.** The team conducted online research to identify and then reach out to more than 200 individuals and 150 local and international organizations, including ministries of education; curricula and standard-setting institutions; curricula evaluation entities; civil society organizations, networks, and think tanks specializing in educational policies and practices or with expertise in public financial management; academic institutions; and development partners. On the basis of the responses received, additional inputs regarding practices for promoting budget literacy were solicited by e-mail and telephone.

3. **Documentation.** A standard template was created to compile and document 35 cases. Data was collected through online research and inputs from outreach efforts. Because information on the depth and range of curricula and initiatives that support budget literacy varies across countries, some case studies are more detailed than others.

4. **Analysis.** The synthesis of key findings was based on a qualitative review of: (1) standard elements of curriculum learning frameworks—learning outcomes, content, pedagogical approaches, teaching materials, and assessment methods; and (2) details available for out-of-classroom initiatives and beyond school initiatives. Information presented in chapter 3 ("Lessons Learned") relies heavily on insights and experiences from numerous practitioners, some of which were shared or gathered during the "Lessons from International Experiences in Strengthening Budget Literacy: Developing a Budget Literacy Curriculum in Russia" workshop, jointly organized by Russia's Ministry of Finance and the World Bank on April 2–3, 2015.

This report is structured as follows: chapter 1 (this chapter) outlines the rationale and objectives of the study and explains the scope and methodology of the stock-taking exercise. Chapter 2 details key findings regarding school-based initiatives promoting budget literacy, including approaches for integrating budget-literacy education in school curricula, purposes and learning outcomes of imparting knowledge of budget literacy to youth, pedagogical strategies for instruction fostering budget literacy, and assessment approaches for classroom-based and out-of-classroom initiatives promoting budget literacy. It also provides an overview of findings from beyond-school initiatives that may have educative implications for promoting budget literacy among young people. Finally, chapter 3 presents lessons that may be useful with regard to the development, improvement, or scaling up of initiatives promoting budget literacy.

Notes

1. The review was conducted as part of a technical support program to the Russian Federation's Ministry of Finance by the World Bank to assist in the design and piloting of a training program on budget literacy to support and inform the development and testing of a secondary-school budget-literacy curriculum for the country.
2. The countries include: Australia, Austria, Brazil, Canada, Chile, Costa Rica, the Czech Republic, the Dominican Republic, Estonia, France, Germany, Guatemala, Hong Kong SAR China, India, Ireland, Japan, Luxembourg, Namibia, New Zealand, Peru, the Philippines, Poland, Singapore, South Africa, the United Kingdom, the United States, and Uruguay.

References

Alton, Martin Luis, and Sanjay Agarwal. 2013. "Increasing Accountability through Budget Transparency at the Subnational Level in Cameroon." Budget Transparency Initiative, World Bank, Washington, DC.

Bellver, Ana, and Daniel Kaufmann. 2005. "Transparenting Transparency: Initial Empirics and Policy Implications." Policy Research Working Paper, World Bank, Washington, DC. http://siteresources.worldbank.org/intwbigovantcor/resources/transparenting _transparency171005.pdf.

Clark, J. R., M. C. Schug, and A. S. Harrison. 2009. "Recent Trends and New Evidence in Economics and Finance Education." *Journal of Economics and Finance Education* 8 (2).

Davies, Peter. 2006. "Educating Citizens for Changing Economies." *Journal of Curriculum Studies* 38 (1): 15–30.

Etizoni, Amitai. 1967. "Mixed-Scanning: A Third Approach to Decision Making." *Public Administration Review* 27 (5): 385–92.

Forsyth, Anita. 2006. "Economic Literacy—An Essential Dimension in the Social Education Curriculum for the Twenty-First Century." *The Social Educator* 24 (2): 29–33.

Gonçalves, Sónia. 2014. "The Effects of Participatory Budgeting on Municipal Expenditures and Infant Mortality in Brazil." *World Development* 53: 94–110.

Marri, Anand R., Meesuk Ahn, Margaret Smith Crocco, Maureen Grolnick, William Gaudelli, and Erica N. Walker. 2011. "Teaching the Federal Budget, National Debt, and Budget Deficit: Findings from High School Teachers." *Social Studies* 102 (5): 204–10.

Melo, Marcus Andre, and Gianpaolo Baiocchi. 2006. "Deliberative Democracy and Local Governance: Towards a New Agenda." *International Journal of Urban and Regional Research* 30 (3): 587–600.

Miller, Steven L., and Phillip J. VanFossen. 2008. "Recent Research on the Teaching and Learning of Pre-Collegiate Economics Education." In *Handbook of Research in Social Studies Education*, edited by L. Levstik and C. Tyson, 284–306. New York: Routledge.

Mosher, Frederick C. 1980. "The Changing Responsibilities and Tactics of the Federal Government." *Public Administration Review* 40 (6): 541–48.

Schug, Mark C., David Dieterle, and J. R. Clark. 2009. "Are High School Economics Teachers the Same as Other Social Studies Teachers? The Results of a National Survey." *Social Education* 73 (2): 71–75.

Schug, Mark C., and William C. Wood, eds. 2011. *Teaching Economics in Troubled Times: Theory and Practice for Secondary Social Studies.* New York: Routledge.

Touchton, Michael, and Brian Wampler. 2014. "Improving Social Well-Being through New Democratic Institutions." *Comparative Political Studies* 47 (10): 1442–69.

Walstad, William B. 1997. "The Effect of Economic Knowledge on Public Opinion of Economic Issues." *Journal of Economic Education* 28 (3): 195–205.

World Bank. 2011. "Global Stock-Take of Social Accountability Initiatives for Budget Transparency and Monitoring: Key Challenges and Lessons Learned." World Bank, Washington, DC. http://www.worldbank.org/en/topic/socialdevelopment/publication/budget-transparency-initiative.

## CHAPTER 2

Main Findings

School-Based Initiatives

Approaches to Integrating Budget Literacy in School Curricula

This review across several countries finds a range of approaches to incorporating budget-literacy education into curricular frameworks. Content can be integrated into existing curricula or introduced as standalone courses on public budgets. Aspects of budget literacy can be introduced through national or subnational curricula, which may be a part of school instruction for all, most, or a small number of students. Budget literacy can be introduced using a gradual, tiered approach that begins in primary school or by introducing public budgets for the first time in secondary school. Students can either be exposed to the fundamentals of public budgets, or they can explore an in-depth study of fiscal policy making. Such approaches can be discrete or one or more of them can overlap.

Cross-Curricular versus Standalone Approach

Most countries in this study have adopted a cross-curricular approach, which involves instruction about budgets in two or more existing subjects, as opposed to a standalone approach, which adopts curricula specifically designed to impart knowledge on public budgets. This finding is not surprising because secondary-school curricula are generally crowded. A cross-curricular approach may also encourage effective student learning about budgets across a range of subjects. Subjects that incorporate budget literacy include the following:

- Economics, with a focus on core economic principles or a combination of economics and other disciplines such as law, management science, business, or politics (India, Austria, France, and the United States)
- Business studies (Ireland and Namibia)
- Mathematical literacy and essential mathematics (South Africa and Canada)
- Social sciences and social studies (Estonia, Japan, New Zealand, and Singapore)
- Civics and citizenship (Canada, the United Kingdom [England only], Poland, and the United States)
- Politics and governance (the Philippines)

- Subjects oriented toward building practical life skills and knowledge of contemporary issues, such as man and society (the Czech Republic), life and society (Hong Kong SAR, China), and life skills (Namibia), which incorporate
lessons that reinforce budget literacy.

National versus Subnational Approach

For countries included in this study, budget literacy has been introduced in
national and subnational curricula. At the national level, it has been integrated
into the curriculum, with learning content and standards mandated like other
courses. In Hong Kong SAR, China, for example, budget-literacy education is
provided through the life and society curriculum, which is approved by the education bureau. At the subnational level, the approach and depth of content for
budget-literacy education varies. In Canada, for example, the emphasis and content of budget-literacy education is not uniform because provinces have jurisdiction over educational curricula and practices. In British Columbia, Manitoba,
New Brunswick, Newfoundland and Labrador, Prince Edward Island, and
Saskatchewan, public budgets are usually featured in the social studies curricula.
By contrast, there is little budget-literacy information in curricula for Alberta,
Northwest Territories, Nova Scotia, Nunavut, Ontario, Québec, and Yukon.

Comprehensive versus Selective Coverage of Students

The number of students receiving budget-literacy education is determined by
whether the subjects examining related concepts are compulsory or elective and,
if they are elective, the proportion of students choosing to study them. For
example, in Poland, budget-literacy instruction is incorporated into two compulsory subjects during secondary school, civics and the basics of entrepreneurship,
which ensures that all senior secondary-school students are exposed to its basic
elements. In Luxembourg, the year eight economics module equips students
with an elementary understanding of their government's budget and the state's
essential functions at a time when the students are deciding what their specialty
will be for the next three years of secondary school. Approximately 40 percent
of students specialize in economics and mathematical sciences or human and
social sciences, which includes a more in-depth exploration of public budgets in
the economics curriculum for year eleven. Ireland's youth are exposed to budget
literacy through the study of optional subjects. In 2013, 56.5 percent of secondary-level students chose to study business studies at the lower-secondary level,
and 9 percent chose to study economics at the senior secondary-school level. It
is therefore likely that the number of students familiar with public budgets in
any depth is limited.

Basic or In-Depth

There are several examples in this study of modules or subjects that provide a
basic introduction to budget literacy. Namibia's mathematics curriculum (years
11–12) teaches students to use data to solve tax- and budget-related problems.
Singapore's upper-secondary social studies syllabus familiarizes students with the

national budget and its relevance to their lives, and introduces concepts to help them better understand the considerations which guide policy making, such as trade-offs and opportunity costs.

Some economics syllabi explored in this study, however, examine public budgets in some depth. India's economics curriculum for grades 11–12 presents the complexity of budget concepts to students, who are then expected to understand and apply them. A unit on the government budget and economy includes graphic representations of the effect of tax policies on aggregate expenditures as well as equations explaining the concept of a tax multiplier. The unit also introduces complex concepts such as built-in and automatic stabilizers and Ricardian equivalence. Students learn how to critically analyze suggested fiscal policies, evaluate the effects of such measures, and understand the rationale for initiatives. The year ten economics and law curriculum in Munich, Germany, illustrates the extent to which youth are expected to absorb and debate social issues pertaining to the public budget. One of its modules on the central aspects of the economic and legal order in the country introduces students to the idea of income tax and its influence on the available income of private households. The question of tax fairness is examined and discussed. Another module on taxes and social security in the social market economy introduces students to the structure of federal and state budgets and social security policy. It encourages them to debate about issues such as tax redistribution and social justice.

Tiered versus Direct Approach

This stock-take finds more frequent and detailed instruction on budget-literacy topics during secondary school, particularly at the higher grades, demonstrating a tiered approach to teaching budget-literacy concepts. Most curricula in the sample broach the broader topics of citizenship and governance, and familiarize students with basic financial literacy concepts before gradually acquainting them with budget-literacy elements during upper-primary and lower-secondary school. Examples include Australia; Canada; the Czech Republic; Hong Kong SAR, China; and the Philippines. Curricula in other countries such as Japan, Peru, and the United States initiate exposure to public budgets earlier—at the lower-primary levels (see box 2.1).

Box 2.1 Teaching Budget Literacy: Examples of a Tiered Approach

Australia

Classes in civics and mathematics at the primary-school level pave the way for a thorough understanding of public budgets during secondary school. In fourth grade (ages 9–10), under the humanities and social sciences category, the civics and citizenship subject aims to improve children's knowledge and understanding of government and democracy. It reviews the purpose of government and familiar services provided at the local level, such as libraries, health, environment and waste services, parks, pools, sports, arts, and pet management; and it

box continues next page

Box 2.1 Teaching Budget Literacy: Examples of a Tiered Approach *(continued)*

describes how local government services affect the lives of students. Budgeting is covered in mathematics courses from fifth grade (ages 10–11) through tenth grade in the money and financial mathematics module, taught with a particular focus on individual financial literacy. In sixth grade (ages 10–11), the same civics and citizenship subject introduces the roles and responsibilities of the three levels of government under Australia's federal system, including shared roles and responsibilities. In secondary school (grades 7–10), economics and business courses successively introduce why and how individuals and businesses plan to achieve short-term and long-term personal, organizational, and financial objectives; the ways that markets operate in Australia; why they may be influenced by government; and the ways that the government manages the economy to improve its performance and the country's living standards. Most of the budget-literacy content is featured in secondary-school economics for the eleventh and twelfth grades. For example, the economics curriculum for New South Wales discusses the budget process, types of budgets (surplus, balanced, and deficit), and revenues and expenditures in the context of introducing the economic functions of the Australian government. The curriculum notes the influence of various stakeholders on government policies, such as political parties, businesses, labor unions, welfare agencies, and the media (Board of Studies NSW 2009).

Japan

Japan's primary school curriculum takes a gradual approach to teaching budget literacy. Young students in the third and fourth grades (ages 8–10) and fifth and sixth grades (ages 10–12) become familiar with budget literacy concepts through the elementary tax education. The third and fourth grade social studies curriculum emphasizes cooperation among agencies and local people to conduct various activities, awareness of oneself as a member of the local community, and the importance of observing rules. The fifth and sixth grade curriculum explains how taxes cover the necessary costs involved in a functioning political system, the relationship between daily life and taxes, and the shared obligation to pay taxes as stipulated in the constitution. Budget literacy is explored in more depth as part of the social studies curriculum in junior high school (grades 7–9) and the syllabi for civics and commerce in senior high school (grades 10–12). For instance, the contemporary society area of study in the civics curriculum describes the government's vital role in the provision of public services in a market economy and the need for taxes, citizens' obligation to pay taxes, and the importance of taxpayers assuming an active interest in how their taxes are spent.

Objectives of Introducing Budget Literacy Education

Policymakers, educators, and civil society organizations are making efforts to increase awareness and strengthen knowledge of public budgets among youth through school-based and beyond-school initiatives that promote budget literacy in pursuit of the following broad objectives:

• **Civic and legal consciousness.** Cultivating and strengthening civic and legal consciousness is a key motivation for introducing budget-literacy education. Familiarity with public budgets is an essential part of Canada's social studies curriculum, which is geared toward understanding rights and responsibilities of citizenship and Canada's democratic system of government, including how decisions are made at the individual, group, local, provincial, and national levels; how to get involved in the political process; and how to express opinions effectively. Budget literacy also lends itself to the Czech Republic's curriculum on man and society, which orients students to various forms of civic engagement and reinforces their sense of personal and social responsibility.

- **Awareness of tax obligations.** Another driver for strengthening familiarity with public budgets is the desire to foster a tax-conscious culture and compliance with tax obligations. Tax authorities, such as those in Japan and Peru, are often particularly keen on mainstreaming tax education at all grade levels. In Japan, the importance of tax education was endorsed by the cabinet in their "Outline of 2011 Tax Reform,"[1] and the National Tax Education Promotion Council[2] was established to develop basic policies about tax education and collaborate with educators and local tax education promotion councils[3] across the country. A key objective of Uruguay's tax education program and Guatemala's permanent program of tax culture is to foster among children and youth an appreciation for the importance of taxes in terms of economic development and social progress.

- **Comprehension of economic and social roles.** To develop an appreciation of what is expected of them in terms of contributing to a democratic society, it is helpful for young people to have some knowledge regarding public budgets. The economics standards in the United States, including those related to budget-literacy, are aimed at preparing students to be full and effective participants in a complex global economy. The life and society curriculum in Hong Kong SAR, China, encourages students to reflect on questions such as the influence of public opinion on public spending, the extent of expenditures on welfare benefits, and possible ways for the government to finance housing and medical expenditures for the elderly.

- **Knowledge of policy formulation.** A familiarity with fiscal and monetary tools for policy making enables students to acquire a more solid grasp of policy formulation. The contents of Austria's economics and geography curriculum are intended to teach students about fundamental economic interdependencies at the company, national, and global levels, and to comprehend macroeconomic mechanisms, structures, and challenges. Hong Kong SAR, China and India are similar in this regard, emphasizing the student's ability to analyze the positions of various stakeholders toward public finance so they can develop into rational and responsible citizens.

- **Participation in fiscal policy processes.** Efforts by the governments of Brazil and Costa Rica to mainstream fiscal education in school curricula reflect their intent to build the capacity of their citizens to effectively participate in the execution and oversight of public budgets. Brazil's national program of fiscal education aims to foster a positive relationship between citizens and the state and to provide incentives for citizen engagement in the execution of public resources, and Costa Rica's Tax Education Strategy is designed to encourage citizens' appreciation of a responsible fiscal culture. In the Philippines, parts of the secondary-school curricula are intensely focused on building civic consciousness and budget literacy, which establishes the groundwork for an increasing reliance on participatory planning and budgeting processes to formulate the national budget.

- **Developing economic competence.** Budget literacy education endows students with the ability to make informed economic decisions and engage in policy processes. In Australia, budget-literacy concepts are intended to inform effective economic thinking, which contributes to socially responsible and competent decision making in a changing economy. In India and France, familiarity with public economics enables students to understand state actions with regard to the economy.

- **Building real-life skills.** Encouraging learning about public budgets is also based on the premise that students must develop skills for managing the practicalities of life beyond school. In South Africa, such knowledge is expected to enable learners to analyze and solve problems as well as to equip them with real-life skills for personal and community development. In Estonia, familiarity with public budgets is part of the general entrepreneurship competence formed over the course of the learning process. Unlike the goals of fiscal education programs and beyond-school initiatives specifically geared toward imparting knowledge of public budgets and promoting oversight of public resources by youth, objectives regarding budget literacy for the majority of classroom-based initiatives translate into a subset of the broader learning outcomes for the respective curricula. For example, the specifications for Ireland's business studies syllabus focuses on improving students' understanding of the business environment and developing students' ability to identify and understand basic economic concepts as they relate to personal finance, enterprise and the Irish economy through its three inter-connected strands on personal finance, enterprise and our economy.

Learning Outcomes of Budget Literacy Education
The team's review of learning outcomes for several curricula reveals that as part of the broader goals for each subject, their budget literacy aspects are conducive toward developing specific types of knowledge, competencies, values, and attitudes that these subjects intend to foster among students (see table 2.1).

Some class assignments for Austria's seventh-grade economics and geography curriculum are clearly intended to augment students' written expression and gauge their ability to discuss and analyze government economic and sociopolitical objectives and measures. Examples include the following: "Describe the fundamental tasks of fiscal policy" and "Assess whether a budget is societal policy

Table 2.1 Dimensions and Learning Outcomes of Budget Literacy Education

Dimension	Learning outcomes
Knowledge	Role of government

- Examine the important role of government with regard to its spending and taxing powers, which, by targeting economic objectives, can affect the allocation of resources and the level of economic activity (Tasmania and Australia).
- Learn how the government redistributes income (Namibia).

System of government revenues and expenditures

- Describe major revenue categories of municipal, provincial, and federal budgets (United Kingdom).
- Define progressive, proportional, and regressive taxation, and determine whether different types of taxes (including income and sales) are progressive, proportional, or regressive (United Kingdom).
- Describe major expenditure categories for local, provincial, and federal budgets (United Kingdom).
- Interpret federal budget data (New South Wales).
- Predict the effect of a budget deficit or surplus on economic activity (New South Wales).
- Assess government budgetary decisions and their effect on government debt (United Kingdom).

Fiscal policy

- Explain the concept of *fiscal policy* (Germany).
- Discuss state budget drafting, tax policy, and income redistribution (Estonia).
- Analyze how the government uses taxing and spending decisions to promote price stability, full employment, and economic growth (Canada).
- Propose solutions for addressing issues in a community or region through fiscal policy (Canada).

Policy making

- Explain the relationship between budgetary and monetary policy, and analyze how the policies may be used to achieve key economic goals and improve living standards (Australia).
- Discuss how monetary and fiscal policies can be used to stabilize economic activity (New South Wales).
- Make informed predictions about the operation of economic policies using economic models and past and current key economic data (Australia).
- Explain the government's fiscal and monetary policies, describe the different types of taxes, discuss how the government uses taxes to influence business activities, and examine the role of the budget (Namibia).
- Discuss and analyze the government's economic and sociopolitical objectives and measures (Austria).
- Formulate conflicting objectives and various positions regarding economic policy (Austria).

Economic competence

- Appreciate the trade-offs faced by the government in prioritizing the country's needs with scarce resources (Singapore).
- Know and understand fundamental economic concepts and theories (India).
- Apply economic concepts and theories to explain real-world situations (Hong Kong SAR, China).
- Understand the government's constraints as well as the short- and long-term economic and social impact of public finance (Hong Kong SAR, China).

Practical skills

- Explain how to file a tax return, usually to pay income taxes, and how to carry out basic tax calculations (Czech Republic).
- Calculate the cost of social and health insurance (Czech Republic).
- Describe the method for calculating a household's subsistence minimum and applying for social benefits for which they are eligible (Estonia).

table continues next page

International Practices to Promote Budget Literacy • http://dx.doi.org/10.1596/978-1-4648-1071-8

Table 2.1 Dimensions and Learning Outcomes of Budget Literacy Education *(continued)*

Dimension	Learning outcomes
	Civic awareness
	• Understand the social function of taxes, stimulating the voluntary compliance of fiscal obligations, and creating the necessary conditions to develop a critical sense of the use of public resources (Brazil).
	• Participate in issues regarding the use of public resources and their control and oversight with the goal of improving social and economic development (Brazil).
	• Acquire a sense of responsibility for and consciousness of the social value of taxes and their important role in social development (Costa Rica).
Competencies	• *Literacy.* Learn to examine and interpret budget data, to effectively use the language and terminology of public budgets when applying concepts to contemporary issues and events, and to communicate conclusions to a range of audiences through a range of multimodal approaches (Australia).
	• *Numeracy.* Apply numeracy knowledge and skills to display, interpret, and analyze fiscal data; draw conclusions; make predictions; and forecast outcomes. Appreciate the ways numeracy knowledge and skills are used in society and apply them to hypothetical and real-life experiences (South Africa).
	• *Information and communications technology.* Develop information and communication technology capabilities in terms of accessing and using digital technologies as investigative and creative tools. Locate, evaluate, research, plan, share, and display budget data and information (Namibia).
	• *Critical thinking.* Develop critical and creative thinking to identify, explore, and determine questions clarifying budget issues and events. Apply reasoning, interpretation, and analytical skills to data and other information (Dominican Republic).
	• *Intercultural understanding.* Develop an understanding and appreciation of the different ways countries respond to issues and events related to budget and fiscal-policy (Canada)
	• *Oral and written expression.* Augment oral and written expression skills by analyzing fiscal sources and data, interpreting this information to make arguments, and clearly communicating ideas and findings (Luxembourg).
Values and attitudes	• Gain the confidence and conviction to participate in decision making and play active roles as effective citizens in public life (United Kingdom).
	• Think proactively about economic phenomena (Luxembourg).
	• Participate as informed persons in the discussion of economic issues and decision making (Hong Kong SAR, China).
	• Contribute as active citizens to the well-being of the local community, the nation, and the world (Hong Kong SAR, China).
	• Strengthen understanding and fair judgment on issues surrounding politics, the economy, and international relations (Japan).
	• Understand the perspectives of a range of different stakeholders regarding economic activities (India).
	• Adopt a critical approach to initiatives for a fair distribution of income and wealth, human rights, and responsibilities (South Africa).
	• Successfully apply theoretical knowledge to the current economic situation; do not succumb to superficial judgment; have the ability to correctly analyze the situation and react to it (Czech Republic).
	• Develop analytical and quantitative skills as well as qualities and attitudes to prepare for the challenges, opportunities, and responsibilities of adult and working life (United Kingdom).
	• Make sense of, participate in, and contribute to the twenty-first century world, which is characterized by numbers, numerically-based arguments, and data represented and misrepresented in a variety of ways (South Africa).

converted into numbers." In the United Kingdom's citizenship curriculum, class debates on topics such as funding extra health spending with income taxes or value-added taxes and income redistribution to mitigate economic inequality hone students' understanding of how citizens actively participate in the United Kingdom's system of government, their skills to think critically and debate political questions, and their ability to present cogent arguments.

Other factors with the potential to influence the learning outcomes of budget-literacy education include requirements and pedagogical approaches for specific subject curricula, education level, and the age and ability of respective pupils, as well as their earlier experiences with similar subject curricula and exposure to public budget issues outside the classroom.

Content of Curricula Advancing Budget Literacy

An analysis of primary- and secondary-school curricula confirms that while knowledge of public budget processes and outcomes is concentrated at the secondary-school level, it is dispersed over a range of subjects addressing specific topics in varying depths and, depending on whether or not they are part of core or elective courses, may be imparted to a substantial or limited proportion of secondary-school graduates.

Economics

In Australia, Austria, Germany, South Africa, and the United States, budget-literacy content is introduced in lower-secondary school (grades 7–9) with differing areas of focus; the subject is covered in more depth in grades 9–12.

In the United States, eighth-grade economics lessons in lower-secondary school refer to sources of revenue and areas of expenditure for state and local governments in the context of describing market failures and the role of government. The politics and economics curriculum for Hannover, Germany does the same but with the intent of endowing students with a sound understanding of local-level political processes.

In Austria, Western Australia, and New South Wales, the year 7 economics curricula broach the subject differently, highlighting the government's role and specific fiscal and social policies. For example, Western Australia's module on economic policies and management examines the government's economic functions in detail, including provisioning goods and services, redistributing income through taxes and spending, regulating business enterprises, and stabilizing the business cycle in addition to the budget policy process and the effect of fiscal policies on economic activities.

At the upper-secondary level, topics and modules on the government's role in the economy; macroeconomics; and economic, fiscal, and monetary policy tend to feature budget-literacy content in some detail. The content is anchored in a broader subject framework to enhance familiarity with politics, economics, and society (Austria); micro- and macro level economic concepts and theories (India); macroeconomic issues (Hong Kong SAR, China); and overall public sector interventions in the economy (France).

International Practices to Promote Budget Literacy • http://dx.doi.org/10.1596/978-1-4648-1071-8

Most upper-secondary economics curricula cover topics such as the government's economic functions, including income redistribution and provision of goods and services; the public budget process; revenues and expenditures; and fiscal policy options, in addition to other aspects of budget literacy more specifically related to the context and learning outcomes of the respective courses.

Estonia's economics and business studies curriculum analyzes the government's economic policy in the context of ensuring economic stability and even goes a step further, referring to the consequences of economic policies for national defense and social security. In France, the economics module on how the state budget influences the economy presents the economic functioning of the public sector and its actions at various levels (state and central administration, social security institutions, and territorial administrations), and familiarizes students with the economic weight of their respective budgets, demonstrating the ways they influence choices made by economic actors.

Requirements for some state curricula in Germany stand out in contrast to that of other countries. Bayern's economics and law curriculum introduces students to income taxes, their influence on the available income of private households, and ways to solve simple tax-related problems. It also addresses the issue of tax fairness, the basics of social security policy, and its key principles. Brandenburg's economic sciences curriculum analyzes the origins, consequences, and economic limits of state indebtedness, including an international comparison of state debt. Saarland's economics curriculum introduces the welfare state, emphasizing its financing challenges. Luxembourg's module on the state's economic and social role presents additional fiscal mechanisms, such as structural, social, environmental, and budget policies in the European Union framework.

A less-frequently explored aspect of budget literacy is the public sector's role in managing economic policy and service delivery. South Africa's economic and management sciences curriculum examines the issue from the perspective of socioeconomic rights, environmental protection, social security, the United Nations' Convention on the Rights of the Child, and compensation for human rights abuses.

Social Sciences

The lower-secondary school (grades 7–9) social sciences curricula in Estonia and New Zealand introduce budget-literacy concepts. The topic is featured in a broad context in Estonia's basic-education civics and citizenship curriculum in the modules on economy, society, and social relations, and state and governance. Students are introduced to the role of the state in the economy; the state budget; taxes, including the fair payment of them and principles of taxation; and social benefits and insurance. Students are expected to be able to explain the principles of the current market economy, the role of business and the state, the purpose of taxes, the effectiveness of taxes in Estonia, and the rights and responsibilities of individuals with regard to taxes. However, New Zealand's tax education and citizenship curriculum at this level is narrowly geared toward helping students understand the decision-making process regarding the expenditure of revenues acquired through taxes.

In upper-secondary school (grades 9–10) in Japan, New Zealand and Singapore, budget-literacy content in the social sciences curricula emphasize the relevance of taxes and the civic responsibility to pay them. Japan's civics module for ninth grade contains more detail on this issue, introducing tax mechanisms, the various types and classifications of taxes, and how tax revenues can be effectively and equitably distributed. The framework adopted for Estonia's curriculum (grades 10–12) is different in that it presents public finances as part of a module on managing the economy of society, which comprises three parts: job market and employment, consumption and investing, and the state and the economy.

The depth of budget-literacy material in upper-secondary-level social sciences curricula is determined by the intended learning outcomes. New Zealand's tax education and citizenship curriculum is more elementary—it aims at strengthening students' understanding of the country's tax system and its purpose. Singapore's social studies curriculum expects students to assess the consequences of the mismanagement of financial resources and develop awareness of the need to responsibly manage financial resources. The social science curricula in Japan and Estonia are more extensive and nuanced, requiring that students have a more detailed understanding of public finances and are able to deliberate on how they would resolve fiscal policy issues, such as securing financial revenues in an aging society.

Civics and Citizenship

In the broader context of describing the levels and functions of government, the foundations of the political system, and the role of citizens, civics and citizenship curricula for lower-secondary school, which are mandatory in Poland and voluntary in the United States, introduce public finance concepts in some detail.

At this stage, the level of budget literacy acquired by students in Poland and the United States is comparable. Students are expected to explain why taxation is necessary to pay for government, identify major sources of revenue for the national government, recognize the chief uses of the tax revenues received by the national government, and be familiar with the main responsibilities and sources of revenue for state and local governments. Students in the United States are also expected to be able to identify provisions of the United States Constitution that authorize the national government to collect taxes. In Poland, learning outcomes for students include a familiarity with sources of funds in the European Union budget as well as their allocation and an understanding of how European Union funds have been utilized by Polish citizens, businesses, and institutions.

A substantial part of the 2013 citizenship curriculum in the United Kingdom (England only) discusses personal budgeting and financial services, a change from the more astute focus on budget literacy in the 2007 curriculum that explained where public money comes from, who decides how it is spent, and how economic decisions are made regarding the collection and allocation of public monies. Curricula on citizenship for upper-secondary school contain more information on public budgets in the United States and the United Kingdom (England only) than in Poland. The United Kingdom's 2015 elective curriculum for the General Certificate of Secondary Education Citizenship Studies, for example, incorporates key citizenship ideas and concepts, including democracy, government, justice, equality, rights, responsibilities, participation, community, identity, and diversity, and it provides an avenue for young people to think deeply and critically about a wide range of political, social, economic, and ethical issues and questions facing society in local and global contexts. It also teaches students how public taxes are raised and spent by the local and national government and how governments manage complex decisions about the allocation of public funding. In the United States, the *National Standards for Civics and Government* address budget-literacy concepts in the context of explaining the roles and responsibilities of national, state, and local governments. Students are expected to explain the history of taxation in the United States, why it is necessary to pay for government, and the provisions of the U.S. Constitution that authorize the federal government to collect taxes. In addition to identifying types of taxes, students are expected to evaluate the equity of taxes and other major sources of revenue for state and local governments.[4]

In Poland, content for the civics curriculum in upper-secondary school is reminiscent of the lower-secondary-school curriculum, including the role of local governments, European integration, and Poland's role in the European Union.

Life Skills and Contemporary Issues

In Hong Kong SAR, China, the Czech Republic, and Namibia, beginning in the seventh or eighth grades, budget-literacy education is included in courses dealing with contemporary issues and practical skills for adult life. Given the discretionary nature of this learning area, there is great variation in content and learning outcomes.

At the lower-secondary level, the life and society curriculum in Hong Kong SAR, China strives for students to acquire a preliminary understanding of the financial management principles of the government and the effect of public finance on society and the economy as well as to make reasoned comments on government budgeting practices. In addition to key features of the government budget, it discusses the role of taxes and the provision of social services to demonstrate the relationship between government and citizens as well as the differences between Hong Kong SAR, China and other developed economies regarding tax classification and rates. At the discretion of the teacher, a session can be added to specifically review the state of Hong Kong SAR, China's public finances in light of the challenge of its aging population.

The Czech Republic's man and society curriculum for eighth and ninth grades is oriented toward helping students to develop civic consciousness, reinforce their sense of social responsibility, and motivate them to participate in a democratic society. Toward this end, the civics module introduces students to sources of state revenue and areas of state expenditures as well as allowances and benefits that citizens receive from the state budget. It also familiarizes students with the functions of the state administration and local government bodies and institutions.

At the upper-secondary level, the purpose of teaching budget literacy ranges from increasing student awareness about types of taxes (Namibia), the significance of their participation in political processes (Japan), and introducing the fundamentals of professional and economic life (the Czech Republic). While Japan's contemporary society curriculum and Namibia's life skills curriculum highlight tax obligations and the importance of assuming an active interest in how taxes are utilized, the Czech Republic's course on man and the world of work describes fiscal, monetary, and social policies.

Mathematical Literacy and Essential Mathematics
In Manitoba (Canada) and South Africa, the mathematical literacy and essential mathematics curricula aim for 10th- to 12th-grade students to become literate citizens, able to use mathematics to contribute to society and to think critically about the world by developing the ability to reason, make decisions, solve problems, manage resources, and interpret information. Both courses only feature a limited amount of information about public budgets.

The home finances section in Manitoba's essential mathematics course includes determining the property tax for a house. The section on business finances expects students to demonstrate an awareness of government tax forms and the procedures involved in owning a business. South Africa's mathematical literacy guidelines intend for students to use their acquired skills to perform calculations involving personal, provincial, and national budgets and to critically engage in data-handling (statistics and probability) to understand and demystify public budgets.

Business Studies
Based on the premise that it is increasingly difficult to make political and economic choices without a basic level of economic awareness, Ireland's lower-secondary-school business studies course partly relies on student knowledge of public budgets to develop their awareness of the significant role of the state in economic affairs and to appreciate the importance of acquiring basic economic literacy to make informed political choices. The specifications for junior-cycle business studies focus on improving students' understanding of the business environment and on developing skills for life, work, and further study through three inter-connected strands: personal finance, enterprise, and our economy. The economy strand enables students to understand the dynamic relationship between the local, national, and international economic situation. It develops students' ability to identify and understand basic economic concepts as they relate to personal finance, enterprise, and the Irish economy.

The approach of Ireland's business curriculum at the upper-secondary level is geared toward improving student understanding of the overall environment in which businesses function. Its objectives include students being able to take into account the effect of the economy on business—such as the general state of the economy, inflation, interest rates, taxes, and grants; the effect of business on the economy at the local and national levels—such as employment and tax revenues; and the interaction between business and the wider economy. The business studies curriculum in Namibia at this level is more business-centric and explains budgets in the context of their overall usefulness and key accounting notions (for example, profit-and-loss account, balance sheets, and cash flow forecasts).

Fiscal Education Programs

Established with the support of EuroSocial, as of June 2013, the Fiscal Education Network, a collaboration seeking to develop and implement country tax education policies, comprises 10 Latin American governments: Bolivia, Brazil, Chile, Costa Rica, El Salvador, Guatemala, Paraguay, Peru, Honduras, and Uruguay (see box 2.2).

Box 2.2 Introduction to Fiscal Education Programs in Latin America

Brazil. The National Program of Fiscal Education (*Programa Nacional de Educação Fiscal or PNEF*) is supported by multiple government agencies: the Ministry of Finance, the Ministry of Education, the General Comptroller's Unit, the Secretary of Federal Budget, the Internal Revenue System, the National Treasury Secretariat, the Attorney General of National Finances, the Secretaries of Finance and Education of the States, the Federal District and Municipalities, and the Superior School of Public Financial Administration.

The objectives of PNEF are to: (1) create citizen awareness around the socioeconomic function of taxes, (2) share knowledge with citizens regarding public administration issues, (3) provide incentives for citizen engagement in the execution of public resources, and (4) nurture an environment that fosters a positive relationship between citizens and the government.

Chile. As part of its fiscal education program, Chile's Internal Revenue Service developed the *Servicio de Impuestos Internos* (SIIEduca) portal, providing students with fiscal education information to prepare them for the responsibilities of adult life. The fiscal education is not merely about paying taxes—it is also aimed at developing positive social attitudes regarding taking responsibility for and committing to achieving a common social good.

To enhance fiscal education, the Internal Revenue Service based its pedagogical approach on three pillars: social values, citizenship, and culture. The goal is to develop content that can be easily understood by students and citizens and to demystify the world of taxes and fiscal issues.

Costa Rica. The Ministries of Finance and Education in Costa Rica created a fiscal education program with the objective of promoting a positive culture among citizens around fiscal issues. The Department of Fiscal Education and Culture, part of the Directorate of Taxation within the Ministry of Finance, implements the program, which aims at providing tools to students and teachers that allow them to become agents of social change.

There are a variety of teaching resources and materials to support teachers and promote fiscal education in schools. Pedagogical materials seek to infuse the values of public

box continues next page

Box 2.2 Introduction to Fiscal Education Programs in Latin America *(continued)*

responsibility, honesty, solidarity, cooperation with financing common needs, adequate management of public issues, and monitoring of public expenditures.

Guatemala. As part of Guatemala's educational system, the Tax Administration Department has partnered with the Ministry of Education to promote a positive tax culture. It has prepared guidelines for teachers that include group exercises, cases studies, and tools to teach citizenship and tax-related cultural values in the classroom. These guidelines, which are aligned with the national curriculum, propose monthly activities to help students develop social competencies.

Peru. Peru's National Tax Administration Office—SUNAT (Superintendencia Nacional de Administración Tributaria)—is leading efforts to raise fiscal consciousness among its citizens by developing educational activities at the national level and by mainstreaming a positive tax and customs culture at all levels of the educational system. Its tax-culture program supports capacity building for teachers across the country, which enables them to teach students about fiscal issues as part of the national curriculum. Activities in support of teachers include lectures and workshops on citizenship and tax culture, implemented in partnership with the Ministry of Education.

Uruguay. Uruguay's tax education program, an initiative of the Ministry of Economy and Finance's Tax General Directorate, is intended to promote fiscal consciousness among citizens. Its objectives include promoting values and civic attitudes such as solidarity, justice, equality, and responsibility among children and youth; encouraging responsibility and participation of children and youth in public and community life; and fostering the understanding of the socioeconomic role of taxes.

Pedagogical Strategies for Initiatives Promoting Budget Literacy

A rich variety of learning and teaching strategies are being used in school-based initiatives to strengthen knowledge of public budgets both inside and outside of the classroom.

- **Direct instruction.** In some instances (for example, economics courses in Austria and Luxembourg), more traditional teaching methods are employed that rely on a textbook-based approach. Teachers lead the learning process and control the pace of learning. Students follow the learning activities designed by the teachers, and step-by-step achieve the expected learning outcomes as defined by the teachers. In most cases however, the textbook approach is combined with interactive activities, such as discussions and debates. Helpful materials include graphics and statistics (Luxembourg) and real budgets and documents from the Ministry of Finance (Austria).

- **Enquiry learning.** Several curricula are teaching budgets by using enquiry learning through inductive approaches. New Zealand's social inquiry approach[5] relies heavily on student participation and leadership to address specific topics.

Enquiry learning emphasizes learning through practice, experience, and problem solving. Based on their prior knowledge regarding a topic, students gain knowledge through exploration, hypotheses, and reflection.

- **Values clarification.** Values clarification methods are useful in guiding students toward thinking critically and examining their assumptions about budget issues. These methods help students reflect on differing opinions and viewpoints regarding public finances, empowering them to make reasoned judgments. Examples include writing assignments and group discussions that invite students to argue for or against differing approaches to fiscal policy.

- **Participatory learning.** When teachers organize and arrange for students to participate in budget-literacy activities, they provide them with opportunities for first-hand observations and direct contact with people and things outside of school. Through such experiences, students gain a better understanding of the political, economic, and social factors that influence government budget processes and outcomes.

Overall, the types of teaching approaches and supporting materials that are being used to impart budget-literacy concepts are based on one or a combination of pedagogical strategies. See appendices B and C for a list of materials for primary- and secondary-school students.

Classroom-Based Initiatives: Pedagogical Approaches and Materials
A rich variety of compelling pedagogical approaches and materials are being used to impart budget-literacy education to students.

Simulations
Several courses examined for this study are increasingly drawing on simulations that allow students to develop an appreciation of the reasoning and decision-making skills required to formulate and adopt public budgets. South Australia's 2014 economics assessment asks students to put themselves in the shoes of Australia's treasurer and make reasoned choices to encourage economic recovery from a range of suggested policies, including budget cuts and tax increases. A variation of the activity in Canada's economics curriculum simulates the budgetary decision-making process of a multimember organization, such as a town, a city council, or a company's board of directors, to determine the potential effect of their decisions on individuals.

Many pedagogical resources are available to support this type of activity, including a worksheet about city budget simulations for teachers in Canada[6] and copies of budget documents from various levels of government to facilitate student analysis of how tax monies are spent. A three-hour role-playing game[7] allows youth to experience the stages involved in determining a municipal budget. Students play the role of citizens advocating for vying interests.

They debate and must finally agree on using the municipal budget to implement a specific project.[8] The Cyber-Budget game[9] enables players to adopt the role of the minister of finance to prove their knowledge of budgetary issues, going through all the steps of the budget process with the goal of balancing public finances. The game ends with a short video message from the actual finance minister, adapted to the player's results.[10]

Role-Playing

Pedagogical approaches using role-play are fairly routine. They are featured in a number of curricula to depict fiscal issues at the municipal and national levels. In Hessen, Germany, students are asked to represent conflicting fiscal interests. In Canada, students are asked to pretend that they are councilors of a small municipality charged with making decisions regarding expenditures based on expected revenues for the fiscal year. Students also pretend to be advisors to the minister of finance, contending with national-level fiscal dilemmas, such as high unemployment and low economic growth. In the United Kingdom, students present arguments to government ministers as to why certain departments should receive a larger share of an upcoming budget than others. In the United States, students try to explain the social security program to a confused aunt or uncle.

Scenario Analysis

This teaching method involves presenting students with hypothetical or real-life scenarios that they need to resolve by utilizing their analytical and problem-solving skills. In Hong Kong SAR, China, students tackle the issue of a narrow tax base caused by an increasingly older population. In the United Kingdom, examples of fiscal scenarios include policy changes announced in the current budget and how they could affect economic goals, as well as a rise in unemployment and declining income tax receipts and how these affect cyclical or structural deficits.

Fact-Finding Efforts and Analysis

Fact-finding exercises increasingly rely on information that is available online. In Canada, youth are asked to locate the website of the Department of Finance to identify tax and spending priorities from the latest budget and to compare amounts spent on various sectors and programs using Microsoft Excel® and data on federal government spending from the website of the Bureau of Economic Analysis. Students in other countries also conduct research on budget-literacy issues, such as in New Zealand, where students walk around their local communities and identify features paid for by the government or local council. Another activity is the design of a survey to discover how people in the school or community feel about taxes, followed by a discussion and cross-comparison by students. Examples of these exercises include instructions and lesson plans, such as "Why Cities Provide Tax Breaks Even When they are Strapped for Cash"[11] and "What Do You Get for Your $1,818,600,000,000?"

Using Real-Life Situations

The study found several courses using an enquiry-based approach by dealing with real-life situations and by working with authentic materials to address budget-literacy issues, including some in the Czech Republic, Hong Kong SAR China, and New Zealand.

In New Zealand, to make budgets tangible to students, school budget charts[12] encourage them to understand the school's budget and the effect of tax spending on this budget. A suggested activity for classes in Hong Kong is to prepare a display board exhibiting the salient features of the national budget after it is announced in February or March and, by way of comparison, a board exhibiting the draft central and local budgets that are presented by the Ministry of Finance annually in March.[13]

In India, teachers ask students to watch the finance minister present the national budget on television and to identify what the budget allocates for specific sectors of the economy, such as agriculture, industry, and services. The next day, students engage in class discussions and analyze the potential impacts of the budget on various sectors of the economy.

Some activities focus on tax implications. An exercise from the United Kingdom asks students to conduct online research regarding value-added tax rates (general sales tax), compiling a list of the five countries with the highest and lowest rates and determining the actual cost of a chocolate bar with a price of 60 pence (pre-sales tax) for each country. An exercise from the United States has students analyze a sample paycheck stub and answer questions about the types of taxes deducted from the check and the gross and net amounts of pay. Students are also asked to calculate sales tax and compare the effect of different tax rates on the total price paid.

In Singapore, after the release of the annual budget, the Ministry of Education's Curriculum Planning and Development Division follows up with a just-in-time resource package to help teachers guide students toward a deeper understanding of the budget from a range of perspectives and to spark classroom discussions about fiscal measures.

Other useful resources in adopting real-life teaching methods include materials from the life and society curriculum in Hong Kong SAR, China,[14] which suggest numerous textbook exercises for students, budget speeches available through relevant ministries of finance online, and newspaper articles about the current-fiscal-year budget.

Debate and Discussion

Some teachers and educators trying to engage students in discussions about budgets and values clarification exercises utilize current fiscal concerns or budget-literacy topics that are likely to elicit student interest and enthusiasm.

In Victoria, Australia, students convene a summit to review Australia's tax policies; inquire into what makes a tax "good"; evaluate a range of taxes using criteria based on the inquiry; and based on their deliberations, recommend changes to the government. Students are expected to take into account factors such as the suitability of the current tax mix and the use of taxes to achieve goals related to equity, sustainability, and economic growth.

There are several examples of using relevant topics in classroom discussions from the United Kingdom, including a class debate centered on the stories of eight characters that students are asked to consider and determine whether or not their circumstances make them worthy of government expenditures. Another example involves students discussing the types of expenses that Parliament members claim and exploring differing views around the issue.

Supporting materials for lessons on government spending,[15] expenses of Parliament members[16] (the United Kingdom), and Europe's debt crisis[17] (the United States) are available online.[18]

Interaction with Relevant Authorities

To familiarize students with government budgets, schools in several countries encourage class interaction with relevant and well-informed experts and authorities to explain the context and details of the budget process. The interactions include:

- In New Zealand, a school principal or treasurer provides feedback on the students' estimations of school expenses and financing mechanisms and answers questions about the school's income and expenditure patterns.
- In Canada and New Zealand, local Parliament members discuss current fiscal and monetary policies and identify the government's goals regarding such measures.
- Officials from finance ministries explain their role and functions and their relevance to the provision of public goods and services by the government. In Costa Rica, Ministry of Finance officials use a game called "Around the Country," which uses mimic games and drawing to teach students about taxes and the investments required to maintain public spaces and deliver public goods.
- In the United States, students write letters to their elected representatives about items they would like to see prioritized regarding federal spending and/or revenue. A politics and governance course in the Philippines conducts a similar exercise (see box 2.3).

Box 2.3 Student Engagement with Elected Representatives in the Philippines

In the Philippines, the politics and governance course (grade 10) is focused on citizenship in practice. Learners are expected to identify issues related to political engagement and youth empowerment, identify and assess existing programs that address such issues, and conduct research for a draft proposal on a project about them. Students learn to identify the different levels of the Philippine local government, explain the roles and functions of the local government unit, and examine how decentralization affects governance. Learning competencies

box continues next page

Box 2.3 Student Engagement with Elected Representatives in the Philippines *(continued)*

for this course include original activities centered on the active participation of students and their direct engagement with their political elected representatives.

Suggested activities for this learning process include:
- Articulate or advocate for a position to a Philippine legislator through formal correspondence;
- Appraise the effect of the congress's performance on development in the Philippines;
- Conduct interviews with *barangay*[a] officials about community programs; and
- Evaluate the performance of a local government unit.

Source: Republic of the Philippines. 2014.
a. A *barangay* is the smallest administrative division in the Philippines. It is the native Filipino term for a village, district, or ward.

Teaching materials that may be useful in these contexts include a template called "Write a Letter to Your Congressperson"[19] and supporting materials for the politics and governance course in the Philippines.

Write-Ups, Essays, and Reports
In several contexts, students are encouraged to utilize their writing skills to analyze and state their arguments regarding specific budget issues. Examples include:

- In the United States, students prepare a "five-minute write"—a brief written piece about the federal government's responsibility for ensuring secure and stable standards of living for the elderly.
- In the United Kingdom, students write an essay on whether to fund extra health care spending from income tax or value added tax.
- In the United Kingdom, students review Her Majesty's Revenue and Customs website for stories of tax evasion convictions and describe such activities in writing.
- In approximately 1,000 words, South African students discuss the effect of the budget on fostering entrepreneurship and on the education sector.

Useful materials include lesson plans on tax avoidance,[20] social security, governance, and the national debt.

Contests and Quizzes
Introducing competition to budget-literacy efforts has proven useful in engaging students. Prior to the release of its annual budget, Singapore's Ministry of Finance launches an online budget quiz that allows students to compete for prizes for themselves and their schools. It is a fun and interactive learning opportunity for students to understand Singapore's national budget process; some of its economic, social, and tax policies; and budgetary measures. The 2015 quiz began with three weekly quizzes that helped participating youth prepare for the "Budget Master Challenge." In addition to receiving prizes, players with the highest scorers are featured in the "Hall-of-Fame."[21]

The Dominican Republic's Internal Revenue General Department organized a national contest called "Create a Campaign to Promote a Tax Culture," which motivated students to create an innovative and creative campaign reflecting their thoughts about taxes and the responsibilities of citizens. Winners received monetary prizes.

Art and Cartoon Analysis

In some cases, students are encouraged to use art to improve their familiarity with budget-literacy issues. In the United Kingdom, in an exercise distinguishing between current and capital government expenditures and progressive, proportional, and regressive taxes, students design images to represent various types of expenditures and taxes. The Tax Education Promotion Council in Toyama Prefecture, Japan, organizes a poster competition about taxes at the local level. Winning posters receive prizes and are featured on the council's website: Hello! Let's Study Tax.[22] In the United States, a lesson on taxes and the national debt[23] includes two cartoons that are used in combination with questions to facilitate class debate in favor of taxes—for example: Why does society need taxes?—or against too many taxes—for example: Can taxes be harmful to the individual or to the economy? Students share their interpretations and responses to such trigger questions and are encouraged to challenge, question, and cross-check with each another to provide the best possible responses to such questions.

Other Methods and Materials

Less-frequently-used teaching methods include record keeping and audit training. As part of Newfoundland and Labrador's (Canada) curriculum, students are encouraged to maintain records of all personal and household taxes paid by themselves and their families over a one-month period to determine the extent and effect of taxes on their daily lives. Since its inception in 2010, the Youth Auditors program in Peru has trained more than 200,000 secondary-school students at the national level who have conducted more than 3,700 social audits of their schools and other entities, improving educational services and the conditions of educational infrastructure.

Because of the emphasis on tax education in several countries, a broad range of pedagogical materials are available to acquaint young people with taxes. In 2015, for example, Her Majesty's Revenue and Customs, the United Kingdom's tax, payments, and customs authority, released "Tax Facts," a comprehensive set of materials designed to introduce the tax system to students ages 14–17.[24] Earlier, the authority had produced a number of resources for teachers, including detailed lesson plans and guidance as well as four short, animated videos to teach students about some of the key tax issues they will face as they begin their working lives. Teaching materials produced by New Zealand's tax and citizenship curriculum, Japan's tax education promotion councils, and members of the Fiscal Education Network are also reliable sources of tax information.

Schools and educators depend on various media, including audio, television, and the Internet to teach budget literacy to students (see appendices B and C).

Out-of-Classroom Initiatives: Pedagogical Approaches and Materials

Classroom-based budget-literacy activities and materials are often driven by the ministries of education which prioritize competencies and learning outcomes necessary for achieving broader curricular objectives. They are complemented by a host of out-of-classroom initiatives advancing budget literacy for youth that are led by other stakeholders and which are intended to:

- Facilitate a hands-on understanding of how public money is administered;
- Foster a sense of civic duty and social responsibility regarding tax obligations and the use of public resources;
- Encourage political debate and dialogue and enhance the voice and choice of the youth in the budgetary process; and
- Support teachers endeavoring to achieve their goals, consistent with the overall objectives of the curricula, including budget-literacy components.

Stakeholders such as ministries of finance, comptroller general's offices, tax authorities, broadcasting associations, academics, educators, think tanks, and civil society organizations have developed a variety of rich and innovative pedagogical resources to acquaint young people with budget-literacy issues and to provide learning support to teachers and students. A summary of key approaches and materials follows.

Field Trips and Study Tours

In Brazil, Sao Paulo's Open Treasury program seeks to familiarize students with the operations of the National Treasury Secretariat and facilitate a hands-on understanding of how public money is administered. The program organizes lectures on fiscal education issues for groups of primary- and secondary-school students who attend public and private schools as well as for their teachers, followed by visits to the National Treasury Secretariat. More than 25,000 students and teachers participated in the program between January 2001 and July 2004.

Japan's National Tax Association has made similar efforts. The Tax Space Ueno[25] facility in Tokyo's Ueno local tax office organizes study tours and tax education classes. As of September 2011, over 10,000 students and teachers had visited the facility since its opening in June 2003. In 2014, students from 34 junior high schools and six high schools visited this facility.

Contests

SUNAT—Peru's national tax administration office—launched a national-level "payment receipt" contest to teach children about the importance of requesting an invoice or payment receipt every time they make a purchase to ensure that there is a tax record of the transaction so that it will contribute to tax revenue. Children are encouraged to submit as many payments receipts as possible to SUNAT. Winners receive monetary prizes.

Uruguay's Tax General Directorate launched a contest for secondary-school students to propose a video game to help their classmates learn about taxes.

Participants were directed to conduct preliminary research about Uruguay's tax culture and combine their findings with positive elements of responsible citizenship in the design of their video game. Suggested topics included the national budget, taxation based on citizens' needs, and combating tax evasion.

In Japan, the Toyama Prefecture's Tax Education Promotion Council organizes a tax-related poster competition at the prefectural level. Winning posters are featured on the Council's Hello! Let's Study Tax website.[26]

Quizzes

A variety of quizzes in the United States, Japan, Singapore, and other countries are geared toward improving young people's awareness of budget issues. For example:

- In the United States, the National Council of La Raza's Social Security VideoQuiz provides basic information about social security and includes material especially relevant to Latino youth.
- In Japan, the 2013 Hello Tax Quiz, which targeted sixth-grade students from the Kyoto Prefecture, awarded prizes for perfect scores.

Public Events and Activities

Peru's National Tax Administration Office makes use of public events and activities and sets up booths in parks, plazas, playgrounds, and other public places to share information and pedagogical resources for tax and fiscal issues with children. This approach is often complemented with games and contests implemented in schools at the request of principals.

In Guatemala, the "Strength Lies in Numbers" Annual Festival uses musical events, talent shows, plays, and information stands to educate citizens about the social significance of taxes. Children learn about tax and citizenship issues through activities such as puppet shows and spending a day at work with the Superintendent of the Tax Administration Department and other tax officials.

Cartoons and Comic-Book Characters

Cartoons and comic-book characters successfully engage youth in discussions about budget literacy. Brazil's Ministry of Finance draws on the stories of a character known as *Leãozinho* ("little lion") to foster citizen participation in social and fiscal control issues. Leãozinho's stories take place at school, the library, the movie theater, and the park, among other places, showing children and youth that fiscal education can be interesting and easy to understand.

Among the materials the Brazil Comptroller General's Office uses is a comic book series about public budgeting that is presented in simple language, which can be understood by students in elementary school. The main character is Sofinha, a girl who, along with her family, friends, and classmates, learns about the budget. The stories refer to budget-literacy issues that are helpful for understanding the budget, budgetary law, the role of the Secretary of the Federal Budget, the oversight of public expenditures, and participation in the budget process.

In Peru, characters Mateo, and Clarita, along with Ayni—a penguin mascot—jointly participate in learning activities for children, contributing to the popularity of activities organized by Peru's National Tax Administration Office.

Television Shows and Videos

In partnership with Novasur (educational television under the National Council of Television), Chile's Internal Revenue System launched a television program to teach students about citizenship and economic concepts like taxes. The story is about four young musicians who participate in a rock concert. The initial run comprised four episodes—each about ten minutes long—that communicated the fundamentals of fiscal education.

A television program launched by the Japan Broadcasting Corporation, 10-minute-box,[27] devoted a number of episodes to public finances and taxes. For example, the ninth episode introduced the role of national and local governments, a breakdown of public expenditures, and challenges facing public finances. The tenth episode emphasized the obligation of citizens to pay taxes and described different types of taxes, such as income and corporate. The program concluded with an overview of taxes in other countries and future tax-related challenges.

The Student Budget Consultation Program website of CIVIX, a national, nonpartisan charity in Canada promoting civics education, presents video tutorials[28] that feature the minister of finance outlining the concepts of revenues, expenditures, surplus, deficit, and debt as well as interviews[29] with major national stakeholders and political party leaders who share their priorities and discuss their preferred use of government budget surpluses.

The Making Sen$e with Paul Solman video series in the United States is another excellent resource to apprise youth on fiscal issues. Topics include "Taxes: How High Is Too High?"[30] and "What Do Tax Rates' Ups and Downs Mean for Economic Growth?"[31]

Games

A number of innovative approaches have been used to create video, online, and other types of games to make learning about budgets and fiscal issues fun. In the San Jose Kid's Museum in Costa Rica, a game room called Tribute to My Country was created to teach youth about the culture of citizenship and the social role of taxes and public spending. With video games, a child can adopt the role of an adult professional and learn about the most common taxes in Costa Rica and how to pay them. One section of the game room highlights the role of Parliament in determining the allocation of public resources. Another section introduces the process of investing taxes.

A wide range of interactive games on fiscal issues has been introduced in the United States, including:

- The Federal Budget Challenge,[32] an interactive web survey tool that enables participants to learn about major public policies and their effect on the fiscal future of the country; make decisions regarding the budget; read a real-time budget meter indicating the overall national debt based on their policy choices; and receive a summary report of their decisions by completing this budget challenge.

- Build a Better Budgets Game[33] enables users to set their own spending priorities for federal programs, including education, job creation, entitlement programs like Social Security and Medicare, and the military.
- Budget Hero,[34] an interactive budgeting game, allows users to allocate tax dollars to government programs and observe the long-term effects of this allocation on the budget deficit and the national debt.
- Budget Explorer[35] enables students to change the priorities of the federal budget and learn how to balance the federal budget and reduce the national debt.
- Your Federal Income Tax Receipt[36] simulates federal government expenditures of taxes paid by individuals during a tax year.
- The Open Budgets Game[37] by the International Budget Partnership investigates whether public resources are being used to fight poverty and improve the lives of poor and marginalized people.

"Finance Roulette,"[38] introduced by Finance Land,[39] the website of the Ministry of Finance in Japan, is a game that teaches children about the basics regarding taxes through a game of roulette.

¡Clink!—Uruguay's Tax Education Portal's featured video game—presents a scenario to secondary-school students in which a natural disaster has befallen their city, and they are in charge of collecting and allocating resources for reconstruction. The comptroller general's office in Brazil includes Ludo Game and Memory Game in the activities prepared for school children.

Participatory Budgeting

Based on examples from Canada, Poland, Germany, and France, student engagement in school-, district-, and municipal-level participatory-budgeting initiatives is emerging as a prevalent trend.

In 2005, the Poitou-Charentes region in France introduced participatory budgeting for students in 93 public high schools and created the impetus for the Nord Pas de Calais and Ile-de-France regions to engage secondary-school students in similar exercises in 2010 and 2011. Since 2008, the participatory-budgeting process has been extended to all private schools in Poitou-Charentes, and this process has resulted in the funding of almost 1,600 projects. Between 2011 and 2014, the number of high schools in Ile-de-France engaging in participatory budgeting increased from 30 to 40. Since 2011, 30–160 students from each high school have participated in the meetings of the "general assembly (comprised of pupils, parents, teachers and school employees from high schools across the region). An impact evaluation[40] found that, as a result of the participatory budget process, 73.8 percent of parents and 56.6 percent of students believed that communications at the school had improved.

Germany's Marzahn-Hellersdorf district introduced participatory budgeting for students in 2005. Participation rates in the budget process among children and teenagers has continued to increase through the online platform Mischen Sie mit!

In 2014–15, approximately 700 online messages were submitted by children and teenagers (about 18 percent of all messages received). Forty suggestions from the 2010–11 participatory budget have already been implemented, notably including the construction of a playground.

Examples of pedagogical materials that may serve as useful references include a flyer[41] explaining to youth the process for getting involved in the budgetary process online, a dedicated Facebook® page,[42] and a blog[43] created by the Marzahn-Hellersdorf district. The Bertelsmann Foundation, which organized a school participatory budgeting in the City of Rietberg and published an informative project report[44] and a comprehensive handbook for schools,[45] has expressed interest in implementing a student participatory budget.

Budget Voting and Youth Budgets

Examples from Canada, India, and the United Kingdom attest to the increasing popularity of budget voting and youth budgets.

The Chance to be Chancellor/Youth Budget Initiative provides students ages 14–18 from across the United Kingdom the opportunity to develop their own alternative budgets based on three taxation areas: work, consumer, and business; and seven spending areas: employment, health, education, welfare, public protection, environment, and government and the economy. The program reached 90,000 young people in 2012–13, 1,400 of whom submitted budgets. It received a 94 percent approval rating for its effect on the economic literacy levels of teachers and a 72 percent approval rating for its effect on youth.

Relevant pedagogical materials for similar initiatives include:

- The Citizenship Foundation's free lesson plans, which are designed to stimulate discussions around economic and public spending issues such as health, environment, transport, education, and employment (the United Kingdom);
- Lesson pathways and resources on budgets, the federal government's budget, and political perspectives and budget priorities prepared by CIVIX (Canada);
- A budget preparatory kit by Model Youth (MY) Parliament,[46] consisting of articles, editorials, and other items from newspapers, magazines, and books (India);
- MY Parliament *Budget Insights 2015/16*—presents a more detailed report on budget allocations and policy changes (India); and
- A 2015/16 primer issued by the government that includes highlights and features of the budget (India).[47]

Other potentially useful pedagogical materials include:

- **Web portals.** Uruguay's Tax Education Portal is a useful example because it conveys concepts about taxes to children and youth using a number of methods, including video games, graphics, and interactive activities. The section "Complying with Tax Duties" provides information about why taxes are important to society, the role and history of the Tax General Directorate, statistics and regional comparisons on tax evasion, and information about public expenditures.

The web portal of Brazil's Office of the Comptroller General—the Children's Portal for Social Control—offers interactive tools to foster the values needed to become a good citizen. Content includes games, cartoons, a display of winning entries from a drawing and composition contest, and links to other youth-centered websites promoting citizenship. Guidance for teachers is also available.

- **Student notebooks and activity magazines.** Brazil's Office of the Comptroller General has created notebooks that include exercises, stories, questionnaires, and activities. There are blank spaces for drawing pictures and writing stories and evaluations of the activities. An "activities" magazine included crosswords, coloring pages, word search puzzles, connect-the-dots, and labyrinths to reinforce the topics of citizenship and social control of the use of public resources.

Policy Workshops

Workshops to impart knowledge of fiscal policies or to solicit suggestions from students on fiscal policy issues have also been useful to develop budget literacy. For instance, Officials from the Ministry of Finance in Costa Rica visit schools and conduct workshops for students to explain the role and functions of the ministry and its relevance to government-provided public goods and services. A game used at the workshops, called Around the Country, includes mime and drawing while teaching youth about tax revenues and investments that are required to maintain public spaces and deliver public goods.

The New Zealand Treasury convenes workshops with young people to seek their input on specific policy projects, which also serves to provide experiential learning experiences for youth and as opportunities to engage in policy debates that they might not have had otherwise. For instance, students who participated in the December 2012 LongTermNZ workshop prepared the "2012 Youth Statement on New Zealand's Long-Term Fiscal Position 2012–2052,"[48] which prioritized fiscal policy areas as the means to attain the vision for New Zealand in 2052 and that they presented to treasury officials. (Krieble and O'Dwyer-Cunliffe 2013).

Assessment of Budget Literacy Education

There are two assessment approaches in the countries and economies included in this stock-take: curriculum-based formative assessments to gauge the knowledge of individual students about public budgets and survey information used by out-of-classroom budget-literacy initiatives. Useful examples of curriculum-based assessments measuring the progress of secondary school students with respect to budget literacy are available but not widespread because pertinent learning outcomes and objectives are only defined in the context of much broader curricula and because budget literacy is not taught as a independent subject (see boxes 2.4–2.7).

Box 2.4 Using Multiple Choice Questions to Test Budget Literacy

Several countries, including India, Ireland, New Zealand, and the United Kingdom, utilize multiple choice questions in examinations and quizzes to test student understanding of budget-literacy concepts. Following are examples of test questions:

India

The government budget has a revenue deficit. This gets financed by:

A. Borrowing
B. Disinvestment
C. Tax revenue
D. Indirect taxes

(a) A and D
(b) C and D
(c) A and B
(d) C and D

New Zealand

Which of these isn't paid for by taxes?

(a) Building and maintaining roads
(b) Building and running hospitals
(c) Building and running schools
(d) Building shops and parks

Who makes decisions about what taxes are spent on?

(a) The Prime Minister
(b) Government Departments
(c) The government
(d) The person paying chooses where the money goes

Sources: (1) Sample Question Paper for Economics (030) Class XII (2014–15). Directorate of Education, Government of the National Capital Territory of Delhi. http://www.edudel.nic.in/welcome_folder/sqp_mas_15012015/SQP12/economics.pdf and (2) Level 5 Unit–Learning Experience 1. "Quiz: How Does Tax Relate to Me?" Online Resources for Tax Education and Citizenship, Ministry of Education, New Zealand, available at http://taxcitizenship.tki.org.nz/Resources.

Box 2.5 Using Data Interpretation Questions to Test Budget Literacy

Data interpretation questions are intended to test students' numeric, analytical, and data-literacy skills. This approach has been adopted in the economics syllabus for the United Kingdom, the mathematical literacy curriculum in South Africa, and textbook exercises for the life and society curriculum in Hong Kong SAR, China (see below).

box continues next page

Box 2.5 Using Data Interpretation Questions to Test Budget Literacy *(continued)*

Kevin is a 45-year-old man who works for a tourism company. He earns a gross salary of R28 754,50 per month and a 13th cheque at the end of the company's financial year. The following are deducted from his salary on a monthly basis:

- 7.5% of his salary toward his pension
- R1 434.70 for his medical aid

1. Calculate Kevin's monthly contribution toward his pension. (3 marks)
2. Calculate Kevin's annual medical-aid contribution. (2 marks)
3. Kevin's taxable income for the year of assessment ending 28/02/2013 was R330 713,02. Describe how Kevin's taxable income was calculated. (5 marks)
4. The table below shows the tax rates for individuals for the year of assessment ending 28/02/2013.

Tax Rates (Year of Assessment Ending February 20, 2013)

Tax bracket	Taxable income (in rand)	Rate of tax (in rand)
A	0–160,000	18% of taxable income
B	160,001–250,000	28,800 + 25% of taxable income above 160,000
C	250,001–346,000	51,300 + 30% of taxable income above 250,000
D	346,001–484,000	80,100 + 35% of taxable income above 346,000
E	484,001–617,000	128,400 + 38% of taxable income above 484,000
F	617,000 and above	178,940 + 40% of taxable income above 617,000

Rebates	
Primary R6 390	R11 440
Secondary (65 years old and above)	R6 390
Tertiary (75 years old and above)	R2 130

- Determine Kevin's tax bracket. Write down only the letter (A–F) corresponding to Kevin's taxable income. (2 marks)
- Write down Kevin's rebate. (2 marks)

Assessment questions with written responses demonstrate the students' knowledge of budget-literacy concepts. Students describe concepts, interpret budget data, and respond to open-ended questions.

Source: Mathematical Literacy Exemplar 2014. Grade 12, Department: Basic Education, Republic of South Africa. http://www .education.gov.za/Portals/0/CD/Computer/Mathematical%20Literacy%20P1%20GR%2012%20Exemplar%202014%20Eng .pdf?ver=2014-03-28-101522-000.

Box 2.6 Using Description of Budget Concepts to Test Budget Literacy

Students are expected to be familiar with issues related to public budgets, such as taxes, revenues, expenditures, and fiscal policies. Depending on the overarching approach and content of the curricula, budget-literacy concepts being tested are basic (such as in Canada and India) or more complex (such as in Austria and Ireland).

box continues next page

Box 2.6 Using Description of Budget Concepts to Test Budget Literacy *(continued)*

Ireland

- Explain two reasons why a government prepares a national budget.
- Describe positive and negative consequences of the current budget deficit.

Newfoundland and Labrador (Canada)

- Describe major revenue categories of municipal, provincial, and federal budgets.
- Define progressive, proportional, and regressive taxes.
- Given relevant information, determine whether different types of taxes (including income and sales) are progressive, proportional, or regressive.

Sources: "Tax and Government Finance." Senior Cycle Economics–Curriculum Resources. Ireland Professional Development Services for Teachers. http://www.pdst.ie/node/4299; Social Studies. *Canadian Economy 2203.* A Curriculum Guide September, Government of Newfoundland and Labrador 2004.
http://www.ed.gov.nl.ca/edu/k12/curriculum/guides/economiced/can_econ2203-04.pdf.

Box 2.7 Using Open-Ended Questions to Test Budget Literacy

Open-ended questions are helpful to test students' abilities to use their knowledge of public budgets to propose hypotheses and make relevant arguments.

Austria

- Assess the expression "A budget is societal policy converted into numbers," with specific reference to the Austrian situation.
- "Tax policy is a reflection of social power relations." Discuss.

Hong Kong SAR, China

- Some people think that although Hong Kong SAR, China is a highly developed economy, its welfare services and policies are still insufficient compared with those of affluent countries. Therefore, some people suggest that the government should learn from the developed countries by raising the tax rate, imposing new taxes to increase government revenue, and providing more welfare benefits to the citizens. Do you agree? Please explain.

Sources: Austrian Federal Ministry of Education and Women's Affairs website: https://www.bmbf.gv.at/schulen/unterricht/lp /lp_ahs_oberstufe.html; "Public Finance of Hong Kong Foundation Part: Economic and Social Consequences of Public Finance of Hong Kong—Core Module 12" (July 2014) at the Learning and Teaching Materials of the Research and Development Project on the Life and Society Curriculum Resources page of the Government of the Hong Kong SAR, China's Education Bureau website: http://www.edb.gov.hk/en/curriculum-development/kla/pshe/references-and-resources /life-and-society/life-and-society-resources.html.

Classroom-Based Assessment

The most commonly used assessment tools appear to be tests, examinations, and quizzes, including multiple-choice questions and written responses. The majority of multiple-choice questions are geared at verifying a student's practical knowledge of taxes (for example, New Zealand) and conceptual knowledge regarding government revenues and expenditures. Data interpretation questions rely on graphs and charts that present information about budgets. They focus on testing a student's ability to read and interpret budget data in order to correctly respond to questions.

Out-of-Classroom Assessment

Out-of-Classroom initiatives, such as the Chance to be Chancellor/Youth Budget program in the United Kingdom and the youth-focused participatory-budgeting process in Boston, Massachusetts (the United States) use evaluation processes to determine the education outcomes of their activities. Both programs draw on a combination of quantitative and qualitative assessment methodologies, including online surveys, evaluation forms for specific trainings and events, interviews and focus group discussions for the list of questions used by the Chance to be Chancellor/Youth Budget program (see appendix A).

The findings of the 2012–13 evaluation for the Chance to be Chancellor/Youth Budget program confirm that 94 percent of teachers believe that their knowledge of and confidence to teach students about economic awareness, including public budgets, has increased. Ninety-two percent of teachers rated their lesson plans' effectiveness in terms of raising student awareness of economic issues as *good* or *very good*. The majority of youth participants rated the program as a *good* or *very good* way to learn about and promote the opinions of youth regarding public budgets (see figure 2.1).

Figure 2.1 Chance to Be Chancellor/Youth Budget Program: Ratings by Participants

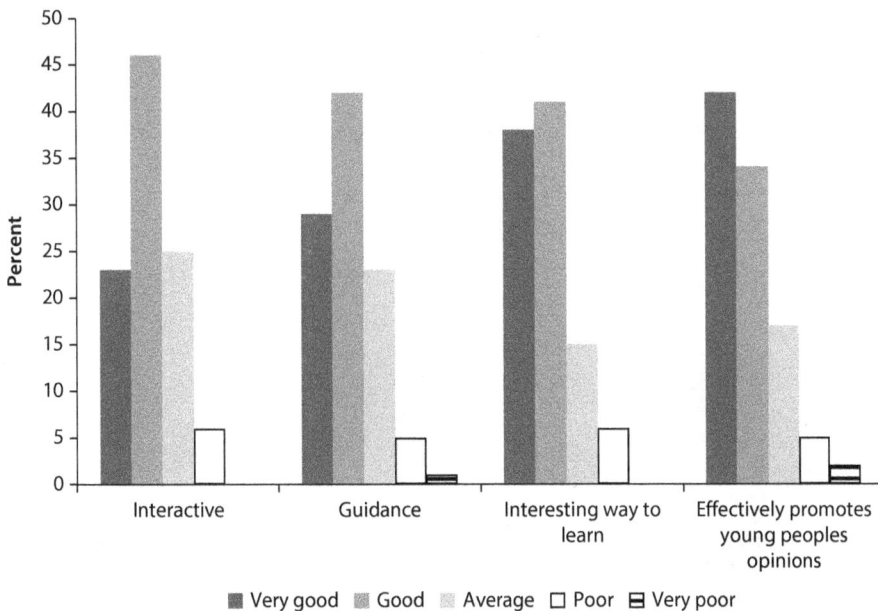

Source: Citizenship Foundation 2013.

International Practices to Promote Budget Literacy • http://dx.doi.org/10.1596/978-1-4648-1071-8

Feedback from the participants of Boston's youth-focused participatory-budgeting program attests to their impression that the process increased their knowledge regarding the rationale and procedures for allocating public funds as well as nuances of the negotiation and decision-making process, the composition of capital costs, and budget choices faced by the government in a context of scarce public resources and competing priorities. Figure 2.2 provides a breakdown of survey responses by youth about how their involvement in the participatory-budgeting process contributed to their sense of empowerment and civic consciousness. Categories of survey respondents were: youth who only voted

Figure 2.2 Participants' Feedback: Boston's Youth Participatory-Budgeting Process

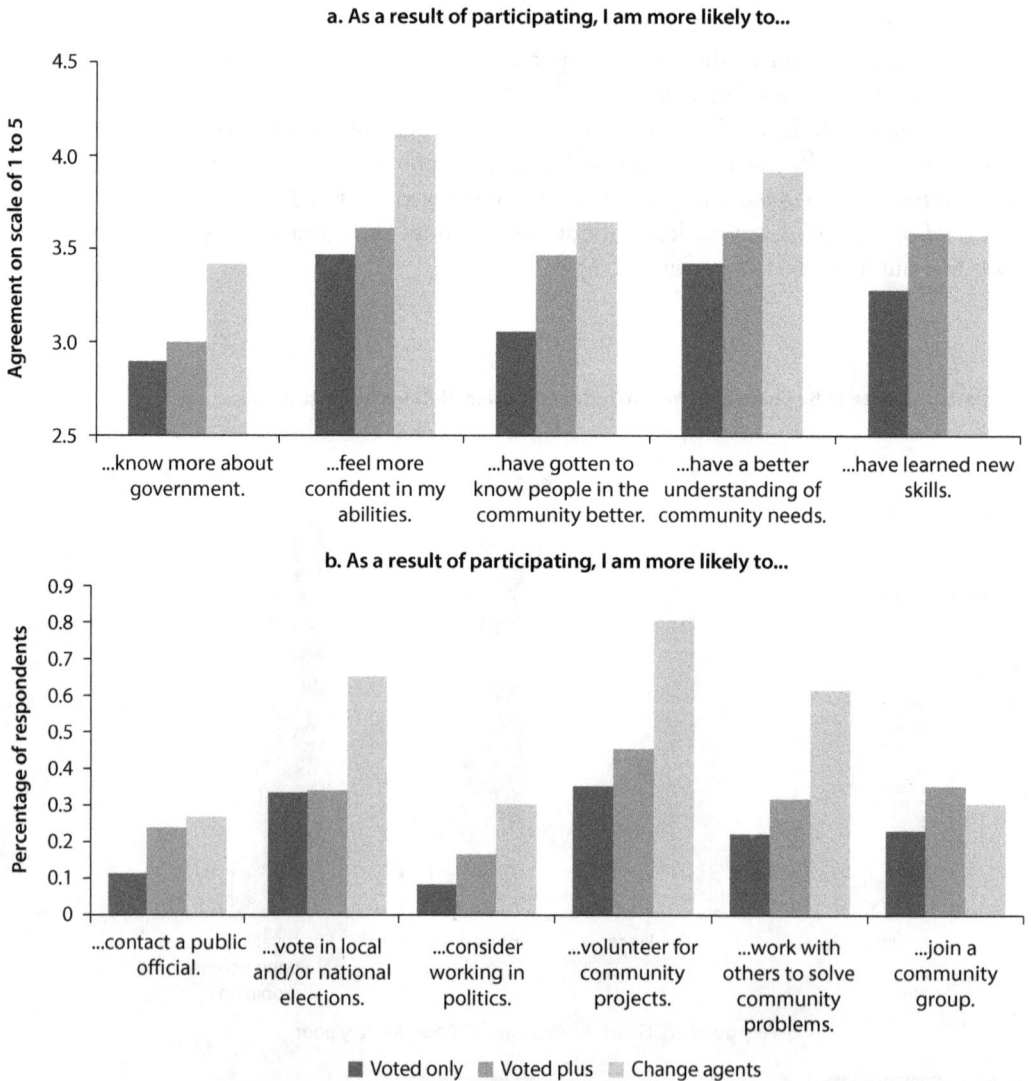

a. As a result of participating, I am more likely to...

b. As a result of participating, I am more likely to...

■ Voted only ■ Voted plus ▨ Change agents

on project proposals, youth who were also involved through the steering committee or idea-generation assemblies, and youth who had served as change agents to develop the actual proposals being put to a vote. The survey results found that those who engaged more intensively in the process were more likely to report being influenced by it in various ways (Grillos 2014).

Beyond-School Initiatives

The role of youth initiatives in promoting the management and oversight of public resources is well documented, but less scrutiny has been given to their implications for youth education. Still, the instructional aspects of participating in democratic decision-making processes proposed by Pateman (1970) and Dewey (1963) as well as the participatory learning approach promulgated by the 2004 Active Learning for Active Citizenship Framework (Mayo and Rooke 2008) are quite relevant. Schugurensky's 2006 study is even more pertinent because it highlights the role of participatory budgeting as a school of citizenship which has the potential to foster budget literacy and instrumental, analytic, social, and deliberative skills (Schugurensky 2006).

The sample of beyond-school budget literacy initiatives for this report have not only been successful in conveying awareness and appreciation among young people about the relevance of public budgets, but have also been instrumental in providing them with the agency to engage in budget planning, execution and, audits. In the context of budget planning, for example, in 2014, 2,693 children from 71 countries participated in a global survey and consultations to provide inputs that informed the March 2015 UN Human Rights Council Resolution "Towards Better Investment in the Rights of the Child." In Nicaragua, the Network of Municipal Governments–Friends of Children has been instrumental in creating spaces such as child councils and lobby events for children to engage in municipal-level budget processes and in ensuring that children are involved directly in the discussions and approval of projects benefitting them.

Some aspects of the budget literacy education that youngsters have acquired through such initiatives overlap with the knowledge imparted through school-based approaches. For instance, trainings convened by Plan Ghana and ISODEC (Integrated Social Development Centre) in Ghana have introduced young people to family budgets, routine budget calculations, and the budget cycle at the local and national levels—all of which are themes that have been incorporated in several curricula. Similar to some out-of-classroom initiatives, children have learned to conduct gap analyses and develop funding proposals in Nicaragua and acquired the basics of project management and life skills in Zimbabwe. However, they have also been able to learn about other facets of public budgets that have not featured as prevalently in the curriculum-based education featured in this report. For instance, child-led groups in Zimbabwe have been trained on children's rights and how states report to the UN Committee on the Rights of the Child; the workshops for children's groups in South Africa have devoted attention to advocacy concepts and strategies, engagement in the budget presentation process in parliament, and preparation of responses to the draft budget; and youth conducting social audits in Kenya were expected to review project financial documents and bills of quantities, scrutinize community projects based on objectives and standards stipulated in the project documents and on feedback from project committees and project beneficiaries, and prepare reports on budget implementation practices.

Budget initiatives led by children and youth have utilized a range of pedagogical approaches to equip them with skills to engage in the budget process.

Awareness raising. In Ecuador, there was a significant focus on raising awareness and mobilizing interest among youth to engage in participatory budgeting through radio, television, and print media (including posters and flyers); camps; games; painting competitions; and neighborhood meetings organized by municipal agents, parents, school directors, and community leaders.

Games. In South Africa, children took part in treasure hunts to learn about budget books, did puzzles to understand their constitutional rights, and played the game *Jeopardy!* to learn about human-rights instruments.

Exposure visits. In República Bolivariana de Venezuela, an exposure visit to France was organized for a delegation of children and youth to help familiarize them with urban consultations. Similarly, a group of children from South Africa participated in a children's budget project run by Cedec (*Centro de Defesa da Criança e do Adolescente do Ceará*—Ceará Children's and Youth Defence Centre) in Fortaleza, Brazil.

Surveys. The Centre for Children's Rights at Queen's University, Belfast, led the development of a global survey to solicit the views of young people ages 10–18 on public spending to realize children's rights. In Ciudad Guyana, República Bolivariana de Venezuela, a survey of development priorities of over 4,000 school-going children and adolescents was conducted focused on five themes: school, home, the community, the neighborhood, and the city.

Primary field-based research. The Youth Budget Advocacy Group of Awutu-Senya District in Ghana planned community field trips to gather baseline empirical data on education, health, water, and social protection for young people; and youth social audit teams in Kwale, Kilifi, and Nairobi counties in Kenya have organized site visits to assess the relevance, cost-effectiveness, and quality of schools, health centers, and water services.

Feedback and validation meetings. Youth social audit teams have shared their audit findings in "feedback" meetings with stakeholders, including beneficiary communities and youth, which have informed detailed action plans on how to improve public services and facilities. In Ghana, youth groups have utilized validation meetings to share their initial data and findings on issues affecting children, such as education, health, water, and social protection.

Peer learning. Several youth-led budget initiatives have relied on peer learning and leadership to promote knowledge of public budgets, including peer facilitation of children's groups in South Africa; youth training of trainers on budget planning and tracking in Ghana; and the election of youth and child delegates for the cantonal congresses in Cotacachi, Ecuador.

Several beyond-school child and youth-led budget processes have resulted in a range of behavioral, process and policy outcomes that bode well for the application of budget literacy education and closing of the budget transparency feedback loop over progressive budget cycles.

For instance, the fact that some of the youth budget advocacy groups were later invited to participate in a civil society forum to provide inputs for the 2011 Ghana budget statement and the fact that Youth Council members in Kenya are now increasingly perceived as having the competence to contribute to their communities through social audit processes are clear manifestations of behavioral changes on the part of other stakeholders.

In Zimbabwe, the efforts of the Child Friendly National Budget Initiative contributed to the important process outcome of increasing budget allocations for the welfare of children—that is, from 2010 to 2011, budget allocations increased by 69 percent for the Ministry of Education, Sports, Arts and Culture and by 63 percent for the Ministry of Health. In Ecuador, after active engagement by youth and children in the cantonal congresses of Cotacachi in 2000, the municipal government allocated funds for child and youth participatory budgeting in subsequent years.

With regard to policy outcomes, in Nicaragua, the number of municipalities with child rights plans increased from seven municipalities in 2010 to 60 in 2011, with 30 of them also releasing a municipal policy for children. Moreover, inputs provided by young people for the report "Towards Better Investment in the Rights of the Child: The Views of Children" informed the adoption of the UN Human Rights Council resolution on better investments in children, which calls on states to make continuous efforts to sustain investments in children at the national and subnational levels and highlights the importance of child participation in budgetary processes.

Notes

1. The outline is available at http://www.cao.go.jp.
2. The council comprises MEXT, the Ministry of Internal Affairs and Communications, and the national tax agency.
3. As of May 1994, the tax education promotion councils at the prefectural level existed in all 47 prefectural and city governments; as of March 2011, there were 738 tax education promotion councils at the municipal level.
4. National Standards for Civics and Government. http://www.civiced.org/standards?page=912erica.
5. See http://taxcitizenship.tki.org.nz/Level-4-unit/Social-inquiry-overview-Level-4.
6. See http://schools.yrdsb.ca/markville.ss/history/economics/act11-1.sim.pdf.
7. See http://www.dekade-thueringen.de/media/public/pdfs/Planspiel_BHH.pdf.
8. This material was created by the Federal Centre for Political Education (*Bundeszentrale für politische Bildung*) in Germany in 2008. It was used in the framework of a 2008 "Young Politics" festival in Berlin.

9. See http://www.performance-publique.budget.gouv.fr/sites/performance_publique /files/files/flash/cyber-budget/minefi_start.swf.

10. This simulation game was created in 2007 by Paraschool for the Ministry of the Economy, Finances, and Industry in collaboration with the Budget Directorate.

11. See http://www.econedlink.org/lessons/index.php?lid=273&type=educator.

12. See http://taxcitizenship.tki.org.nz/Level-4-unit/Learning-experience-1-What-is -tax-for.

13. See http://www.edb.gov.hk/attachment/en/curriculum-development/kla/pshe/Econ %20C&A%20Guide_updated_e_20140212.pdf.

14. See http://www.edb.gov.hk/attachment/en/curriculum-development/kla/pshe/l&s _curriculum_guide_eng.pdf.

15. See http://www.teachitcitizenship.co.uk/index.php?CurrMenu=3439&resource=11503.

16. See http://www.teachitcitizenship.co.uk/index.php?CurrMenu=397&resource=12685.

17. See http://teachufr.org/admin/europe%E2%80%99s-debt-crisis.

18. See http://teachufr.org/admin/europe%E2%80%99s-debt-crisis; http://teachufr.org.

19. See http://www.nationalpriorities.org/budget-basics/educator-toolkit/peoples-guide -federal-budget/write-letter-your-congressperson.

20. See http://www.taxmatters.hmrc.gov.uk/Pdf/KS3_Citizenship_Lesson_Plan.pdf.

21. See http://www.singaporebudget.gov.sg/budget_2014/budgetquiz/quizwinners.aspx.

22. See http://www.pref.toyama.jp/sections/1107/sosuikyo.

23. See http://teachufr.org/admin/taxation-and-the-national-debt.

24. See http://www.tes.com/teaching-resource/tax-facts-teachers-pack-11075252.

25. See http://www.nta.go.jp/tokyo/shiraberu/gakushu/taiken/01.htm.

26. http://www.pref.toyama.jp/sections/1107/sosuikyo/.

27. See http://www.nhk.or.jp/syakai/10min_koumin/?das_id=D0005120357_00000.

28. See http://www.civix.ca/sbc/learn.

29. See http://www.civix.ca/sbc/debate.

30. See http://www.econedlink.org/interactives/index.php?iid=235&type=educator.

31. See http://www.econedlink.org/interactives/index.php?iid=182&type=educator.

32. See http://www.federalbudgetchallenge.org/budget_challenge/sim/budget_master.html.

33. See http://www.buildabetterbudget.org/?code=NPP.

34. See http://budgethero.publicradio.org/widget/widget.php.

35. See http://www.kowaldesign.com/budget/index.html.

36. See http://www.nationalpriorities.org/interactive-data/taxday.

37. See http://formula-d.co.za/IBP/GAME.

38. See http://www.mof.go.jp/kids/life/index.html.

39. See http://www.mof.go.jp/kids/index.php.

40. See http://www.iledefrance.fr/sites/default/files/mariane/RAPCP14-670RAP.pdf.

41. See http://www.berlin.de/imperia/md/content/bamarzahnhellersdorf/haushalt/ buergerhaushalt/2014_2015/flyer_kinder.pdf?start&ts=1346238863&file=flyer _kinder.pdf.

42. See http://www.facebook.com/misch.mit.mahell.

43. See http://buergerhaushalt.wordpress.com.
44. See http://www.bertelsmann-stiftung.de/fileadmin/files/BSt/Publikationen /GrauePublikationen/ZD_Schuelerhaushalt_Infobroschuere_2015.pdf.
45. See http://www.bertelsmann-stiftung.de/fileadmin/files/BSt/Publikationen /GrauePublikationen/ZD_Schuelerhaushalt_Handbuch_2015.pdf.
46. See MY Parliament is a civic engagement platform established so that youth can engage with governance and public policy processes with the aim of strengthening participatory democracy.
47. See http://indiabudget.nic.in/ub2015-16/bh/bh1.pdf.
48. See http://longtermnz.org/wp-content/uploads/20130131-Youth-Statement2.pdf.

References

Citizenship Foundation. 2013. "Youth Budget—Chance to Be Chancellor Evaluation 2012–13." Citizenship Foundation, London, U.K. http://www.youthbudget.org.

Dewey, John. 1963. *Democracy and Education*. New York: Macmillan.

Grillos, Tara. 2014. "Youth Lead the Change: The City of Boston's Youth-Focused Participatory Budgeting Process Pilot Year Evaluation." Harvard University, Boston, MA.

Mayo, Marjorie, and Alison Rooke. 2008. "Active Learning for Active Citizenship: Participatory Approaches to Evaluating a Programme to Promote Citizen Participation in England." *Community Development Journal* 43 (3): 371–81.

Pateman, Carole. 1970. *Participation and Democratic Theory*. Cambridge, MA: Cambridge University Press.

Republic of the Philippines. 2014. "K to 12 Senior High School Humanities and Social Sciences Strand—Philippine Politics and Governance." K to 12 Basic Education Curriculum for Philippine Politics and Governance, Department of Education. Republic of the Philippines, Manila, Philippines. http://www.deped.gov.ph/sites /default/files/HUMSS_Philippine%20Politics%20and%20Governance%20CG.pdf.

Schugurensky, D. 2006. "This is Our School of Citizenship': Informal Learning in Local Democracy." *Counterpoints* 249: 163–82.

CHAPTER 3

Lessons Learned

The practices presented in this review reveal that concerted approaches to mainstream budget literacy into primary and secondary school curricula are relatively recent and quite limited. However, a global trend of increasing fiscal transparency and accountability is resulting in expanding opportunities for citizens to participate in the budget cycle, and governments are increasingly recognizing the role and long-term benefits of budget literacy. Key lessons from this exercise that could be relevant to practitioners and project teams advocating for and integrating interventions promoting budget literacy—in or out of the classroom or beyond school—are summarized below.

Setting Strategic Objectives

Chart Clear Objectives for Imparting Budget Literacy Education

Clarity and foresight regarding the rationale for instruction supporting budget literacy are critical to emphasize its relevance to policy makers and educators, to identify entry points for strategically incorporating it without overburdening existing curricular frameworks, and to establish standards that make it possible to assess associated learning outcomes. Fiscal education programs in Latin America provide helpful examples because they identify distinct objectives, such as promoting fiscal consciousness; infusing values of public responsibility, honesty, solidarity, and cooperation; and monitoring public expenditures.

Emphasize Links between Budget Literacy and Public-Service Delivery

A number of curricula reviewed for this report allude to issues of economic inequality and social justice, but there is much room to hone in on the link between knowledge of public budgets and the effectiveness of service delivery as an overarching objective for classroom-based budget-literacy education. Out-of-classroom initiatives promoting budget literacy (for example, participatory budgeting) as well as beyond-school initiatives (for example, social audits) that recognize this link would help inform this dimension of budget literacy.

Incorporating Budget Literacy Education into School Curricula

Use Existing Subject Curricula as Entry Points to Teach Budget Literacy

The choice of subjects and corresponding budget-literacy content should be driven by the rationale for introducing budget-literacy education. If the goal is to emphasize civic aspects of budget literacy, then the citizenship curriculum from the United Kingdom (England only) or the social studies curriculum in Singapore might offer appropriate entry points. Economics curricula might be best suited to impart detailed and technical information about public budgets and economic policies (for example, Austria's geography and economics curriculum); life skills curricula might be best suited for highlighting tax obligations and explaining how to file taxes (for example, the contemporary society curriculum in Hong Kong SAR, China); and entrepreneurship programs may be best suited for anchoring budget literacy in a business context (for example, Ireland's business studies curriculum).

Adopt a Gradual, Tiered Approach to Educating Students about Public Budgets, Beginning in Primary School

This type of approach ensures that youth acquire the needed technical skills to analyze public budgets. For example, primary-school students might be introduced to budget literacy through stories, comics, or activity books on fiscal education. Students in the seventh and eighth grades may be exposed to more detailed information on the budget cycle, tax policy, and the importance of paying taxes. They may have increased access to budget-literacy materials, such as presentations, guidebooks, and booklets.

This approach has also been used successfully in beyond-school budget-literacy initiatives, such as the project on "Budget Monitoring within a Rights-Based Framework: Children Participating in Governance" in South Africa. Adult facilitators charged with teaching children about public budgets adopted the principle of building on what children already knew. For example, when adult facilitators wanted children to understand government budgets, they started by reflecting on pocket money or household budgets. Once there was a basic understanding of a concept, they built on this knowledge by changing the context. After children understood household budgets, opportunities were provided for them to visit community projects and interview staff to understand their organizations' budgets.

Continue to Rely on a Tiered Approach to Budget-Literacy Education during Secondary School

Rather than delve into an in-depth study of public budgets during the final years of secondary school, concepts related to public finance can be introduced in the upper-primary or lower-secondary curriculum, establishing the basis for a more in-depth study of economics, social sciences, and other subjects. From a pedagogical standpoint, a tiered approach is more likely to strengthen the acquisition of knowledge among students compared with studying budgets during only one level of school. For example, the curriculum in the Philippines includes budget-literacy elements as part of its social studies courses in lower-secondary school, as part of its economics and contemporary issues courses in junior high school, and as part of its applied economics and politics and governance courses in senior high school.

Emphasize Civic Competence and Technical Knowledge to Capture the True Essence of Budget Literacy

In the United States and Luxembourg, the curricular approach suggests that matters related to public budgets are out of the hands of everyday citizens. Students are not presented with ways they might influence the budget or voice their preferences. In Namibia, however, an emphasis is placed on individual responsibility to contribute to the state income and budget rather than on a critical analysis of state expenditures. A balanced approach that includes both components would be better.

Use Budget-Literacy Content to Convey Interesting Facts, Initiate Stimulating Discussions, and Pose Real-Life Challenges to Students

Budgets can seem boring; they rarely lend themselves to stimulating content, especially if limited to a presentation of public revenues and expenditures. But several curricula reviewed for this study have overcome these limitations. For example, to help students understand the government's budgetary constraints and choices, the life and society curriculum in Hong Kong SAR, China offers international comparisons, stressing the specifics of the government's tax policy. As part of New Zealand's social sciences curriculum, students design surveys to discover how people in the school or community feel about taxes and to conduct perception-based interviews with adults on taxes and tax use by the government. This is followed by class discussions and cross-comparisons. Guidelines for India's economics curriculum suggest that teachers acquaint students with the particulars of the national budget by asking them to watch the annual budget announcement on television and to participate in subsequent group discussions analyzing the impact of the budget on various sectors of the economy.

Developing Diverse Methods and Materials for Teaching and Assessing Budget Literacy

Use Instruction Methods That Make Learning about Public Budgets Relevant and Compelling for Students

Educators can draw on a range of pedagogical approaches and strategies that enable youth to identify with budget issues. For example, the online budget quiz launched by Singapore's Ministry of Finance is a fun and interactive learning opportunity to help students understand the national budget process, the country's economic, social, and tax policies, and budgetary measures. The quiz includes a series of weekly mini-quizzes, leading up to a final quiz in which

International Practices to Promote Budget Literacy • http://dx.doi.org/10.1596/978-1-4648-1071-8

participants with perfect scores compete with each other to earn prizes for themselves and for their schools. In Brazil, the Secretary of the Federal Budget has prepared a series of comics about public budgeting. Sofinha, the main character, learns about the public budget along with her family, friends, and classmates. The stories address budget-literacy topics, such as the public budget, budgetary law, the role of the Secretary of the Federal Budget, the oversight of public expenditures, and participation in the budget process. In Peru, the Youth Auditors program was established in 2010 by the General Comptroller's Office and the Ministry of Education to equip youth with social-auditing skills. To date, Youth Auditors have conducted more than 3,700 social audits for schools and other agencies. Their efforts have improved education and public infrastructure.

To the Extent Possible, Arrange for Students to Receive Feedback on Their Contributions to the Budget Process

Closing the feedback loop by responding to student suggestions can serve as an important incentive for learning about public budgets. Feedback is particularly important to experiential learning methods that rely on tools like participatory budgeting and student voting on public budgets. Youth benefit by witnessing the outcome of their contributions in the form of a new park or recreation center, for example, or by receiving acknowledgement and responses from policy makers, such as the minister of finance or members of Parliament. For example, every year, a group of Canadian youth participating in the Student Budget Consultations Program are given the opportunity to present a summary report to senior officials, such as the minister of state or the parliamentary secretary to the minister of finance, of the survey results on the federal budget priorities of high school students across the country.

Provide Learning Opportunities That Will Improve Confidence

While implementing the project on children's participation in budget monitoring in South Africa, adult facilitators trained and then served as reference points for young peer facilitators leading the trainings, thereby demonstrating their confidence in the children's abilities. Children's experiences from Zimbabwe's Child-Friendly National Budget Initiative convey that adults should be prepared to listen to young people and include them in decision-making processes so they can develop the confidence to learn and meaningfully engage in the budget process. In Nicaragua, the preliminary results of a diagnostic on adults' perception of children's capacity to participate in governance processes revealed that only five percent thought that children were able to say anything concrete or rational. Two years after the Network of Municipal Governments-Friends of Children started working with children to provide their inputs to the budget process, the results of a similar diagnostic analysis showed that 35 percent of adults believed that children had the required capacity to contribute to governance processes.

Adopt Assessment Approaches That Can Keep Pace with the Diversity of Materials and Pedagogical Approaches Being Used to Teach Budget Literacy

In addition to exams and quizzes, teachers can use tools such as participation, learning journals, oral presentations, poster designs, project learning, and field studies. These assessments can be implemented in groups, with teachers assessing students' generic skills, behavior, attitudes, and learning progress by observing how they collaborate, communicate, and get along with other students; how they exercise critical thinking skills; what attitudes they display in response to the views of others; and the factors they consider when evaluating different opinions.

A self-assessment element that would allow students to apply their acquired knowledge to teacher-assigned tasks and activities could also be introduced. After completing the activity, it would be helpful for students to reflect on their abilities and progress, using teacher feedback as a reference point for improvement. In addition, peer assessments can be useful in this regard, particularly for complex learning and teaching activities that require a division of labor such as role-play, project learning, and debating. Because each student is responsible for a particular role or task, they must collaborate with one another to complete the assigned task. These aspects can be reflected and evaluated in peer assessments, allowing students to learn from the observations and insights of their classmates.

Develop Pedagogical Materials That Can Accommodate Varying Levels of Budget-Literacy Knowledge Among Educators

Supporting budget-literacy materials should account for and build on the existing knowledge base among secondary-school teachers of subjects other than economics, since many educators are not familiar with budget literacy. For example, South Africa's mathematical literacy curriculum draws heavily on exercises that are based on actual national and subnational public budgets in order to assess the students' understanding of mathematics content. The business studies syllabus in Ireland also uses budget-literacy content as a bridge to connect basic financial literacy and business education for individuals and households. Some history curricula lesson plans in the United States explore budget legislation and proposals for dealing with long-term deficits and compare national debt trends with the national deficit.

Building Capacity to Promote Budget Literacy Education

Design Assessment Methods That Are Exclusive to Budget-Literacy Education

Because budget-literacy learning outcomes only constitute a subset of curricular priorities, it is difficult to assess whether or not approaches to systematize relevant instruction have been successful at inculcating the required knowledge, competencies, and values among youth. Based on objectives and standards for budget-literacy instruction at different levels of schooling for a variety of subjects, there is a clear imperative for research to inform the design and testing of assessment methods that are appropriate and—more importantly—exclusive to this topic.

International Practices to Promote Budget Literacy • http://dx.doi.org/10.1596/978-1-4648-1071-8

Collaborate with Relevant Stakeholders in the Design and Implementation of Measures for Strengthening Budget Literacy

Small-scale as well as more expansive efforts at the international, national, and subnational levels would benefit from this approach, and there are examples that attest to this. At the school level in Germany, for example, successful participatory budgeting relies on collaboration among teachers (for help with designing and facilitating the participatory-budgeting process); parents (for funding and in-kind support); administrators (for oversight of selected projects); and external advisors (for technical assistance and guidance). In Japan, the mainstreaming of tax education across all levels of schooling depends on continued support from the Ministry of Education, Culture, Sports, Science and Technology, the National Tax Agency, and Tax Education Promotion Councils at the national, prefectural and municipal levels, as well as other entities including the Ministry of Finance and the Board of Audit. At the international level, the EuroSocial Network has been instrumental in providing a platform for strengthening tax education in several Latin American countries, with a joint effort among the respective ministries of finance and education to promote awareness of tax obligations and effective budget management.

Explore Various Means of Providing Ongoing Support to Educators

In-class instruction techniques and materials for teachers should be complemented by online and printed resources for budget literacy education. For example, the United Kingdom's Citizenship Foundation finds that the impact of their budget-literacy training workshops for teachers could be improved by directly marketing them to school networks and by offering in-person and online options for receiving instruction. In the United States, Columbia University's Teachers College established the Understanding Fiscal Responsibility Network, a platform of websites created by teachers using the curriculum called "Understanding Fiscal Responsibility" to showcase budget-literacy content, post questions and activities, and allow students to respond in a variety of ways.

Evaluation Resources for the Chance to be Chancellor/ Youth Budget Program in the United Kingdom

*The following are questions asked of educators who have used the "**Paying for It**" resources and youth who have participated in the "**Chance to be Chancellor**" challenge. They were part of the assessment methodology for the 2012–13 evaluation of the Chance to be Chancellor/Youth Budget Program.*

Questions for Teachers about "Paying for It" Teaching Resources

General Questions

1. Do you teach *citizenship* as a subject? If *yes,*
   a. Are you aware of the new draft curriculum? If *yes,*
   b. What are your impressions of it?
   c. How do you feel about the inclusion of the subject of finance in the curriculum?
   d. What support would you find useful for implementing the curriculum?
2. For what subjects and in what classes did you use the *Paying for It* resources?
   a. Why were these subjects and classes selected?
   b. If you do not teach *citizenship* as a subject did you find the citizenship focus useful and relevant?
3. How do you source the resources you use?
   a. What formats are they in/which do you prefer?
   b. Do you use websites inside lessons?
4. Regarding some of the better teaching resources you use …
   a. What are their main strengths and how could they be improved?
   b. What is missing/where are the gaps?

5. What, if any, challenges do you face when teaching about economic and financial issues?
6. What types of economic and financial issues do you think are the most important and relevant to your students?

Paying for It

7. Which *Paying for It* resources have you used, if any?
   a. Did you used them to contribute to a scheme of work on the economy? *If you did not use any:* How could the Citizenship Foundation help you deliver such a scheme?
8. Lesson plans:
   a. Which lesson plans did you use (including teachers' notes)?
   b. Did you use the accompanying presentation slides?
   c. Which did you prefer and why?
   d. Which did you like least and why?
9. Chance to be Chancellor:
   a. Was it in conjunction with the lesson plans? *If not,* why not?
   b. The Citizenship Foundation is planning to develop whole class activities and a General Election 2015 version—are there any other ways we could develop it?
   c. How best can the Youth Budget be used as a follow up to the Chance to be Chancellor Challenge?
10. Chance to be Chancellor: How could we best support you in getting your students involved in Chance to be Chancellor?
11. How have you used the *Paying for It* website?
    a. How would you rate it?
    b. What would you like to see on it?
    c. Do you use the news and/or term newsletter?
    If yes:
    – How would you rate them?
    – How would you improve them?
    d. What other supplementary materials would you find useful?
12. The *Paying for It* website provides lesson plans, teacher training, regular e-newsletters, and news to address the subject of public finance through real life examples and develops economic awareness in curricula.
    a. How else could the Citizenship Foundation help you develop an economic awareness in the curriculum?
    – What other types of resources could we provide?
    – What other issues and topics could we cover?
13. Any last things you would like to say?

Questions for Chance to be Chancellor Participant Focus Groups
General Questions
1. We are interested in engaging young people online in economic issues. Thinking about your Internet use, do you …
   a. Visit youth-orientated websites?
   b. Visit websites covering social or political issues?
   c. Use social media to follow issues or political campaigns?
2. If the answer is *yes* to any of the above …
   a. What is it that you find appealing about them?
   b. How would you improve them?
3. Have you ever been involved in an initiative like Chance to Be Chancellor before?
   a. If *yes*, what did you enjoy and what did you dislike about it/them?
   b. If *no*, are you aware of any such programs?
4. Are the current economic challenges a concern to you and your friends?
   a. If *yes*, what are your main concerns?
5. Are the views of youth represented in the public debate about the U.K. economy?

Chance to be Chancellor
1. What did you enjoy about participating in Chance to be Chancellor?
2. How would you improve the program?
   a. Survey findings suggest that the most participants would like more opportunities to come up with their own ideas. How could this best be done?
3. How can we reach young people outside of school with the Chance to be Chancellor Program?
   a. How could we make better use of social media?
4. Did anyone here enter the video competition?
   a. If *yes*, how did you find it? What would you improve?
   b. If *no*, why not?
5. How can the Chance to be Chancellor and the Youth Budget programs better address the concerns of youth regarding the economy and encourage youth to participate in the public debate?

Pedagogical Resources for Primary School

Type of resource	Example	Country
Activity books	Coloring books: public places, school, hospital, Ministry of Finance, theater, museum, firemen *Source:* http://educa.hacienda.go.cr:8080/costarica_prod/index.php/pagina/17.html.	Costa Rica
	• We build a better country *Source:* https://issuu.com/dgii/docs/cartilla_construyamos_un_mejor_pa ___d66d0d6948f14d/0.	Dominican Republic
Interactive games	• Memotest *Source:* http://educa.hacienda.go.cr:8080/costarica_prod/uploads/juegos/memotest .html.	Dominican Republic
	• Granitos de maize • Melose de memoria • Dando y dando *Source:* http://portal.sat.gob.gt/culturatributaria/?page_id=222.	Guatemala
	• Finance roulette *Source:* http://www.mof.go.jp/kids/life/index.html.	Japan
	• People's pie *Source:* https://www.icivics.org/node/33765/resource.	United States
Posters/pictures	• Social change mural *Source:* http://portal.sat.gob.gt/culturatributaria/?wpfb_dl=87.	Guatemala
Resources for teachers	• Tax guide for primary schools *Source:* http://portal.sat.gob.gt/culturatributaria/?page_id=216. Lesson plans • "No Funny Money, Honey. … I Want the Real Thing!" *Source:* http://www.econedlink.org/teacher-lesson/460/. • "Who Pays for City Hall?" *Source:* http://www.econedlink.org/teacher-lesson/281/. • "Community Helpers are at Your Service!" *Source:* http://www.econedlink.org/teacher-lesson/454/. • "Clean Land-Thanks to us!" *Source:* http://www.econedlink.org/teacher-lesson/372/. • "TIC TAC Taxes!" *Source:* http://www.econedlink.org/lessons/index.php?lid=370&type=educator. • "Making Sense of the Census" *Source:* http://www.econedlink.org/teacher-lesson/410/. • "Free Ride" *Source:* http://www.econedlink.org/teacher-lesson/198/.	Guatemala United States

table continues next page

Type of resource	Example	Country
Storytelling	• Forest story of DanaHappy Blue BalloonThanks Guys *Source:* https://www.nta.go.jp/osaka/shiraberu/gakushu/dana/top.htm.	Japan
Television shows, clips, and songs	• Simon Tax Series *Source:* http://portal.sat.gob.gt/culturatributaria/?page_id=607. • Micos and Pericos television series *Source:* http://portal.sat.gob.gt/culturatributaria/?page_id=140.	Guatemala
Websites and web portals	• PlanetaSII portal *Source:* http://www.planetasii.cl/index.html.	Chile
	• Finance Land *Source:* http://www.mof.go.jp/kids/index.php. • Budget and Taxes • The Board of Audit of Japan Kids	Japan

Pedagogical Resources for Secondary School

Type of resource	Example	Country
Blogs	• Budget Matters Blog	United States
	• Understanding Fiscal Responsibility Blog	
Comic books and cartoons	• Sofinha and her Gang	Brazil
	• O Menino Quero Saber e o Professor Sabe tudo Sobre Educação Fiscal	
	• Choices	New Zealand
	• What's Tax?	
	• What's in it for Us?	
Crossword puzzles	• Economic Framework Crossword	Ireland
	• National Budget Crossword	
Datasets on public spending	• A Scuola di OpenCoesione	Italy
	• Budget Stories	Moldova
	• A Mi Penzünk	Hungary
	• Local Spending Data: Follow Tax Dollars in Your Community	United States
Glossaries, primers, and calendars	• Glossary	Canada
	• Taxpayer Calendar, June 2015	Dominican Republic
	• Tax Glossary	
	• Primer for New Citizens	Guatemala
	• The ABC of Taxes	
	• Tax Series	
	• Model Youth Parliament Primer on the Basics of the Budget	India
	• Q&A on Taxes and Finance	Japan
	• Tax Education Glossary	New Zealand
	• Inland Revenue Timeline	
	• Federal Budget Glossary	United States
	• Glossary of Common Terms	
	• Glossary	Uruguay

table continues next page

Type of resource	Example	Country
Interactive games	• Declaring My Taxes	Costa Rica
	• Somos Equipo	
	• Pictofrases Tax Culture	Dominican Republic
	• You formasílabas	
	• Sudoku Tax	
	• Word Search	
	• Online Simulator for Public Finances	France
	• CyberBudget Game	
	• Role-Playing Game-Deciding a Municipal Budget	Germany
	• Social Security VideoQuiz	United States
	• The Federal Budget Challenge	
	• Build a Better Budgets Game	
	• Budget Hero	
	• Budget Explorer	
	• Your Federal Income Tax Receipt	
	• Open Budgets Game	
	• People's Pie	
	• Visualize Your Taxes	
	• Detectivate Ivan vs. Evatrones	Uruguay
	• Invincible	
Interactive budget tools	• Local Spending Data	United States
	• Your Tax Receipt	
	• Faces of the Budget	
	• Build a Better Budget	
Online training courses and programs	• Entrepreneur's Skills Certificate	Austria
	• Model Youth Parliament-Online Policy Workshop Curriculum	India
Participatory-budgeting guides	• Participatory Budgeting Implementation Guide	France
	• Handbook for Schools to Implement Student Participatory Budgeting	Germany
	• Flyer on Youth Engagement in Participatory Budgeting	
	• Welsh Government Participatory Budgeting Toolkit	United Kingdom
PowerPoint® presentations	• The Federal Government's Budget	Canada
	• The Federal Government's Expenditures	
	• The Federal Government's Revenues	
	• International Comparisons	
	• Economic Framework	Ireland
	• National Budget	
	• Budget Taxation and Government Finances	
	• Role of the Government	
	• National Debt	
	• Government Finances	
	• Government and the Economy	United States
	• Taxation	
	• Government Spending	

table continues next page

Type of resource	Example	Country
Posters, graphics, and wordles	• Income Wordle	Ireland
	• Expenditure Wordle	
	• Budget Wordle	
	• Economic Framework Wordle	
	• National Budget Wordle	
	• Tax Expenditure Interactive Graphic	Uruguay
Quizzes, trivia, and surveys	• Political Spectrum Quiz	Canada
	• Budget Consultation Quiz	
	• Taxes Trivia	Dominican Republic
	• Economic Awareness Quiz	Ireland
	• Economics Quiz	
	• Tax Education and Citizenship Survey	New Zealand
	• Budget Quiz	Singapore
Resources for educators	• Teaching Guide for Seminar on Tax Culture	Guatemala
	• History of Taxation in Guatemala	
	• Guide for Educators	Canada
	• Past Exam Questions-Junior Cycle Business Studies	Ireland
	• Past Exam Questions: Taxation-Senior Cycle Economics	
	• Past Exam Questions: Economic Policy-Senior Cycle Economics	
	• Teaching Manuals on Taxation	Japan
	• Supplementary Teaching Materials	
	• Just-In-Time (JIT) Resource Package: Learning about Budget	Singapore
	• HM Revenue and Customs' Tax Fact Teachers Pack	United Kingdom
	• Citizenship Foundation's "Paying for It" Lesson Plans	
	• A People's Guide to the Federal Budget	United States
	• Educator Toolkit	
	• Lesson Plan: Government and the Economy	
	• Lesson Plan: Taxation	
	• Lesson Plan: Government Spending	
	• Lesson Plan: Where Does the Money Come From?	
	• Tax Time Scavenger Hunt	
	• What Do You Get for Your $1,818,600,000,000?	
	• Fiscal and Monetary Policy Process	
	• National Budget Simulation	
	• Why Cities Provide tax Breaks Even when they are Strapped for Cash	
	• The Role of Government: The Federal Government and Fiscal Policy	
Videos and webinars	• Introduction to the Budget	Canada
	• Videos: Overview, Expenditures & Revenues	
	• Developing the State Budget: How Does it Work?	France
	• Developing a Municipal Budget: How Does it Work?	
	• Video clips on taxation issues	Guatemala

table continues next page

Type of resource	Example	Country
	• Tax Education Classes	Japan
	• Web-TAX-TV	
	• Online introductory video: "what is tax for?"	New Zealand
	• National Priorities Project Video Library	United States
	• National Priorities Project Webinars	
	• UFR Tools: Video-Driven Discussion	
	• Budget Deficit and Public Debt	
	• Youth Participatory Budgeting	
	• Lectures on the state (of) pensions, environmental taxation and labor supply and taxes	United Kingdom
Television shows and media clips	• 10-minute-box (vol 9 and 10)	Japan
	• C-Span Classroom: Economics	United States
	• PBS Learning Media: Government Revenues and Spending	
Web portals	• Citizen Child: The Brazilian Office of the Comptroller General Children's Portal for Social Control	Brazil
	• Leãozinho (Little Lion) Website	
	• SIIEduca portal	Chile
	• Think about the Finance of Japan	Japan
	• You can be Dr. Tax, too	
	• Exciting City Tax Class	
	• Our Life and Taxes	
	• Hello! Let's Study Tax	
Worksheets and handouts	• Government All Around Worksheet	Canada
	• Government and Budgets Worksheet	
	• Government Expenditures Worksheet	
	• Government Revenues Worksheet	
	• What are the sources of government revenue?	Hong Kong SAR, China
	• Government expenditure in Hong Kong SAR, China	
	• The trend of public revenue and spending of the Hong Kong SAR, China government	
	• Comparison of tax rates	
	• Young People and Tax: Consequences	New Zealand
	• How does tax relate to the concept of economic decision making?	

Summary of Case Studies on School-Based Budget Literacy Initiatives

				Classroom-based initiatives		
#	Country	Level	Implementer(s)	Subject/program	Grade level/year and typical age range	Out-of-classroom initiatives
D1.1	Australia	National and subnational	Departments of Education of the States and Territories	Economics	• Grade 11 (ages 16–17) • Grade 12 (ages 17–18)	n.a.
D1.2	Austria	National	Federal Ministry of Education and Women's Affairs	Geography and Economics	• Grade 3 (ages 8–9) • Grade 7 (ages 12–13)	• The Entrepreneur's Skills Certificate® • Beste Bildung • Next Generation • Money and the Like
D1.3	Brazil	National, subnational, and local	Multiple state agencies	National Program of Fiscal Education	• Years 1–9 (ages 6–14) • Years 10–12 (ages 15–18)	• Leãozinho website • EasyBudget website • The Chamber of Deputies' budget website • Children's portal • Drawing and writing contest on ethics and citizenship • Citizen Child Day
D1.4	Canada	Subnational and local	Provincial Ministries of Education; CIVIX; Ridgeview School (Vancouver)	• Social Studies (British Colombia) • Social Studies (Manitoba) • Social Studies (Newfoundland and Labrador) • Economics (New Brunswick • Economics (Manitoba) • Essential Mathematics (Manitoba)	Grade 11 (ages 16–17) Grade 6 (ages 11–12) and Grade 9 (ages 14–15) Grade 11 (ages 17–18) Grade 12 (ages 17–18) Grade 12 (ages 17–18) Grade 12 (ages 17–18)	• CIVIX's Student Budget Consultation • School Participatory Budgeting in Vancouver
D1.5	Chile	National	Internal Revenue Service; Ministry of Education	Fiscal Education Program	Primary School—Years 1–8 (ages 6–13) Secondary School—Years 1–4 (ages 13–17)	Television series including The Debut of the Gang and The Adventures of Ivo the Chinchilla

table continues next page

#	Country	Level	Implementer(s)	Classroom-based initiatives		Out-of-classroom initiatives
				Subject/program	Grade level/year and typical age range	
D1.6	Costa Rica	National	Ministry of Finance; Ministry of Public Education	• Social Studies and Civics • Civics Education • Education for Everyday Life	• Grades 1–6 (ages 6–12) • Grades 7–12 (ages 13–18) • Grade 9 (ages 14–15)	Tribute to My Country Games Room
D1.7	Czech Republic	National	Ministry of Education, Youth, and Sports	• Man and Society • Man and the World of Work	Grades 8–9 (ages 13–15) and Grades 10–12 (ages 16–19)	n.a.
D1.8	Dominican Republic	National	Internal Revenue General Department	Fiscal Education Program	Primary School. Years 1–8 (ages 7–13) and Secondary School. Years 1–4 (ages 14–18)	n.a.
D1.9	Estonia	National	Ministry of Education and Research	• Social Sciences • Economic and Business Studies	• Grades 1–12 (ages 7–18) • Grades 10–12 (ages 16–18)	n.a.
D1.10	France	National and subnational	Ministry of Education; Ministry of the Economy, Finances, and Industry; regional councils	• Basic Principles of Economics and Administration • Economics • Sciences and Technologies of Management and Administration	• Grade 10 (ages 15–16) • Grade 11 (ages 16–17) • Grade 12 (ages 17–18)	School Participatory Budgeting
D1.11	Germany	Subnational and local	Regional education ministries and municipalities	• Economics (Baden-Württemberg) • Economics (Thüringen) • Economics (Bremen)	• Grade 10 (age 15) • Grades 11–12 (ages 16–17 years) • Grades 11–13 (ages 16–18 years)	School Participatory Budgeting

table continues next page

	Classroom-based initiatives			
#	Country	Level	Implementer(s)	Subject/program	Grade level/year and typical age range	Out-of-classroom initiatives

#	Country	Level	Implementer(s)	Subject/program	Grade level/year and typical age range	Out-of-classroom initiatives
				• Economics (Berlin)	• Grades 11–13 (ages 16–18 years)	
				• Economics (Hamburg)	• Grade 10 (age 15 years)	
				• Economics (Saarland)	• Grades 11–12 (ages 16–17 years)	
				• Economics (Schleswig-Holstein)	• Grades 7–8 (ages 12–13 years)	
				Economics and Law (Bayern)	• Grades 9–10 (ages 14–15)	
				• Social and Economic Sciences (Berlin)	• Grades 9–10 (ages 14–15)	
				• Economics and Social Sciences (Rheinland-Pfalz)	• Grades 9–10 (ages 14–15)	
				Economic Sciences (Brandenburg)	Grade 10 (age 15)	
				Social Sciences (Hessen)	Grade 7 (age 12)	
				Politics and Economics (Niedersachsen)	Grades 8 and 9 (ages 13–14)	
				Internal Revenue Service, Law, and Economics (Sachsen)	Grade 10 (age 15)	
D1.12	Guatemala	National and local	Tax Administration Department; Ministry of Education	Permanent Program of Tax Culture	• Primary School: Years 1–6 (ages 7–13) • Middle School: Years 1–3 (ages 13–16) • Secondary School: Years 1–2 (ages 16–18)	• Strength Lies in Numbers Annual Festival • Tax Dramas • Forums

table continues next page

				Classroom-based initiatives		
#	Country	Level	Implementer(s)	Subject/program	Grade level/year and typical age range	Out-of-classroom initiatives
D1.13	Hong Kong SAR, China	National	Education Bureau	• Life and Society • Economics	• Secondary Years 1–3 (age 12–14 years) • Secondary Years 4–6 (age 15–16 years)	n.a.
D1.14	India	National	National Council of Educational Research and Training; Model Youth (MY) Parliament	Economics	Grades 11–12 (age 16–18 years)	Model Youth Parliament
D1.15	Ireland	National	Educators as advised by the National Council for Curriculum and Assessment and the Professional Development Service for Teachers	• Business Studies • Business • Economics	Lower secondary school. Years 1–3 (ages 12–15 years) Upper-secondary school. Years 1–2 (ages 16–18)	n.a.
D1.16	Japan	National/provincial/local	Ministry of Education, Culture, Sports, Science and Technology; Ministry of Finance; National Tax Agency; Board of Audit; Cabinet Secretariat; Japan Broadcasting Corporation; Tax Education Promotion Councils	• Internal Revenue Service • Civics • Commerce	Primary School. Grades 5–6 (ages 11–12 years) and Junior High School. Grades 1–3 (ages 12–15 years) High School. Grades 1–3 (ages 16–18 years)	• Finance Land website • Study tours and tax-education classes • Poster and essay contests about taxes • Hello Tax Quiz
D1.17	Luxembourg	National	Ministry of National Education, Childhood, and Youth	Economics	Grade 11 (ages 18–19 years)	n.a.
D1.18	Namibia	National	Ministry of Education	• Economics • Life Skills	• Grades 11–12 (ages 18–19 years) • Grades 8–10 (ages 14–15 years)	n.a.

table continues next page

71

#	Country	Level	Classroom-based initiatives		Out-of-classroom initiatives
			Subject/program	Grade level/year and typical age range	
D1.19	New Zealand	National	Ministry of Education; New Zealand Treasury	• Social Sciences • Economics	• Years 7–10 (ages 13-15 years) • Years 11–13 (ages 17–19 years)	• Essay contests • Policy Workshops • Visits and Lectures with the Treasury Department
D1.20	Peru	National	National Tax Administration Office; Ministry of Education; General Comptroller's Office	Tax Culture Program	Grades 1–6 (ages 6–12 years) and Grades 7–12 (ages 13–18 years)	• Payment Receipt Raffle • Youth Auditors
D1.21	Philippines	National	Department of Education; Philippines Center for Civic Education and Democracy	• Economics • Contemporary Issues • Applied Economics • Politics and Governance	Grades 7–10 (ages 12–15 years) Grades 11–12 (ages 16–17 years)	• Civic Education Training Seminar • Project Citizen
D1.22	Poland	National	Ministry of Education, Youth and Sport	• Civics • Basics of Entrepreneurship	• Lower secondary school. Years 1–3 (ages 13–16 years) and Upper secondary school. Years 1–3 (ages 16–19 years) • Upper secondary school. Years 1–3 (ages 16–19 years)	• Educational program on taxes and state funding of basic activities • School Participation Project
D1.23	Singapore	National	Ministry of Education; Ministry of Finance	• Social Studies • Economics	• Grades 9 and 10 (ages 15–17 years) • General Certificate of Secondary Education (ages 13–17 years) and General Certificate of Education Advanced Level (ages 17–19 years)	n.a.

table continues next page

				Classroom-based initiatives		
#	Country	Level	Implementer(s)	Subject/program	Grade level/year and typical age range	Out-of-classroom initiatives
D1.24	South Africa	National	Ministry of Basic Education	• Economics and Management Sciences • Mathematical Literacy • Economics	• Grade 8 (age 13–14 years) • Grades 10–12 (ages 16–18 years) • Grade 10 (ages 15–16 years)	n.a.
D1.25	United Kingdom	National/subnational/ local	Department of Education; Oxford, Cambridge and RSA (OCR); HM Revenue and Customs; Citizenship Foundation	• Citizenship/Citizenship Studies • Economics	• Grades 7–11 (ages 11–16 years)/ General Certificate of Secondary Education (ages 11–16 years) • General Certificate of Secondary Education (ages 11–16 years) and General Certificate of Education Advanced Level (ages 16–18 years)	Chance to be Chancellor/Youth Budget Initiative
D1.26	United States	National, subnational, and local	Teachers College Columbia University; National Council for the Social Studies; Council for Economic Education; iCivics; City of Boston–Department of Youth Engagement and Employment	• Civics and Government • Economics	• Grades 9–12 (ages 14–18 years) • Grade 12 (ages 17–18 years)	Boston's "Youth Lead the Change" Participatory Initiative
D1.27	Uruguay	National	General Tax Directorate of the Ministry of Economy and Finance; the Ministry of Education and Culture	Civics and Social Education	Secondary School. Years 1–3 (ages 12–16 years)	• Tax Education Portal • Video Games Contest

Note: n.a. = not applicable.

D1.1 Australia

Country: Australia
Level: National and Subnational
Implementers: Departments of Education of the States and Territories

Context

In Australia, the Curriculum Assessment and Reporting Authority is responsible for developing the national curriculum, called "Foundation Year to Year 10," but states and territories are responsible for its implementation (ACARA n.d.; NCEE 2013).[1] Echoing the 2011 National Consumer and Financial Literacy Framework, the curricula (ASIC 2011) crafted by the states and territories primarily emphasize consumer and financial literacy among students, but some components of the *humanities and social sciences* and the *mathematics* curricula relate to budget literacy as well. The overall purpose of teaching budget-literacy content is for students to develop the necessary knowledge, understanding, skills, values, and attitudes necessary to engage in competent, effective, and socially responsible thinking and decision making around economics (Board of Studies NSW 2009).

A number of classes at the primary- and lower-secondary-school levels pave the way for a more thorough understanding of public budgets during senior-secondary school. In the *humanities and social sciences*, this aim is served by the curricula for *civics and citizenship* (ACARA 2012b) and *economics and business* (ACARA 2012a). During year 4, the *civics and citizenship* curriculum builds student knowledge and understanding of the government and democracy by exploring the benefits and services provided by local governments, including libraries, parks, health services, environmental protection, and waste disposal. In the sixth year, students are introduced to the roles and responsibilities of the three levels of government under Australia's federal system, demonstrating the interrelated nature of *economics and business* through four overarching and interconnected key ideas: resource allocation and making choices, consumer and financial literacy, enterprising behaviors and capabilities, and work and business environments. Budget literacy is covered in *mathematics* courses in years 5–11 (SACE Board of South Australia 2016). The section on *money and financial math* is taught with a specific focus on personal finances. In some states and territories, the bulk of budget-literacy content is in the *economics* curricula for years 11 and 12.

Classroom-Based Budget-Literacy Initiatives

Youth are introduced to the subject of public finances in years 11–12. Relatively sparse information is available on public budgets in the curricula for Queensland, South Australia, and the Northern Territory,[2] but Tasmania, Victoria, Western Australia, and New South Wales devote a significant part of their curricula to budget-literacy education under the *economics* framework (Board of Studies NSW 2009).

Curriculum

In Tasmania's 2010 curriculum, budgets are presented in a module on *government objectives and policy* (TQA 2010). In Victoria's 2009 *economics* curriculum (currently being revised—the new course will be implemented in 2017), budgets are featured in the fourth unit, which reviews *economic management*, including four weeks of instruction about *budgetary policy*. The Western Australian curriculum, which dates back to 2008 and was updated in 2013, is structured into sections, with the first unit introducing personal economics and finance, the second covering macroeconomics, and the third exploring economic policies and management. Together, these units help students understand public budgets (SCSA 2014a). In the 2011 curriculum for New South Wales, 20 percent (24 hours) of the preliminary course on economics is dedicated to the topic of *government in the economy* (Board of Studies New South Wales).[3]

Learning Outcomes

Tasmania. Students should be able to describe key facts and concepts about Australia's economic system and to use, interpret, and make connections between economic terms and concepts to describe the economic system in detail (TQA 2010).

Victoria. After completing the *economic management* unit, students are required to be able to explain the nature and operations of government macroeconomic policies, explain the relationship between budgetary and monetary policy, and analyze how policies can be used to achieve key economic goals and improve living standards (VCCA 2014).

Western Australia. Students are introduced to ways that the government can affect the allocation of resources and economic activities by targeting economic objectives through its taxing and spending powers (unit 2: *macroeconomics*). They learn how to make informed predictions about economic policies using economic models and past and current economic data (unit 3: *economic policies and management*). Students learn to apply this knowledge in developing a critical perspective on the role of current economic policies in the government policy mix (unit 3) (SCSA 2014b).

New South Wales. Students are expected to be able to examine economic issues and understand the need for government interventions in a market economy; evaluate the impact of taxes on the distribution of income and the allocation of resources in the economy; investigate sources of revenue for governments; apply economic skills to determine whether a specific tax is progressive, proportional, or regressive; interpret federal budget data; predict the impact of a budget deficit or surplus on economic activities; and discuss the impact of monetary and fiscal policies (Board of Studies NSW 2009).

International Practices to Promote Budget Literacy • http://dx.doi.org/10.1596/978-1-4648-1071-8

Content

Tasmania. Key budget-literacy content includes defining *fiscal policy*; exploring the role of automatic stabilizers (for example, welfare payments and progressive taxes) recognizing the impact of different budget outcomes on aggregate demand, and understanding the strengths and weaknesses of fiscal policy instruments (TQA 2010).

Victoria. Content on public budgets describes the nature and operations of budgetary policy (for example, the level and composition of government receipts and expenditures), the role of automatic and discretionary stabilizers, methods of financing a budget deficit or using a budget surplus, and the relationship between monetary and budgetary policy in the management of aggregate demand (VCCA 2014).

Western Australia. The first unit of the *economics* curriculum links personal budgets and the role of government by looking at each in turn and examining how government affects personal finances, notably by providing income support (welfare payments), by taxing individuals, and by supporting long-term personal investments. The second unit explores the role of government more deeply, describing the types of taxes; the size of the government sector in the Australian economy; and the composition of government revenue and spending at the national, state, and local levels. The third unit examines monetary and fiscal policies and how the government can use them to pursue specific economic policy objectives. Australia's recent fiscal policy approaches are also discussed (SCSA 2014b).

New South Wales. The *economics* curriculum discusses the budget process, types of budgets (surplus, balanced, and deficit), and revenues and expenditures in the context of introducing the economic functions of the Australian government. The curriculum notes the influence of various stakeholders on government policies, such as political parties, businesses, labor unions, welfare agencies, and the media (Board of Studies NSW 2009).

Pedagogical Approach

Teaching budget-literacy concepts is part of a broad pedagogical approach to foster knowledge of the Australian economic and political system. It seeks to integrate budget literacy into the curriculum rather than conveying it through separate, external programs.

This approach is also characterized by the use of contemporary examples, issues, and events that make budget concepts relevant to students, facilitating their learning. In South Australia's curriculum, one assignment in an *economics*[4] course requires students to put themselves in the shoes of the Australian treasurer and make a reasoned choice among a range of suggested policies to encourage economic recovery, including budget cuts and tax increases. This exercise encourages students to directly identify with government policy makers. In Victoria's *economics* curriculum, a range of teaching methods are being used including:

- Simulating the type of decision making required when the Treasury Department meets to advise the treasurer on preparations for the commonwealth's annual budget.
- Investigating policy changes announced for the commonwealth's current budget and outlining how these changes could affect key economic goals.
- Convening a summit to review Australia's tax policies and recommending changes to the government based on the deliberations. Students must consider aspects such as the suitability of the current tax mix and the use of tax policy to achieve the goals of equity, sustainability, and economic growth.

Lessons Learned
- Fiscal and monetary policy are often linked or jointly presented in curricula as complementary levers of government action (for example, in Tasmania).
- The use of contemporary issues and events in the teaching and learning program significantly increases understanding among students and enables them to apply their knowledge across a broad range of contexts.

D1.2 Austria

Country: Austria
Level: National
Implementer: Federal Ministry of Education and Women's Affairs

Context

The motivation behind including budget literacy in the Austrian school curriculum is to equip students with sound skills in economics. Students are expected to understand fundamental economic interdependencies at the national and international levels from the perspective of business entities, as well as macroeconomic mechanisms, structures, and challenges. Economic policy is an essential part of politics, and students are expected to learn how to assess economic models and their implementation in diverse contexts.

Classroom-Based Budget-Literacy Initiatives

Budget literacy is taught at the national level as part of the third-grade (ages 8–9) and seventh grade (ages 12–13) *geography and economics* course. There were 83,224 students in the third grade and 98,093 students in the seventh grade in Austria in 2013–14.[5]

Curriculum

The third-grade *geography and economics* curriculum, which dates back to 2004,[6] focuses on the interaction between production and consumption, offer and demand, mechanisms of price formation, private sector and national economic processes, and how they are at the center of questions regarding markets and economic circles. In seventh grade, budget literacy is addressed in a module on *macroeconomics and economic and social policy*.

Learning Outcomes

During third grade, students are expected to learn basic economic concepts relevant to private households and financial planning. Students are exposed to macroeconomic concepts and learn about the fundamental relationships and interdependencies of market economies and market processes. Using practical examples, they learn to recognize how the public sector influences the economy and how political and structural measures, notably those in cooperation with the European Union (EU), foster regional development.

The desired learning outcome for seventh grade is for students to comprehend the specificities of Austria's economic and social policy. Using the budget, they should be able to discuss and analyze the government's economic and sociopolitical objectives and formulate conflicting objectives and positions regarding economic policy. Data literacy is also enhanced because students learn to determine how key economic data is computed and can assess its relevance.

Content

In the third grade, students are introduced to content about private household economies and Austria's economic relations with the rest of Europe. Lessons about private households include *financial planning, consumer protection in a market economy*, and the *advantages to customers of a common EU currency*. Topics addressing Austria's economic position include the public sector's influence over the economy and strengthening cooperation with the EU with regard to economic policy making.

In the seventh grade, students focus on the general objectives of economic policy and the "magic square"—a model that illustrates the main goals of economic policy to maintain stable prices, high employment rates, balanced foreign trade, and economic growth. Other topics include fiscal and tax policies, social policy, and the effectiveness of Austria's policy instruments.

Pedagogical Approach

Budget literacy is part of a broader framework for familiarizing students with politics, economics, and society. The pedagogical approach that has been adopted seems to be primarily a textbook one, although budget documents from the Ministry of Finance are also being used in the classroom, and teachers are encouraged to use didactic games, online tools, projects, and case studies.[7]

Out-of-Classroom Budget-Literacy Initiatives

The *Entrepreneur's Skills Certificate*®[8] is an online training program created by the Bit Media Group for the Austrian Federal Economic Chamber. The University of Economics in Vienna, the Ministry of Education, educators, and representatives from the private sector were involved in the design of its content. This voluntary course offers a supplementary qualification beginning in the eighth grade. It is assessed through standard, online examinations and culminates in a certificate that is recognized across Europe.

Module A, which students can begin in the eighth grade, covers fundamental economic concepts and relationships. Modules B and C are usually offered to upper-level secondary-school students (ages 14–19). They address budgets, national finances, and the basics of business administration. The fourth module, Module UP, covers taxation (value-added tax, income tax, corporate tax, tax returns, and so forth), personnel (costs, taxes, payroll, social security) and other aspects related to accounting, financing and marketing and commercial law. Each module concludes with an examination, and the final module concludes with a board examination. Students who pass the four examinations do not have to take the otherwise required entrepreneur's examination for regulated crafts and trades[9].

Pedagogical Approach

An introduction to public budgets is presented as part of an overall approach to teaching about entrepreneurship with a focus on taxes, the key functions of the state, debt, and external budget constraints. Didactic materials are provided through an online training program. Students are issued a certificate after they successfully complete the four modules.

Outcomes

The *Entrepreneur's Skills Certificate* was offered at 254 schools across Austria during the 2013–14 school year. The program's flexible structure allows students to study the first module as early as in lower-secondary school, and to complete the remaining modules in upper-secondary school. As of January 2014, students had taken more than 45,000 module examinations in Austria. The final module, called "UP" can be studied at an adult learning institution after a student finishes school[10].

This certificate has been translated and adapted in Germany, France, the Czech Republic, Albania, Kosovo, Mali, and Ethiopia. Tens of thousands of students are trained and certified every year in Austria, Germany, France, and the Czech Republic.

Another initiative led by the Federation for Austrian Industries is *Beste Bildung*,[11] which calls for agreed-upon standards for graduates of all upper-secondary schools on a basic understanding of economics (*wirtschaftliches Grundverständnis*) and the fundamentals of science, technology, engineering, and mathematics.

Next Generation[12]—a business plan competition led by the Ministry of Education and Women's Affairs, is aimed at two categories of upper-secondary students. Between the ages of 14–17, students are expected to develop an idea for a business start-up that draws on cost calculations and other economic literacy concepts. Students ages 17–19 prepare complete business plans, including detailed marketing and financial arrangements.

Finally, a number of private banks are active in fostering financial literacy among youth. One initiative that includes teaching materials on budgetary issues is called *Money and the Like* (*Geld und so*). Launched by Erste Bank, it provides teachers with media excerpts, cartoons, worksheets, and exercises to familiarize students with budgetary issues ranging from the budget process to spending priorities, the Austrian budget, state debt, and European public debt.

Lessons Learned

Curriculum

The Austrian curriculum places an emphasis on demonstrating interdependencies (for example, between the national and the regional levels) and the conflicting objectives of various interest groups with regard to economic policy design. The curriculum also highlights how budget repartition is fundamentally a political exercise involving various interest groups and conflicting priorities.

The Entrepreneur's Skills Certificate

E-learning offers new opportunities for scaling-up the program across schools, regions, and even countries. These opportunities are not confined to students—they can also be accessed by adults.

D1.3 Brazil

Country: Brazil
Level: National, Subnational and Local
Implementers: Multiple State Agencies

Context

Brazil's 2015 Open Budget Survey score of 77 percent on transparency and 71 percent on public participation demonstrates that the public has access to a substantial amount of budget information and ample opportunities to engage in the budget process.[13]

Education in Brazil is regulated by the Cabinet of Brazil through the Ministry of Education, which defines the guiding principles for organizing educational programs. Local governments are responsible for establishing state and educational programs that follow guidelines issued by the Ministry of Education, using federal government funding. As of 2010, primary education has a duration of nine years for children aged 6–14 years, and secondary education is for a period of three years for students aged 15–18 years. Primary education is compulsory and free at public institutions. Although preprimary and secondary education are not compulsory, they are also available for free at public institutions. Higher or university education in Brazil is divided into two levels: undergraduate and graduate.[14]

Instruction in support of budget literacy among youth is featured as part of the *Programa Nacional de Educação Fiscal* (PNEF), a national program for fiscal education.

Classroom-Based Budget-Literacy Initiatives
National Program of Fiscal Education

PNEF is supported by multiple government agencies in Brazil to promote and institutionalize fiscal education. Established in 1999, its objectives are to create awareness among citizens regarding the socioeconomic functions of taxes, share knowledge regarding public administration issues, create incentives for citizens to engage in the oversight of public resources, and foster an environment that encourages collaboration between citizens and the government.

PNEF is the result of a joint collaboration among several agencies. The Ministry of Finance, by means of the School of Finance Administration-Escola de Administração Fazendária (ESAF), coordinates the PNEF. At the federal level, the programme partners are the Brazilian Federal Revenue Service and the National Treasury Secretariat (Ministry of Finance), the House of Representatives, the Ministries of Education and of Social Welfare, the General Comptroller's Office and the Ministry of Planning, Budget and Management (Federal Budget Secretariat). At the state and municipality levels, the Departments of Education and of Treasury participate in the program.[15]

The PNEF program has five modules that can be adopted by public institutions at the national, subnational, or local level and tailored to their context. The first module, aimed at elementary school students, introduces the basic concepts of fiscal education. These concepts are explored in further detail in the second module, aimed at secondary-school students. The third module is intended to create awareness among public officials of the PNEF program. The fourth module is geared toward college or university students. The fifth module seeks to increase the awareness of civil society organizations and citizens.[16]

Comic Books for Children—Sofinha and Her "Gang"

Based on the understanding that most citizens have difficulty comprehending information about public budgets, the Federal Budget Secretariat developed a comic book series about public budgeting, presented in straightforward language that can be understood even by elementary school students. The main character *Sofinha*, along with her family, friends, and classmates, learns about public budgets. The stories address budget-literacy issues such as the public budget, budgetary law, the role of the Federal Budget Secretariat, the oversight of public expenditures, and participation in the budget process.[17]

A concerted effort was made to popularize this material during meetings with educators and students in the cities of San Sebastian and Recanto das Emas, including a launch event in December 2008, the "First Meeting on Fiscal Education in the Public Schools of the Federal District: Citizens Budget"; national and regional seminars on the public budget; and other meetings and technical visits involving representatives from the Federal Budget Secretariat. Since 2009, about 450,000 copies of the Portuguese version of this material have been distributed in the states of Alagoas, Bahia, Minas Gerais, Roraima, Piauí, Pernambuco, Santa Catarina, Paraná, Amazonas, and the Federal District. More than 70,000 copies of the Spanish, English, and German versions of the materials have been distributed, based on the requirements of states and educators (Ministry of Planning, Budget and Management n.d.).

Virtual School

The Federal Budget Secretariat continues to promote budget-literacy education among public officials and citizens through e-learning courses such as the *basic public budget*, the *public budget and federalism*, and *mentoring and monitoring*.

The *basic public budget* course describes laws, rules, concepts, techniques, and principles that govern the public budget throughout the budget cycle and highlights the importance of popular participation in the management of public resources. The more advanced course on *public budgets* mainly focuses on budget management. Another course offers guidelines on *municipal budget law*, featuring information on drafting municipal- and local-level public budgets.

Table D.1 illustrates the increasing levels of enrollment in the Federal Budget Secretariat's virtual school since 2008.

Courses on institutional strategic planning, performance indicators, and integrated planning and budgets are currently being designed by the Secretariat of the Federal Budget.

Table D.1 Student Enrollment in the Federal Budget Secretariat's Virtual School

Course	2008	2009	2010	2011	2012	2013	2014	2015 (1st Semester)	Total
Basic public budget	–	–	–	1,728	29	1,476	1,653	3,554	8,440
Public budget	50	971	935	663	225	1,907	1,556	1,275	6,026
Development of law on budgetary guidelines	–	–	–	527	–	–	976	1,848	3,351
Federalism	–	–	–	–	–	–	282	1,041	1,323
Ethics and public service	–	–	–	–	–	–	777	1,161	1,938
Total	50	971	935	2,918	254	3,383	3,688	8,879	21,078

Source: Ministry of Planning, Budget and Management n.d.
Note: – = data not available.

Citizen-Centric Budget Publications

Efforts by the Federal Budget Secretariat to prepare citizen-centric budget publications are based on an understanding that increased knowledge of public finances among citizens is useful for improving the preparation and implementation of public budgets and strengthening social control over the use of public resources. Since 2010, the *Federal Budget for Everyone* magazine (renamed *Citizens Budget* in 2014) is distributed alongside the *Annual Proposal of the Budget Law*. Its simplified magazine format features photos and graphics that make it easy to read (Ministry of Planning, Budget and Management n.d.).

The *Citizens Budget* has three sections. The first outlines the budgeting process, including the actors involved and the deadlines for each stage of the budget process. The second, called "Large Numbers of the Budget," presents aggregate information on macroeconomic projections, primary results and goals, social security systems, and personnel expenses and related charges. The third part features policy highlights and associated budget forecasts for the subsequent year. An electronic version of the magazine was launched in 2012, which included links to more detailed information, such as the annual plan for public debt financing, relevant budget legislation, and underlying budget data for each state as well as the federal district.

Sao Paulo's Fiscal Education for Citizenship Program

Sao Paulo is one among several states in Brazil participating in PNEF in order to strengthen budget-literacy education. The Education Secretariat and the National Treasury Secretariat for Sao Paulo collaborated to design and implement the Fiscal Education for Citizenship Program, which aims to engage with students, public officials, and tax-paying citizens to promote and institutionalize learning about fiscal issues.

As part of its efforts to improve the program's outcomes, the National Treasury Secretariat and the Education Secretariat of Sao Paulo have taken steps to mainstream fiscal education into school curricula at the primary and secondary levels. Teachers at selected schools have been provided with training on topics such as fiscal education and the new vision of the school curriculum; the economic, social, and fiscal indices of Brazil and the state of Sao Paulo; sources of public money; and prioritizing public expenditures. Trained teachers are responsible for disseminating materials and relaying fiscal education to their colleagues and students.

Through Sao Paulo's *the Treasury Goes to School* program, members of the National Treasury Secretariat visit schools and share information about fiscal education with the goal of creating awareness among students and teachers regarding the social function of taxes and encouraging a critical approach regarding the use of public resources and voluntary compliance with fiscal obligations. Its *Open Treasury* program is intended to introduce primary-, secondary-, and tertiary-level students to the National Treasury Secretariat. It organizes lectures on fiscal education issues, which are followed by field trips to the secretariat's offices. Students are familiarized with the National Treasury Secretariat's operations and participate in a hands-on learning experience to help them understand how public money is administered.

Rio de Janeiro's Fiscal Education Course
The State of Rio de Janeiro has created a fiscal education course focused on primary- and secondary-level students (grades 1–9). It is embedded in the basic education curriculum and is geared toward increasing citizen participation around the use, control, and oversight of public resources, with the goal of improving social and economic development. Its content includes the public budget, the origin and allocation of resources, tax laws, the relationship between state and society, the role of tax authorities, and oversight of public funds.

Ethics and Citizenship Program
The Office of the Comptroller General's Secretariat of Transparency and Corruption Prevention has launched the *Education Action for Ethics and Citizenship* program—a set of initiatives promoting active citizenship and public participation in the monitoring of public finances. It includes the voluntary school program—*One for All and All for One! For Ethics and Citizenship!*

In 2009, the Office of the Comptroller General partnered with the Maurício de Sousa Institute to develop didactic materials for elementary school students that were subsequently piloted in select public schools. The famous cartoon characters of the well-known Brazilian cartoonist Mauricio de Sousa were brought together under the brand *Monica's Gang* to engage students, teachers, families, and communities to reflect on issues related to the oversight of public resources exhibitions, lectures, and other activities. Distance training is organized for teachers participating in the program to help them conduct relevant classroom activities for their students. Materials produced for this program include teacher guides; student notebooks with exercises, texts, questionnaires, surveys, and activities; cartoons about participatory democracy and budget monitoring; posters and flyers; crosswords; coloring pages; connect-the-dots pages; mazes; memory games; and board games.

Between 2009 and 2014, the *One for All and All for One! For Ethics and Citizenship!* program was voluntarily implemented in 1,600 public schools, involving 400,000 students and 13,000 teachers. A program evaluation revealed that 100 percent of the students enjoyed participating in the program; 97 percent of the schools were glad they participated; and 96 percent of teachers thought the program achieved its goals.

Out-of-Classroom Budget-Literacy Initiatives
Pedagogical Approaches and Materials

Leãozinho Website. As part of its support for PNEF, the Internal Revenue System of the Ministry of Finance launched the *Leãozinho* (little lion) website in 2002, aimed at creating interest and awareness of social and fiscal control issues among youth ages 7–14. The stories take place at the school, the library, the park, and the movie theater, among other places, demonstrating to students that fiscal education can be fun and interesting.[18]

EasyBudget Website. The Brazilian senate's *EasyBudget* website presents 2–3 minute explanatory videos on topics such as the national budget, multiannual budgeting plans, and details on year-by-year amendments to the budget and the legal framework.[19]

The Chamber of Deputies' Budget Website.[20] Aimed at youth, this site explains the public budget, the budget process, and concepts related to public finance. From a pedagogical point of view, it introduces budgeting plans at the family level, then moves on to city, provincial, and state levels. Key issues, such as the relevance of the public budget to individuals, budgetary law and related legislation, and the participatory-budgeting process are explored. An online budget game challenges young players to put themselves in the mayor's shoes and spend public funds in accordance with the public's wishes.

Children's Portal. The Office of the Comptroller General's web portal on *citizenship and public oversight*[21] was launched in 2008 in partnership with the United Nations Office on Drugs and Crime. Geared toward children ages 6–12, the portal addresses civics-related topics, such as the differences between the executive, legislative, and judicial branches of government. It allows youth to participate in monitoring activities, such as the quality of school meals. It adopts a fun and dynamic approach to attract its target audience, including comic characters and educational games. There is also a dedicated pedagogical space offering resources to teachers.

Drawing and Writing Contest on Ethics and Citizenship. The Brazilian Office of the Comptroller General has organized a series of drawing and writing contests on topics such as *ethics, citizenship,* and *participation.* The 2015 contest theme was "Petty Corruption—Say No." Prizes are awarded to students, teachers, and schools; a collection of the best works is published annually. More than one million students have participated in this competition since it began in 2007.[22]

Citizen Child Day. The Office of the Comptroller General, in partnership with the Amazonian Protection System Office, organized "Citizen Child Day" during the same week that "Children's Day" is celebrated in Brazil, with the aim of involving children in the debate on ethics, citizenship, and the fight against corruption. By participating in activities such as storytelling workshops, computer games, dance, and artwork, children learned important lessons on being good citizens in an engaging way. The first Citizen Child Day convened more than 600 children on one day in October 2008, but due to the costs and logistics involved, this initiative has been discontinued.

Lessons Learned
- The chamber of deputies and senate websites explore budget processes and legal frameworks in detail, suggesting that it is important to inform students about the actors involved in budget decision making and the national rules and guidelines regulating the process.
- The efforts of the Office of the Comptroller General in this area indicate that the strong leadership of one state agency, combined with thoughtful design, can significantly raise youth awareness about specific issues. Importantly, the activities implemented include a teacher-training component and an outcome evaluation—cornerstones to building solid programs that advance budget literacy.
- Many of the materials developed in Brazil create a personal link between content and the story of every student. For instance, the notebooks designed as part of the "One for All and All for One! For Ethics and Citizenship!" program accompanies the student throughout the school year. Students can collect all the information received in class discussions, research, activities, interviews, and community experiences. There is space for drawings, photographs, and answers to open-ended questions, where students can express their personal tastes, habits, family histories, living situations, and other personal concerns. The notebook is like a diary, allowing for a more personal relationship to the topic, reinforcing the potential for it to have an enduring impact.

D1.4 Canada

Country: Canada
Level: Subnational and Local
Implementers: Provincial Ministries of Education; CIVIX; Ridgeview School (Vancouver)

Context

Education in Canada is under provincial jurisdiction; curricula are overseen by the provinces. The teaching of budget literacy aligns with the goals of the *social studies* curricula—that is, for students to develop an understanding of:

- The rights and responsibilities of citizenship and Canada's democratic system of government, including how decisions are made at the individual, group, local, provincial, and national levels; how to get involved in the political process; and how to effectively express opinions.
- How economic systems work and what their role is in an interconnected global economy in order to develop an awareness of political, environmental, and economic decisions as well as the trade-offs involved in balancing diverse interests.[23]

Even though Canadian provinces do not have a dedicated course to address the topic of government budgets, mandatory courses introduce students to government responsibilities and functions, paving the way for acquiring an understanding of budget literacy. Public budgets are primarily explored in grades 11–12 (ages 16–18).

Classroom-Based Budget-Literacy Initiatives

Of Canada's 13 provinces and territories, British Columbia, Manitoba, New Brunswick, Newfoundland and Labrador, Prince Edward Island, and Saskatchewan have introduced aspects of budget literacy into their school curricula, usually as part of the social studies courses. Curricula for Alberta, Nova Scotia, Ontario, Québec, Northwest Territories, Nunavut, and Yukon contain limited information related to budget literacy.

In British Columbia, for example, *economics* and *social studies* courses introduce elements of economics to facilitate a better understanding of budget-literacy concepts. Students are introduced to an analysis of the relationship between economic development at the community level and available resources (grade 5), the various ways ancient peoples exchanged goods and services (grade 7), and the influence of resource development and technological innovations on the Canadian economy from 1815 to 1914 (grade 10). Economic concepts are also explored in the *social studies* curriculum, enabling students to develop a comprehensive understanding of concepts related to economics, including scarcity, supply and demand, trade-offs, and opportunity costs.

Financial-literacy elements, such as an introduction to personal and business budgets, are presented in *mathematics* classes (grades 9–12), *health and career* classes (grade 9), *planning* classes (grade 10), and *apprenticeship and workplace* classes (grades 10 and 11). Financial literacy concepts are also addressed in a number of "applied skills" options, such as *business education*.[24]

In New Brunswick, financial literacy is addressed in different subjects across grade levels, particularly in *mathematics* and *social studies* courses as well as in elective courses such as *business organization management* (grades 9–10). Students can also take an elective *economics* course in the twelfth grade.[25]

In Manitoba's *social studies* classes, students learn to identify the main responsibilities of the various levels of government, which serves as a basis for discussion of their respective budgets (grade 6). Students acquire an understanding of how the government affects their daily lives; are able to describe the responsibilities and processes of the legislative, executive, and judicial branches of the federal government; and learn about the division of power and responsibilities across all levels of government (grade 9), which sets the stage for a discussion about revenues and expenses. Approximately half of twelfth-grade students take an optional *essential mathematics* course (grade 12), which includes exercises about taxes, such as property taxes, and explores how they are determined through a budgeting process. Finally, students learn about public budgeting in an optional twelfth-grade *economics* course, which includes a unit on *government and the economy* that helps students develop an awareness of the economic functions of government, their magnitude and purpose, and their suitability and effectiveness.[26]

Newfoundland and Labrador's *social studies* curriculum for high school provides students with a somewhat detailed exposure to public budgets.

Curriculum
As part of Newfoundland and Labrador's 2004 *social studies* curriculum for eleventh-grade students (ages 17–18), the *Canadian economy* module (Government of Newfoundland and Labrador 2004) is highly relevant to budget-literacy education. The overall approach involves imparting knowledge of fundamental principles and economics concepts from national and global perspectives. Sessions dealing with budget literacy begin with an examination of government revenues and expenditures, followed by a review of fiscal and monetary policies and their impact on the economy. Thus, the focus shifts from a static analysis of the government budget to an observation of which budgetary tools can influence policy outcomes (for example, the third unit of Newfoundland and Labrador's *social studies* curriculum is about *macroeconomics*).[27]

Learning Outcomes
Expected learning outcomes regarding knowledge of government budgets include the ability to describe major revenue categories of municipal, provincial,

and federal budgets; to define progressive, proportional, and regressive taxes; to determine whether different types of taxes—including income and sales—are progressive, proportional, or regressive; to assess government budgetary decisions and their impact on government debt; and to describe major expenditure categories in local, provincial, and federal budgets (Government of Newfoundland and Labrador 2004:58). Students are also expected to be able to analyze how the government uses fiscal policy to promote price stability, full employment, and economic growth, and to propose solutions for addressing economic policy issues (Government of Newfoundland and Labrador 2004:60).

Content
The first part of the curriculum deals with concepts regarding government budgets, particularly deficits, debts and surpluses, the basic functions of governments in market economies, and the impact of government choices on the lives of students (for example, through health care or education). The second part delves into the different kinds of taxes. The third looks at fiscal policy (Departments of Education of New Brunswick, Newfoundland and Labrador, Nova Scotia, and Prince Edward 1999:21).

Pedagogical Approaches
Pedagogical approaches adopted to teach budget literacy concepts tend to be interactive and based on student participation. Suggested strategies to acquaint students with government budgets and fiscal policy include the following:

- Maintain records of all personal and household taxes paid by themselves and their families over a one-month period to determine the extent and impact of taxes on their daily lives.
- Pretend to be councilors of a small municipality who decide on expenditures for the year based on expected revenues.
- Assume the role of advisor to the minister of finance and provide advice and fiscal policy suggestions in a context of high unemployment and low economic growth.
- Simulate the budgetary decision-making process of a multimember organization—for example, a town or city council or a company board of directors—to identify potential impacts on individuals.
- Find the Department of Finance website and identify spending and taxing priorities from the latest budget.
- Invite a local member of the House of Assembly or member of Parliament to the class to discuss fiscal and monetary policies currently in place and explain what the government is hoping to achieve with such measures.

Most materials used by teachers can be found in textbooks. Teachers are encouraged to use a combination of print, visual, experiential, and technological resources. Examples include using copies of budgets from various levels of government to facilitate analysis by students of where tax money is spent (Government of Newfoundland and Labrador 2004).

Out-of-Classroom Budget-Literacy Initiatives
i) CIVIX's *Student Budget Consultation*
Context. CIVIX is a national, nonpartisan charity promoting civics education in Canada with the objective of building skills and promoting habits of citizenship among Canadian youth. CIVIX's flagship program—*Student Vote*—is a parallel election coinciding with official elections for youth under the voting age. More than 563,000 students from schools throughout Canada cast "ballots" during the last federal election.

Another CIVIX initiative, the *Student Budget Consultation*, is a *civics* and *financial literacy* program for high school students across Canada. CIVIX facilitates the study of Canada's federal budget and national priorities by providing educators with curricular materials and students with an opportunity to voice their opinions about the federal budget.

Curriculum
Implemented since 2012, the *Student Budget Consultation* is a relatively new initiative focused on engaging students in grades 9–12 (ages 14–18) and grades 10–12 (ages 15–18). Students from all of Canada's ten provinces and three territories have participated in the program, and approximately 5,000 students per year share their political perspectives and budget priorities through CIVIX's annual online survey.

The elective curriculum for the consultation was developed by CIVIX in 2012 and has been modified and updated every year since. With outreach to about 10,000 students per year, it is mainly being utilized in *social studies, politics,* and *civics* classes as well as some *economics, mathematics,* and *accounting* classes.

Situated within a broader framework of *civics* education, the curriculum of the Student Budget Consultation comprises four sections:

- **Learning.** The finance minister leads a nonpartisan video tutorial outlining the concepts of revenues, expenditures, surpluses, deficits, and debt, and their relevance at the federal level of government.
- **Debate.** Representatives from major national stakeholder groups share their priorities and suggestions for the budget. In previous incarnations of the program, a panel of political pundits shared their views on major national issues.
- **Comparison.** Political party leaders and representatives offer their party's perspectives on the budget and fiscal priorities.
- **Consultation.** Students take an online or paper-based survey, and their opinions are compared with the perspectives of other youth from across the country and shared with the national media and the minister of finance.

Learning Outcomes
Students gain an understanding of the government and the budget process; the ability to compare and evaluate viewpoints made by politicians and interest groups; and the capacity to form their own opinions about government spending priorities.

Pedagogical Approach and Materials

The pedagogical approach is based on an experiential learning experience, including participatory learning debates and the use of interactive media. Teaching materials (suggested activities and lesson plans) provided by CIVIX to educators target either the junior- or senior-level *social studies* or *finance* courses. Using the teaching tools, teachers are encouraged to spend two to four classes covering the content and the budget consultation.

Resources provided by the Student Budget Consultation[28] rely heavily on the use of audiovisual and online materials, such as animated video tutorials featuring the Canadian minister of finance outlining the concepts of *revenues, expenditures, surplus, deficit,* and *debt*; video interviews with major national stakeholders and political party leaders sharing their priorities and discussing their preferred use of government budget surpluses; a quiz helping students situate themselves in their country's political spectrum; and feedback from the Department of Finance on the results of the consultation.

Outcomes

A program evaluation of the Student Budget Consultation confirms that it strengthens knowledge of the government and the budgeting process among students. It also increases the students' interest in politics and public policy and their desire to participate more actively in policy debates, including the budget process. Seventy-seven percent of teachers reported an increase in their knowledge and understanding of the Canadian government and the federal budget. Seventy-eight percent reported that the program effectively improved their confidence and capacity to teach about politics, the Canadian government, and civics.

ii) School Participatory Budgeting in Vancouver

In 2005, at the initiative of one of its teachers, Ridgeview School—a public school in West Vancouver with about 380 students in kindergarten through seventh grade—launched a participatory-budgeting project at the elementary-school level. Students made spending decisions based on the parent advisory council budget (monies raised by parents), which set aside $ 2,000 (10 percent of its overall budget) for the exercise.

Pedagogical Approach

The participatory budgeting took place over the course of one month. During the first two weeks, students discussed their needs and identified three top proposals for school projects. In the third week, the school administration reviewed the students' proposals for their feasibility, and every class selected a top proposal. Finally, in the fourth week, students convened at a school-wide assembly where they presented the proposals using prepared posters as illustrations. Students voted on the best idea using paper ballots, and the winning project was implemented in the following year.

International Practices to Promote Budget Literacy • http://dx.doi.org/10.1596/978-1-4648-1071-8

Outcomes

In this instance, students chose to allocate the budget to create a school store, notably because it could potentially support mid- to long-term fundraising efforts. Other ideas included cooking classes, a small indoor climbing wall, a water fountain, new sports equipment, or a school pet that would be cared for by the students (TNI 2006). At the request of the school superintendent, students later presented the project at a district parent-council meeting.

Lessons Learned

Curriculum

- The content of budget-literacy modules can be expanded beyond the analysis of government revenues and expenditures to an analysis of fiscal policy.
- The range of ways in which public budgets are addressed in the school curricula of various states illustrates that there can be several entry points for incorporating elements of budget literacy into school curricula. A choice must be made between splitting elements across classes and modules or presenting them in one specific curriculum.

Student Budget Consultation

- Creating a personal link with students (for example, allowing them to determine their own political preferences by comparing their priorities with those of political party leaders) is an effective method for engaging youth in budget policy discussions.
- An experiential learning opportunity is likely to leave a more lasting impression on students than traditional didactic teaching methods.
- Involving Ministry of Finance representatives, political party leaders, and the media adds visibility and credibility to the initiative.
- It is important to close the feedback loop through mechanisms such as an official response from the Ministry of Finance.

School Participatory Budgeting in Vancouver

- In addition to role-playing games, it is possible to involve students—even young ones—in activities that allow them to see the actual impact or results of their decisions.
- A participatory-budgeting process in a school is likely to require a collaborative, multistakeholder effort between teachers (to help design and facilitate the participatory-budgeting process), parents (to contribute money or in-kind support), administrators (to offer feedback on student proposals and monitor implementation), and possibly external advisors (to provide technical assistance and guidance).
- A participatory-budgeting initiative for a school can be a two-way learning experience and a useful opportunity for teachers and students to learn about one another's perspectives.

D1.5 Chile

Country: Chile
Level: National
Implementers: Internal Revenue Service; Ministry of Education

Context

The results of the 2015 Open Budget Survey reveal that Chile has a budget transparency score of 58 out of 100 and that it provides the public with limited budget information. Based on a score of 23 out of 100 on public participation, survey results also confirm that the government of Chile is weak at providing the public with opportunities to engage in the budget process. The Ministry of Education in Chile is responsible for preprimary, primary, and secondary school education. Primary (ages 6–13) and secondary education (ages 14–17) is compulsory.

Classroom-Based Budget-Literacy Initiatives

Curriculum[29]

Aspects of the primary- and secondary-school curriculum are aimed at fostering a sense of citizenship among students and developing their ability to participate in the democratic process, including compulsory *history, geography, and social sciences* classes and optional *orientation and religion classes*.[30] But the majority of budget-literacy instruction is based on the fiscal education program of the Internal Revenue Service. As part of this program, the Servicio de Impuestos Internos (*SIIEduca*) portal[31] provides students with relevant knowledge of fiscal issues through a series of educational resources.

Learning Outcomes

The primary education *orientation and religion* class seeks to develop students' capacity to participate in public life, especially in their school community, by encouraging them to behave in a responsible, active, and democratic manner. The purpose of the *history, geography and social sciences* courses is to inform students about their role in contributing to a better economy and society. The key learning objective of the *SIIEduca* web portal is to acquaint secondary-school students with essential fiscal concepts, the public budget and the budget process, and their tax responsibilities.

Content

One of the core elements of the *history, geography, and social sciences* classes at the primary-education level is *citizen formation*. Beginning in first grade, students learn about public and private institutions. In the fourth grade, students become familiar with the concepts of *citizenship* and *civic responsibilities*, including *community participation as a way to achieve the common good*—a concept also linked to the respect of the law and compliance

International Practices to Promote Budget Literacy • http://dx.doi.org/10.1596/978-1-4648-1071-8

with fiscal duties by firms and individuals. During the fifth and sixth grades, students learn about democratic institutions, including the state, the constitution, and how public authorities are elected. Students learn about the rights and responsibilities of citizens and about values such as tolerance, mutual respect, and honesty.

Aimed at teachers, parents and tutors as well as the general public, the *SIIEduca* web portal provides information on taxpayer education and offers content suggestions for educators related to tax laws and administration, the annual budget cycle, revenue, public expenditures, public resources, types of taxes, and invoices or payment receipts. The portal also offers materials for technical and professional college education, including modules on entrepreneurship as well as small business management and commercial and tax regulations.

The *Planeta SII* website is directed at primary school children (6 to 13 years old) where they can find information on fiscal issues that complements what they are learning in school. There is one section for students in the first through fourth grades and another for students in the fifth through eighth grades. The site's main characters—*Mayte, Gaspar,* and *Ivo the Chinchilla*—engage youth through games, videos, and stories that reinforce the fiscal education and citizenship values they are learning at school, including the social role of taxes and the importance of asking for invoices and payment receipts.

Pedagogical Approach

Chile's curriculum emphasizes that teachers should take into account the diverse learning styles of students and use a variety of instruments to construct the assessment framework, such as individual and group project research, presentations, oral and written reports, journals and learning logs, and oral and written tests, and depending on the topic, different assessment methods, such as evaluations from observation, self-assessments, and peer assessments).

The pedagogical approach adopted by the Internal Revenue Service to improve the learning of fiscal education issues rests on three pillars: instilling values, building citizenship, and fostering a positive fiscal culture. The Internal Revenue Service intends to develop content that is easily understood by students and citizens and to destigmatize taxes and fiscal issues. It has therefore adopted a range of pedagogical methods, including a play called *Entering the SII Planet*, which has toured various regions of the country; published promotional articles in specialized magazines (Maestra Básica and Aula Creativa); and school visits by public officials who explain taxes in an informative and entertaining way to students and teachers (OECD 2013).

Out-of-Classroom Budget-Literacy Initiatives
Television Series

The Internal Revenue Service, in partnership with Novasur—the National Council of Television's educational television station—launched *The Debut of the Gang* in 2012, a television program about four young musicians performing at a rock concert. It is aimed at teaching students about citizenship and economic concepts, including taxes. By drawing on compelling and accessible media content delivered in four episodes, each ten-minutes long, the show exposes young people to citizenship values and fiscal culture. In addition, educational episodes of the children's television program *The Adventures of Ivo the Chinchilla*, are broadcast by Chile National Television, in which Ivo and his friends develop concepts linked to citizenship and social coexistence.

Lesson Learned
Chile's partnership with an educational television channel highlights one of the ways in which public authorities can foster budget literacy among youth and reach out to children through a variety of channels.

D1.6 Costa Rica

Country: Costa Rica
Level: National
Implementers: Ministry of Finance; Ministry of Public Education

Context

Costa Rica scored 54 out of 100 in the 2015 Open Budget Survey on budget transparency, revealing that it provides limited budget information to the public. It scored 27 out of 100 on public participation, demonstrating that the government is weak in providing the public with opportunities to engage in the budget process.[32]

Costa Rica's political constitution establishes that the Ministry of Public Education is in charge of education at the national level. Primary education (ages 6–12) is compulsory. Students are offered two options for their secondary education (ages 13–18): a five-year academic school or a six-year technical school. They can obtain high school diplomas with either option, which qualifies them for tertiary education at universities. The Division of Curricular Development of the Ministry of Public Education and the Directorate of Taxation of the Ministry of Finance have launched Costa Rica's Tax Education Strategy, which is designed to encourage citizens' appreciation of a responsible fiscal culture. Examples of similar initiatives such as those launched by Argentina's Federal Administration for Public Revenue and El Salvador's Tax Education Unit in the Ministry of Finance have informed this initiative.

Educational authorities and national technical advisors are aware of the importance of promoting tax education, especially in fostering a responsible tax culture from an early age and improving prospects for improved economic growth and public services.[33] As part of this effort to establish a responsible tax culture, training has been provided to primary and secondary school teachers, including through the National University, to apply tax education across the educational syllabus.

Classroom-Based Budget-Literacy Initiatives
Curriculum

The *social studies and civics* curriculum (grades 1–6), the *civics education* curriculum (grades 7–12), and the *education for everyday life* curriculum (grade 9) include content about taxes.

Content

The *social studies and civics* curriculum introduces students to fiscal-education concepts with the aim of instilling a culture of solidarity, participation, and awareness of fiscal responsibilities. Similarly, the *civics education* syllabus promotes a culture in support of tax morale and compliance and values of respect, solidarity, effort, and collaboration through participatory and inclusive classroom methodologies.

The content of the *education for everyday life* course is intended to delve deeper into financial-education concepts as they relate to actions performed in daily life, including conducting transactions, and spending money, paying taxes and acquiring assets.

Pedagogical Approach and Materials

The Ministry of Finance, in collaboration with the Ministry of Public Education, has developed a variety of resources and materials to support and train primary and secondary school teachers implementing the fiscal education program. The *Guidelines for Teaching Fiscal Education in Primary Schools* (Ministry of Finance Costa Rica 2010), for example, include three focus areas: values, citizenship, and the fiscal-education culture. A theoretical framework and class activities are suggested for each topic. Fiscal education content addresses fiscal rules, the national budget, public spending and resources, and the role of the Ministry of Finance. Additional resources for teachers include a glossary of fiscal terms and information on budgetary laws.

A number of educational video games were developed as part of this initiative,[34] including *Memotest*, an interactive game to help children acquire and strengthen their understanding of the basic concepts of tax education and to learn the difference between public institutions and private enterprises. The game *Declarando mis impuestos* enables youth to calculate income taxes by selecting various trades and professions and identifying the portion of their annual income needed to pay their taxes. At the end of the game, players can see that their tax contributions help to maintain and fund hospitals, schools, museums, and parks. Finally, the game *Somos equipo* teaches children about the social rationale for paying taxes and reinforces the notion of the common good—when all members of a community benefit if everybody contributes.

The Ministry of Finance Goes to School

Officials from the Ministry of Finance visit schools and conduct workshops for students to explain the role and functions of the ministry and its relevance to government-provided public goods and services. A game used at the workshops, called *Around the Country*, includes mime and drawing while teaching youth about tax revenues and investments that are required to maintain public spaces and deliver public goods.

Tax Education Week

Tax Education Week is an initiative of the Ministry of Finance and the Ministry of Education to teach students about the importance of paying taxes and to foster values of solidarity, cooperation, and citizen responsibility. Throughout the week, students learn that citizen compliance with tax responsibilities provides the government with the necessary resources to deliver services, such as health, education, water, and electricity.

Out-of-Classroom Budget-Literacy Initiatives

Tribute to My Country Games Room

Located in the Children's Museum (*Museo de los Niños*) in San Jose, the *Tribute to My Country Games Room* is a space created to teach youngsters about civic culture and the social role of taxes and public spending. It incorporates three themes on the introduction and history of taxation; the role of the legislative assembly and how the national budget is approved and distributed; and tax investment and the function of customs authorities. For instance, as part of the *Public Money Path and the Legislative Assembly* exhibit, children pretend to be legislators and distribute tax revenues among various priorities, such as education, health, and infrastructure. As part of the "*La Facturita*" (the little invoice shop) exhibit, by pretending to buy and sell, children learn how taxes work and how to determine which payment receipts are valid (OECD 2013).

Lessons Learned

- As demonstrated by initiatives such as *Tax Education Week*, cooperation between the Ministry of Education and the Ministry of Finance is critical for strategizing, piloting, and mainstreaming budget literacy education for young people.
- The fact that examples of fiscal and tax education programs designed by Argentina's Federal Administration for Public Revenue Resources and El Salvador's Tax Education Unit in the Ministry of Finance informed Costa Rica's efforts in this regard suggests potential for regional and global cooperation to harmonize content and educational standards on budget-literacy issues.

D1.7 Czech Republic

Country: Czech Republic
Level: National
Implementer: Ministry of Education, Youth, and Sports

Context

With a score of 69 percent for budget transparency in the 2015 Open Budget Survey, the government of the Czech Republic provides the public with substantial budget information, but opportunities to engage in the budget process are limited, as reflected by its score of 42 percent for public participation.[35]

The Ministry of Education, Youth, and Sports sets the curricular content for the primary- and secondary-school systems. Knowledge about the state budget is not explicitly expressed as a learning outcome, but concepts related to public revenues and expenditures are featured in the program framework for elementary education (primary lower-secondary level), gymnasiums, vocational education, and training (secondary level).

Students are continuously and progressively introduced to budget-literacy concepts during primary and secondary school, depending on the development of their intellectual abilities and in accordance with the graduate profile in the relevant field of secondary-school education.

Classroom-Based Budget-Literacy Initiatives

Curriculum

Updated in 2007, the curriculum is designed around educational areas. Budget-literacy elements are introduced at the basic educational level in sessions on *man and society* and *man and the world of work* in the eighth and ninth grades (VÚP 2007a) and at the upper-secondary level in the tenth through twelfth grades. In 2010–11, there were 789,486 students in 4,123 primary and lower-secondary schools and 532,918 students in 1,423 upper-secondary schools (Czech Republic 2011).

Learning Outcomes

The *man and society* educational area is focused on helping students orientate themselves to social reality and to successfully participate in social relations and relationships with family, society, economic life, and political bodies and institutions, and to potentially engage in civic life at the individual level. Students develop their citizenship and legal consciousness, reinforce their sense of personal and social responsibility, and are motivated to actively participate in democratic society (VÚP 2007b). Budget literacy is featured in the *man, state, and the economy* unit. Expected learning outcomes include students being able to identify the various sources of state revenues and state expenditures, and to provide examples of allowances and benefits received by citizens from the state budget.

Classes in the *man and the world of work* unit introduce students to the professional and economic life of adult citizens, enabling students to apply their theoretical knowledge to current economic situations and to analyze the information correctly instead of relying on superficial judgments (VÚP 2007b). Based on their study of the unit on the *national economy and the role of the state in the economy*, students are required to be able to explain basic principles regarding state revenues and expenditures, identify the basic types of taxes, file tax declarations, and conduct basic tax calculations.

Students pursuing vocational education and training are expected to be able to explain state budget revenues and expenditures, prepare tax returns (tax declarations), distinguish between direct and indirect taxes, and maintain tax records for payers and nonpayers of value-added taxes.

Content

The program framework for basic elementary education (primary and lower-secondary school) outlines the content of the *civics* module in its fifth educational area, *man and society* (VÚP 2007a). The *state and the economy* lesson in this module teaches students how to identify sources of state revenue and areas of state expenditure and to provide examples of allowances and benefits that citizens receive from the state budget. As part of the *state and the law* lesson, students are familiarized with the roles and functions of the municipal, regional, and state administrations.

The *home economics* module on *man and the world of work*- the ninth educational area—introduces concepts such as budgets, income, expenses, payments, and savings and enables youth to learn how to make simple payments and do household accounting.

The program framework for secondary general education includes a section on the national economy and the role of the state in the economy as a part of its *man and the world of work* module (VÚP 2007b). Students are introduced to basic types of taxes, tax obligations, and procedures for filing tax returns. They are taught how to carry out basic tax calculations to determine the amount owed for social and health insurance. They discuss fiscal policy, including the state budget and tax system; the Czech national bank's monetary policy; and social policy. A subsequent module focuses on personal finances. Students learn how to distinguish between regular and irregular income and costs, create a household budget, solve a budget deficit, and handle a household budget surplus. The macro- and microelements of budgets are therefore intertwined in this curriculum.

The program framework for vocational education and training also includes thematic units relevant to budget-literacy education. The *national economy and the EU* unit focuses on the state budget; the *wages and statutory levies* unit introduces the wage system, salary components, wage regulations, and income taxes; and the *tax system and financial markets* unit teaches students about direct and indirect taxes and tax accounting.

Pedagogical Approaches

The *man and the world of work* educational area places great emphasis on the practical application of the skills acquired, which students are expected to have gained by dealing with real-life situations (for example, carrying out basic tax calculations). Discussions with guest experts on public budgets and other policy issues are recommended for this unit.

By presenting budget-literacy issues in a variety of educational areas, the Czech curriculum weaves budget-literacy education into a range of domains relevant to the students' daily lives, including understanding societal issues, dealing with personal finances, and preparing to become economically savvy and critical young professionals.

Lessons Learned
- The Czech curriculum is a useful example of the multifaceted character of budget-literacy education. On one hand, it clearly focuses on building the students' civic knowledge and ability to understand the sociopolitical environment and, on the other hand, it illustrates how budgets have major economic implications that affect individuals at a very personal level.
- The curriculum's focus on a critical approach to the presentation of economic facts in the media is useful for helping students relate to budget-literacy issues outside the classroom
- An in-depth study of state budgets during secondary school, stemming from an introduction to the topic at the basic educational level, is more apt to strengthen budget literacy than if the issue is only studied during a single school level.

D1.8 Dominican Republic

Country: Dominican Republic
Level: National
Implementer: Internal Revenue General Department

Context

According to the findings of the 2015 Open Budget Survey, the Dominican Republic's score of 51 out of 100 on transparency attests to the fact that the public has access to a limited amount of information on the national budget, and its score of 23 out of 100 on public participation indicates that the government is weak in regard to providing the public with opportunities to engage in the budget process.

The Internal Revenue General Department's Fiscal Education Unit is responsible for planning, coordinating, and supervising efforts to promote a national tax culture and a fiscally responsible citizenry. The unit's efforts are focused on strengthening tax education at primary, secondary, and tertiary levels of education, in addition to other programs that are geared toward promoting awareness, participation, and responsibility among citizens regarding the social role of taxes.

Classroom-Based Budget-Literacy Initiatives

Curriculum

The fiscal education unit sponsors activities to educate all citizens, which includes targeted efforts at educating primary and secondary school students. For example, the unit has contributed to budget-literacy content development for the *civics* course that is part of the national curriculum for primary and secondary education. The unit is also responsible for developing pedagogical materials and organizing educational activities and trainings for university students and educators.

Learning Outcomes

The fiscal education unit's pedagogical materials emphasize the promotion of citizenship values and knowledge of tax obligations.

Content

The Internal Revenue General Department's fiscal education portal[36] presents a compilation of resources on budget literacy intended for students enrolled in the first through eighth grades of primary school. These cover a range of themes, including civic responsibility and compliance with tax obligations for students in grades one through four; main taxes in the country and the public agencies in charge of collecting them for students in grades four through six; and an emphasis on the concepts of *citizenship*, the *common good*, and *social values* for seventh and eighth grade primary school students.

For grades one through four of secondary school, budget literacy materials cover topics such as the types of taxes, tax functions of the Directorate General of Customs and municipal councils, and the benefits of taxation for economic growth and development.

Pedagogical Approach and Materials

Materials for primary school students and teachers include stories, comic books, booklets, and brochures on fiscal education. For example, a calligraphy notebook for students in the fifth and sixth grades helps to introduce terms about citizenship and tax culture. A resource booklet for students enrolled in seventh and eighth grades introduces information about the types of taxes, such as who pays them, why they are important, who collects them, and how they are utilized. Resources prepared for secondary schools include presentations, guidelines, and booklets, which include information on the budget cycle, tax policy, and the benefits of paying taxes. The fiscal education portal helps youngsters to learn about fiscal issues by offering an array of online games, such as *Fiscal Sudoku*, *Alphabet Soup*, and *Tax Trivia* as well as drawing and word games.

Moreover, fiscal education counselors visit secondary schools to speak about topics as diverse as fiscal consciousness focused on the needs of individuals and the community, public budget planning, revenues and expenditures, and taxes. Counselors instruct students about the role of the Internal Revenue General Department, the importance of taxes, the taxpayer's cycle, and the rights and responsibilities of taxpayers. They also visit summer camps where they convene similar discussions and organize activities, such as games, plays, and developing art murals.

Finally, the Internal Revenue General Department created a national contest—"Create a Campaign to Promote a Tax Culture" for fourth-grade students in secondary school. Students were asked to create an innovative and creative campaign reflecting their vision of state taxes and the responsibilities of citizens. Fourteen schools participated; and winners were awarded monetary prizes.

Budget literacy materials for university level students include: the *Charter on Duties of Taxpayers, Tax Management Manuals* (volumes 1–4) and *Practical Study Booklets on the National Register of Taxpayers and Tax Receipts*. Resources for educators include *Tax Management Manual Teaching Guides* (Volumes 1–4) as well as *Educational Tools for Primary and Secondary School Teachers*.

Lessons Learned

- As a complement to teacher training on fiscal issues, external experts—in this case, fiscal education counselors—can be invited to schools to give special lectures on the topic.
- As part of the wider outreach of programs advancing budget literacy, the fiscal education portal of the Internal Revenue General Department includes a dedicated rubric aimed at parents, with advice on how they can help strengthen their children's tax education.

D1.9 Estonia

Country: Estonia
Level: National
Implementer: Ministry of Education and Research

Context

A key priority of Estonia's Open Government Partnership Action Plan 2014–16 (OGP 2014a) is to increase the transparency of public budgeting and financial management. This includes efforts to incorporate fiscal data for the central government and as many other units of the public sector as possible into a designated web-based application about public finances, and compiling guidelines for local authorities to prepare a concise overview of the local budget that citizens can understand.

Oversight of the national curriculum is under the purview of the Ministry of Education and Research. While Estonia has a solid framework for financial education (OECD 2014:28), a review of the 2011 national curricula for basic schools and upper-secondary schools reveals that there is limited explicit focus on strengthening knowledge of public budgets. On the other hand, because there is substantive focus on the development of entrepreneurship competence among students, entrepreneurship education is explicitly recognized at all school levels as a cross-curricular objective. It is taught as part of the compulsory *social sciences* course, and in September 2013, led to the introduction of a separate optional subject, *economic and business studies* (EACEA 2012).

Classroom-Based Budget-Literacy Initiatives

Curriculum

Budget literacy elements are featured in the *social sciences* curriculum at the basic school level (grades 1–9) (Republic of Estonia 2011a) and in the *social sciences* and *economic and business studies* curricula at the secondary level (grades 10–12) (Republic of Estonia 2011b). Curriculum guidelines for these subjects were updated in 2011 (Republic of Estonia 2011a, 2011b).

Budget literacy elements are also embedded into broader *civics and citizenship* education for *social sciences* courses, while the *economic and business studies* curriculum encourages knowledge of public budgets to facilitate understanding of government policies and socioeconomic objectives.

Learning Outcomes

Through their study of *social sciences*, students at the basic level of schooling are expected to be familiar with the concepts of the state budget, state and local taxes, social benefits, security, and insurance; the principles of the current market economy and related roles of businesses and the state; the purpose of taxes; and the rights and responsibilities of individuals in connection with them (Republic of Estonia 2011b:295).

With regard to learning outcomes at the secondary level, students studying *social sciences* are expected to: understand macroeconomics, including tax policies; value tax payments as contributions by citizens and entrepreneurs toward the well-being of society; research and compile information about the economy; and analyze and present their findings based on appropriate statistical methods (Republic of Estonia 2011b).

The secondary *economic and business studies* course is intended to equip students with sufficient knowledge to provide examples of government supplied goods and transfers; appreciate the government's regulatory role in economic circulation and redistribution of income; analyze the government's economic policy in the context of ensuring economic stability, national defense, and social security; and discuss state budget drafting, tax policy, and redistribution of income (Republic of Estonia 2011b:376).

Content

The basic level *social sciences* course depicts public finances as part of the *civics and citizenship* education sequence. Following chapters on *society and social relations, state and governance,* and *civil society,* this module explores the role of the state in the economy as it relates to planning and regulation, the national budget and tax principles, and social benefits and insurance (Republic of Estonia 2011a:295).

The secondary level *social sciences* course[37] presents public finances as part of the module on *managing the economy of society,* which focuses on the concepts of fiscal policy, the state budget, the tax load, and taxes in general (Republic of Estonia 2011b:275).

Finally, the *economics and business studies* curriculum[38] discusses public finances in the *role of the government in the economy* module and describes economic circulation, the drafting of the state budget, the pros and cons of various tax systems and policies, the influence of fiscal and monetary policies, and the cyclical nature of the economy (Republic of Estonia 2011b:376).

Pedagogical Approach

Learning methods suggested for the basic school level curriculum are diverse; they include active learning such as role-play, discussions, debates, and brainstorming; joint activities and volunteer work; project-based learning; compilation of reviews, research papers, opinion pieces and learning portfolios; thematic games; analyses of statistics and reference sources, including legal texts and maps; critical analyses of advertisements, thematic films, and other sources of economic or budget information provided by the media; and field trips (Republic of Estonia 2011a:295).

Lesson Learned

Entrepreneurship education could serve as a useful entry point to introduce students to public budgets across individual, business, and macroeconomic contexts.

D1.10 France

Country: France
Level: National and Subnational
Implementers: Ministry of Education; Ministry of the Economy, Finances, and Industry; Regional Councils

Context

Ranked seventh among the 98 countries included in the 2015 Open Budget Survey, France scores 76 out of 100 on transparency. However, its score of 40 out of 100 on public participation indicates that there is room to improve public engagement in the budget process.

All educational programs in France are regulated by the Ministry of National Education. Budget-literacy education is part of the *economics and social sciences* curriculum in the penultimate and last year of general secondary school. The approach adopted to introduce public budgets to youth emphasizes their knowledge and understanding of the state's role in the economy.

Classroom-Based Budget-Literacy Initiatives
Curriculum

Secondary-school education is divided into two stages: *collèges* that consist of the first four years of secondary education (grades 6–9)—and *lycées* that provide a three-year course of further secondary education (grades 10–12). During the tenth grade, students enrolled in *lycée général* and *lycée technologique* are expected to choose a specialization for their final two years of secondary education; *hard sciences, humanities and economics,* or *social sciences.*

Students who choose to study the optional *basic principles of economics and administration* module in tenth grade (1.5 hours per week) are provided with a preliminary introduction to budget literacy. Students opting for the *economics and social sciences* stream have the opportunity to acquire detailed knowledge of public budgets through the *economics and social sciences* course for grades 11 and 12.[39] Curricula for the baccalaureate in *sciences and technologies of management and administration* or *management-administration* place greater emphasis on personal and business budgeting.

Learning Outcomes

The *economic role of the state* module, a part of the tenth-grade *basic principles of economics and administration* course, aims to facilitate the discovery of economic concepts and sensitize students to questions regarding the economic role of the state.

The eleventh grade *economics* course—in a module entitled "How Can the State Budget Influence the Economy?"—presents an overview of the economic functioning of the public sector and its actions at the central administrative level and across territorial administrations (regions, departments, and municipalities). Students are expected to learn about the relevance and economic weight of public budgets to the respective administrative levels and state institutions and to make reasoned judgments about how they can influence the choices of other economic actors.

The twelfth-grade study stream on *sciences and technologies of management and administration* addresses questions regarding the economic role of the state, such as priorities for economic policy making and the efficiency of state interventions.

Content

The tenth-grade *basic principles of economics and administration* course presents the state's tridimensional economic role as producer, redistributor, and regulator through the use of concrete examples.

The *economics* curriculum for eleventh grade is organized around five chapters; public budgets are addressed in chapter 5: "Regulations and Macroeconomic Disequilibria." Budgets are presented as part of the question about how the public sector can and should intervene in the economy, notably through economic policies. Taxes, public spending, public deficits, and public debt are explored in this context. The module on "How Can the State Budget Influence the Economy?" is divided into three sections: public budgets, structure and financing of public spending, and state action on the economy.

The content for the twelfth-grade curriculum of the *science and technology of management and administration* baccalaureate/high school diploma (*Sciences et Technologies du Management et de la Gestion* [STMG]) addresses 11 key economic questions, two of which are specifically dedicated to the economic role of the state. The first question encourages deliberation on the efficiency of state interventions in the economy. It describes the state's responsibilities to reduce social risk and inequalities, which legitimizes its interventions and presents the concepts of *social policy* and *national solidarity*, reinforcing the notions of *progressive taxes* and *redistribution*. The second question is centered on whether the state has room to implement economic policy. It examines the regulation of economic activities and the adaptation of economic structures to the social and political environment. This section introduces the role of monetary and budgetary policies as tools for state action, to balance the budget, as stimulus or stabilization policy, and for financing the budget deficit and sovereign debt.[40]

Pedagogical Approaches

The pedagogical approaches used to convey budget-literacy concepts draw on multimedia and interactive materials, including:

- Videos: "Developing the State Budget: How Does It Work?"[41] and "Developing a Municipal Budget: How Does It Work?"[42] are available on the *Draw Me the Economy* website, a joint initiative between the newspaper *LeMonde.fr* and economists.
- An online simulator for public finances[43] created by the public policy think tank *Institut Montaigne*, where the user can increase or decrease state revenues and expenditures and instantly observe corresponding repercussions on state debt and state deficit.

In addition, an online quiz[44] developed by the Ministry of Education and the National Institute for Statistic and Economic Studies tests students' knowledge of state revenues and expenditures as well as the budget preparation process, the actors involved, and the legal framework.

More than 400,000 users have already played the *CyberBudget* game,[45] created in 2007 by Paraschool in collaboration with the Budget Directorate. Players assume the role of the minister of finance as they try to balance public finances and prove their knowledge of budgetary issues by guiding the budget process from preparation and planning to parliamentary vote and management. The game ends with a short video message adapted to the player's results from the actual budget or finance minister. A guide to the game is available to teachers.

In 2009, the Ministry of Budget and Finance collaborated with magazines targeting teenagers to publish a special edition called "Why Are We Paying Taxes?" It includes cartoons depicting interns learning about the Ministry of Finance as well as quizzes and comprehensive information about all stages of the budget process.[46]

In 2012, the *Le Figaro* newspaper developed an online animation[47] that enables users to increase or decrease governmental expenditures and income to achieve the desired impact of reducing the government deficit.

Out-of-Classroom Budget-Literacy Initiatives
School Participatory Budgeting
In 2005, the region of Poitou-Charentes introduced participatory budgeting in 93 public high schools. Two other regions—Nord Pas de Calais and Ile-de-France—followed the lead, introducing participatory budgeting at the secondary-school level (*budget participatif des lycées*) in 2010 and 2011, respectively. The rationale for the initiatives has been to contribute to the students' civic education, and help them improve their studying environment by engaging in participative democracy while contributing to the effectiveness of public action. The initiatives also seek to foster the participation of the entire educational community: students, parents, teachers, and administrative and technical staff. Students are tasked with deciding on a project for their high school and charting out related priority actions, generally focused on infrastructure development or building renovation, such as the installation of a new computer room or the building of a new "students' house." Projects costing up to 70,000 euros can be financed through school participatory budgeting.

Pedagogical Approach
A multistakeholder meeting is typically convened in the fall to brainstorm about student needs and to compile suggestions for high school projects. The regional council (an elected assembly) then reviews the suggestions and evaluates them from a feasibility and financial standpoint. In the spring, the project ideas are thoroughly debated, and three priority projects are chosen per high school. The following year, elected regional representatives vote on the financing of each high

school's priority projects within the limit of the available budget. A steering committee composed of high school directors, teachers, students, academy representatives, regional advisors, and the like meets regularly to oversee the implementation of the projects.

Outcomes

Besides the 30 Ile-de-France high schools that had initially engaged in the participatory-budgeting process, 10 additional high schools joined the initiative in 2014. Since 2011, 30–160 students from each high school have participated in a general assembly of project stakeholders. An impact evaluation[48] found that, as a result of the participatory budget process, 73.8 percent of parents and 56.5 percent of students felt that communications within the school had improved.

Since 2008, the participatory-budgeting process in Poitou-Charentes has been extended to all private schools under contract with the state based on their demands and has led to the funding of almost 1,600 projects (Budget Allocator 2014).

Lessons Learned

Curriculum

- The French example is a useful example of a multifaceted approach to budget literacy because it delves into all of the political and legal preparation stages of the national budget and the parliamentary vote.
- The online CyberBudget game provides an experience through which students can identify with the finance minister's tasks and challenges.

Participatory Budgeting

- Participatory budgeting is conducted in collaboration with regional councils. The process stretches out for over a year and involves significant funding because it often leads to the development of infrastructure. Because of its relative complexity and length, the process can offer an excellent illustration of real-life budget processes.
- High school students can witness the results of their participation in the process firsthand and are key actors in the improvement of their learning environment.

D1.11 Germany

Country: Germany
Level: Subnational and Local
Implementers: Regional Education Ministries and Municipalities

Context

In Germany, the rationale for teaching budget literacy is primarily to provide students with a solid understanding of economic matters and of the interplay between politics and economics. Germany scores 71 out of 100 on transparency in the 2015 Open Budget Survey, but its score of 23 out of 100 on opportunities for the public to engage in the budget process is weak.[49] Most programs related to budget literacy for youth are part of secondary-school education.

Classroom-Based Budget-Literacy Initiatives

The educational system in Germany is decentralized. Every federal state (*Bundesland*) is responsible for its own curriculum. Children attend elementary school (*Grundschule*) from first through fourth grades; all students are taught the same subjects. After fourth grade, students attend one of three different types of schools based on their academic ability and personal preferences: *Hauptschule*, which prepares them for apprenticeships or vocational schools; *Realschule*, which prepares them for vocational or higher vocational schools, or *Gymnasium*, which prepares them for further studies at a university. The majority of budget-literacy content is taught to *Gymnasium* students in grades 8–10, and all 16 federal states feature a secondary-school *economics* course.

Subjects that include budget-literacy elements are framed differently from one federal state to another. In some states, budget literacy is part of a module called simply *economics*, in others, the module is referred to as *politics and economics, economics and law, politics, society and economics*, or *economics and social sciences*.

Curriculum

The adopted approach is broad and always makes mention of state budgets in relation to the state's broader objectives, policies, and responsibilities in the framework of the *social market economy*—an economic concept deeply entrenched in Germany since 1948, according to which the state can legitimately intervene in the economy to uphold sociopolitical principles compared with purely capitalistic, free-market economies.[50] The depth of teaching about economic matters depends on the structure of the module, which varies from state to state.

Learning Outcomes

An analysis of budgets is not systematically included in the various curricula, but where it is featured, the presentation of budgets is meant to contribute to the students' understanding of the "bigger picture"—that is, the state's role and action in the economy and how it is made possible through taxation. Alternatively, when municipal budgets are featured, the goal is to equip students with a sound understanding of political processes at the local level.

Content

Curricula vary in terms of content and level of detail. Some only present macro-economic policies and their challenges (for example, Bremen); others drill down into an understanding of the rationale for specific taxes (for example, Bayern). Overall, all curricula focus on providing students with knowledge of economic and political processes and an understanding of how they relate to larger-scale societal debates and values.

A detailed breakdown of the relevant modules and curricular content of the 16 federal states is provided in table D.2.[51]

Table D.2 Relevant Modules and Curricular Content

Baden-Württemberg	The *economics* curriculum for grade 10[a] is structured around four key themes: budgets, private sector entities, the state, and international issues. Budgets are approached from a financial literacy and private sector perspective. The module on *the state* includes topics such as distributive justice and state debt, but does not specifically mention budgets. The learning progression is gradual, moving from a focus on private households and individual consumers in sixth grade to private sector companies in eighth grade to the state and international economics in tenth grade. The government of Baden-Württemberg will soon be rolling out a completely new *economy and professional orientation* curriculum for seventh through tenth grades. Its draft suggests that budget literacy will be an integral part of this new subject.
Bayern	In a module on *social market economy as economic order*, part of the *economics and law curriculum* for ninth grade (10 teaching hours),[b] students are introduced to the idea that free-market economies risk market failures. They examine the necessity of state intervention in the economy, notably to provide public goods and mitigate negative externalities. State redistribution of income and federal and state budgets are introduced in this context, as is the impact that taxes and social contributions have on private household income. In tenth grade, the *economics and law curriculum* includes two modules relevant to budget literacy: • Income taxes (12 teaching hours). In the *central aspects of the economic and legal order in Germany* module, students are introduced to income taxes, their influence on the available income of private households, and ways to solve simple tax-related problems. The situation in Germany is analyzed and compared to that of other countries. The question of tax fairness is examined and discussed. • Taxes and social security in the social market economy (12 teaching hours). In this module, students are confronted with the concept of social justice in a discussion about how state income is redistributed through taxes. The structure of federal and state budgets and the impact of taxes and social contributions on the income of private households are explored. Students are introduced to the government's social security policy, including its key principles: subsidiarity and solidarity.[c]
Berlin	The curriculum for *social and economic sciences* for grades 9–10 introduces the idea of state interventions to correct market failures.[d] The *economics* curriculum in grades 11–13 introduces fiscal policy.[e]

table continues next page

Table D.2 Relevant Modules and Curricular Content *(continued)*

Brandenburg	State budgets are part of the *macroeconomics* and *economic policy* chapter of the economic sciences curriculum for tenth grade. First the state budget is presented; then the concept of state debt, monetary policy, and the European system of central banks. Students are expected to learn to describe the composition and creation of the state budget and to assign essential income and expenditure categories. The origins, consequences, and economic limits of state indebtedness are examined; statistics are analyzed; international state debts are compared; and fiscal policy instruments are discussed.[f]
Bremen	• The *politics* curriculum for grades 11–13, touches on macroeconomic and state economic policy but does not specifically address budgets.[g] • The curriculum for grades 11–13 *economics* takes a similar look at economic policy and theories without mentioning budgets.[h]
Hamburg	• The curriculum for grade 10 *politics, society, and economics* examines participation in democratic processes, including at the municipal level. Students are exposed to budgets for private households but are not introduced to public budgets.[i] • The *economics* curriculum for grade 10 includes a section analyzing Hamburg as an economic player, including the region's economic development, areas of growth, employment structure, infrastructure development, its financing through taxes, regional economic policy, and regional and international competition.[j]
Hessen	• The *politics and economics* curriculum for grades 7–9 introduces private household budgeting skills.[k] • For students in *Realschule* (schools preparing students for apprenticeships and vocational qualifications), the *social sciences* curriculum for grade 7 includes 10 hours of teaching on *municipal life*, which follow two sequences on *school and family life*. The learning objective of this section is to increase students' understanding of the formation of political will at the municipal level, to help them recognize the principles of political decision making and become acquainted with the institutional framework in which these decisions are made. Students learn about the possibilities and limits of influencing these processes and enhance their own capacity to engage. They develop judgment by analyzing possible solutions from different perspectives and the ability to argue for their own positions. The curriculum specifies that this teaching module should be based on a specific, topical case of the students' municipality. The use of documented or simulated cases is discouraged. Using the municipal case study, students are expected to examine a controversial case from different perspectives; identify interests, interest groups, and citizen initiatives; evaluate possible solutions; know who the decision makers are in the municipality; and understand the municipality's responsibilities and budget. Recommended working methods and materials are role-play; projects; debates; and the use of inquiry, surveys, and statistics.[l]
Mecklenburg-Vorpommern	The *economics* curriculum[m] for grades 11–12 includes an introduction to the *social market economy* but does not refer specifically to budgets.
Niedersachsen	• The junior secondary-level *economics* class presents the concepts of *state income* and *expenditures*, which are well anchored in the curriculum for grades 7–10. • In grade 8 of the *politics and economics* curriculum, a sequence entitled "Politics Near To You" looks at the role of municipalities; their status within the federal state; forms of political participation; finances at the municipal level, such as income, expenditures, and budget plans; and the distribution of tax income at various levels. • In grade 9 of the *politics and economics* curriculum, the role of the state in the economy is examined alongside principles and elements of a social market economy and the possibilities and limits of state action. The state is presented as one of the key actors in the economy, along with private households, private companies, and international actors. • A new *politics and economics* curriculum is currently being developed for grades 11–13, which will feature a discussion of the state's core functions and related debates.

table continues next page

Table D.2 Relevant Modules and Curricular Content (continued)

Nordrhein-Westfalen	The *politics and economics* curriculum for grade 8 introduces social policies and their challenges but does not mention budgets.[n]
Rheinland-Pfalz	The *economics and social sciences*[o] curriculum for grades 9–10 *Realschule* students includes a module on taxes called "What Are the State's Responsibilities and How Does It Fulfil Them?" Key concepts for students to learn are taxes, the federal budget, economic cycles and phases, and gross national product. Regarding taxes, teachers are meant to present the role and meaning of tax and social contributions as source of income for public budgets. Role-play is a recommended pedagogical approach in which students must decide who gets taxed, how much, and by what means in an imaginary country where citizens have differing revenue levels, and the state wants to collect a given amount of tax to cover its expenditures. The goal is to stimulate a discussion about tax fairness. Another suggestion is to examine taxes individually and specifically, such as income taxes, added-value taxes, and gas taxes. Regarding the federal budget, students should get an overview of the state's current expenditure patterns. The suggested approach includes using recent graphs to analyze the income and expenditures of the state and of the local municipality, focusing on expenditures related to schools, as an example.
Saarland	The *economics* curriculum for grades 11–12 introduces the welfare state; its financing challenges; and an overview of income and expenditure structures, such as those for the state budget. A discussion about state debt follows.
Sachsen	The *Internal Revenue Service, law, and economics* curriculum for grade 10 includes an elective module introducing communal-level administrative processes and public services, notably by presenting the concept of taxation.
Sachsen-Anhalt	In grades 7–8, private budgets are introduced in the *economics* curriculum.[p] Grades 9–10 delve into economic policy (still in the *economics* class) but do not contain any content specific to budget literacy.[q]
Schleswig-Holstein	The *economics* curriculum for grades 7–8 includes an introduction to private household budgets as well as an introduction to public budgets under the respective titles: "Public Budgets—Where Do Cities and Municipalities Get Their Money from and How Do They Spend It?" and "We Want Youth Meetings, Cycling Paths and Disco Bus: Advisory and Decision-Making Processes in a Municipality."
Thüringen	The *economics and law curriculum* in grades 11 and 12 examines the role of the state. In grade 11, students are taught how to represent key state income and expenditure areas. In grade 12, students learn about direct and indirect taxes, fiscal policy, and deficit spending.

Note: Unless otherwise indicated, these are the curricula for *Gymnasium* students.

a. See http://www.bildung-staerkt-menschen.de/service/downloads/Bildungsstandards/Gym/Gym_W_bs.pdf.

b. See http://www.isb-gym8-lehrplan.de/contentserv/3.1.neu/g8.de/index.php?StoryID=26202.

c. See http://www.isb-gym8-lehrplan.de/contentserv/3.1.neu/g8.de/index.php?StoryID=26202.

d. See http://www.berlin.de/imperia/md/content/sen-bildung/schulorganisation/lehrplaene/sek1_sozialwissenschaften_wirtschaftswissenschaft
.pdf?start&ts=1425461080&file=sek1_sozialwissenschaften_wirtschaftswissenschaft.pdf.

e. See http://www.berlin.de/imperia/md/content/sen-bildung/unterricht/lehrplaene/sek2_wirtschaftswissenschaft.pdf?start&ts=1425461080&file
=sek2_wirtschaftswissenschaft.pdf.

f. See http://bildungsserver.berlin-brandenburg.de/fileadmin/bbb/unterricht/rahmenlehrplaene_und_curriculare_materialien/gymnasiale
_oberstufe/rlp/VRLP_Wiwi_Sek2_BB_2012.pdf.

g. See http://www.lis.bremen.de/sixcms/media.php/13/POL_GyQ_2008.pdf.

h. See http://www.lis.bremen.de/sixcms/media.php/13/WIR_GyQ_2008.pdf.

i. See http://www.hamburg.de/contentblob/2373332/data/pgw-gym-seki.pdf.

j. See http://www.hamburg.de/contentblob/2975708/data/wirtschaft-gym-seki.pdf.

k. See https://verwaltung.hessen.de/irj/HKM_Internet?cid=ac9f301df54d1fbfab83dd3a6449af60.

l. See https://verwaltung.hessen.de/irj/HKM_Internet?cid=f1e079cc428af80d07f4fe2db20fe301.

m. See http://www.bildung-mv.de/export/sites/bildungsserver/downloads/Wirtschaft.pdf.

n. See http://www.schulentwicklung.nrw.de/lehrplaene/upload/lehrplaene_download/gymnasium_g8/gym8_politik-wirtschaft.pdf.

o. See http://lehrplaene.bildung-rp.de/lehrplaene-nach-faechern.html?tx_abdownloads_pi1%5baction%5d=getviewcatalog&tx_abdownloads
_pi1%5bcategory_uid%5d=113&tx_abdownloads_pi1%5bcid%5d=5786&cHash=566e1cb1b416a62c4feec6aae3c2d512.

p. See http://lbssa4.urz.uni-magdeburg.de/index.php?KAT_ID=7405&historyback=1.

q. See http://lbssa4.urz.uni-magdeburg.de/index.php?KAT_ID=7407&historyback=1#art25585.

International Practices to Promote Budget Literacy • http://dx.doi.org/10.1596/978-1-4648-1071-8

Pedagogical Approach

While there seems to be a reliance on a textbook approach, especially when introducing macroeconomic concepts, some curricula also mention role-play, especially with regard to debating about tax fairness (for example, Rheinland-Pfalz) or conflicting interests at the municipal level (for example, Hessen).

Materials

Schools in the respective states are free to choose their textbooks from a list agreed to by the Ministry of Education. In 2008, the Federal Centre for Political Education (*Bundeszentrale für politische Bildung*) developed a three-hour role-playing game[52] for young people to act out the stages involved in deciding on a municipal budget. Students play the roles of citizens defending different interests. They must debate and agree on how to use the municipal budget to implement a specific project. This material was used in the framework of a 2008 festival in Berlin called "Young Politics," but, in theory, it could also be used in a class-room context.

Depending on how they are framed, the modules will likely demonstrate the strongest emphasis on social, economic, or political angles.

Out-of-Classroom Budget-Literacy Initiatives

i) School Participatory Budgeting in the Rietberg

In 2012, to stimulate the students' civic engagement and sense of responsibility and to give them a first-hand experience of democratic processes, the municipal council of the city of Rietberg (East-Westfalia, with 28,000 inhabitants) gave students the opportunity to determine how approximately one-quarter of the year's budget allocated to the city's schools would be used. All secondary schools (general high schools and vocational schools) in the city participated—a total of 2,600 students. The concept for this student budgeting initiative came from the Bertelsmann Stiftung Foundation, which provided support for the project from beginning to end (RegionalWolfenButtel.De 2013).

The project begins in early fall by collecting ideas and debating school priori-ties. In November, students vote for their favorite project. Then implementation plans are developed or refined. In March, students submit and present their plans to the municipal council committee responsible for the use of relevant funds. Not all suggested projects receive funding, though. An example is the introduction of Wifi into the school due to concerns about the legal framework and uncertainty about potential misuse. For proposed projects that have been rejected, teachers can take the opportunity to explain concepts such as limited resources and arbitration among political priorities. Examples of validated projects include additional sporting equipment, lockers, new relaxation rooms, new drink distribu-tors, new tables and chairs, school t-shirts, hammocks, whiteboards, and support for a school newspaper.

The chosen approach primarily relies on building the students' debating, persuasion, and presentation skills as well as their understanding of democratic processes.

Materials

According to the Bertelsmann Foundation, which managed the project, no materials are being used to teach budget literacy specifically because the focus is on experiential learning rather than a textbook approach. However, in 2015, the foundation published an informative project report and a comprehensive handbook for schools seeking to implement a student participatory budget, which detail the steps required for the project.[53]

Outcomes

Between 87 and 93 percent of students in the four schools participated in the vote to determine how the funds would be used. The Bertelsmann Foundation suggested this approach to other municipalities as well, and more than 10 have implemented it. The project is now led by the Service Center for Youth Participation (*Servicestelle Jugendbeteiligung*) in Berlin.[54]

ii) Participatory Budgeting with Youth in Berlin's Marzahn-Hellersdorf District

The Marzahn-Hellersdorf district introduced a participatory budget in 2005 focused on the inclusion of children and youth (ages 14 or older) in this process. The outreach effort proved quite successful, with many suggestions coming in from youth, such as increased financial support for public libraries and the introduction of "graffiti/street art wall" (Bürgerhaushalt 2013).

Pedagogical Approach

Youth are targeted through specific actions and events related to the participatory budget. Examples include workshops in primary schools, the "Get Involved!" (*Mischen Sie mit!*) online portal, the development of materials aimed at multiplying participation in the political process, and measures coordinated by the district's Office for Children and Teenagers (*Kinder-und Jugendbüro*).[55]

One reported challenge involves youth having difficulty distinguishing between levels of responsibility. Some suggestions sent by youths are not really meant for the district but rather for the state, which is responsible for implementation. The pedagogical work of the Office for Children and Teenagers is therefore essential to clarify their respective functions.

To enhance the focus on results, which is understood to be essential for keeping younger participants engaged, the district administration of Marzahn-Hellersdorf has introduced a "traffic light" system to visualize the implementation status of the citizens' suggestions. In addition, all of the previously implemented suggestions are easily available online. For instance, suggestions from youth that were provided for the participatory budget during the 2012–13 academic year are clearly indicated.

Materials

The district administration produced a flyer explaining to children and teenagers the possibilities for getting involved in the budgetary process online. The administration also created a dedicated Facebook® page[56] and a blog with information about expressing opinions regarding public finances. Teenagers can post suggestions online by e-mail or with an easily accessible form that does not require the user to create a profile.

Outcomes
According to a representative from the Office for Children and Teenagers, the participation rate among young people in the budget process through the *Mischen Sie mit!* online platform is increasing. Approximately 700 online messages came from children and teenagers—approximately 18 percent of all sent messages—during the 2014–15 academic year. Forty suggestions from the 2010–11 academic year participatory budget have already been implemented, notably the construction of a playground. Moreover, since 2010, a similar project has been implemented in the Berlin district of Steglitz-Zehlendorf.

Lessons Learned
Curriculum
The frequent association of economics with politics and societal matters demonstrates a strong emphasis on teaching students about the interplay of economic and political actors. Economic issues are not presented in a vacuum. The same holds true for budget-literacy concepts and knowledge. A budget cannot be understood only as a standalone object of examination; it must be embedded in a broader educational framework.

Participatory Budgeting
- Students are able to see the results of their engagement in the budgetary activity first-hand. Interaction with municipal elected representatives appears to be an effective method of reinforcing a sense of active and conscious citizenship.
- Young people are more likely to participate when the issues and possible results affect them and are a part of their local environment (for example, the possibility of the closure of a youth meeting center). Thus, the process should be anchored in the living sphere of the young people and lead to short-term results that will affect their daily lives (Ködelpeter n.d.).
- To reach out to youth, it is important to adopt an effective communication strategy (for example, build on the use of Facebook® or other online platforms used by children and teenagers).
- To foster youth engagement, it is essential to close the feedback loop. The Marzahn-Hellersdorf project has done this by emphasizing the online visualization of implementation stages and results.
- To attract youth, participatory budgeting must be fun. The project should motivate, generate enthusiasm, and spark interest among the teenagers; it should also be challenging.
- Although the role of adults as enablers to support the project and create the relevant material and financial framework is important, it is advisable that they minimize their influence on outcomes.
- Time constraints, age-related criteria, and the involvement of relevant local actors and networks are necessary for the success of participatory methods.

D1.12 Guatemala

Country: Guatemala
Level: National and Local
Implementers: Tax Administration Department; Ministry of Education

Context

Guatemala's budget transparency score of 46 out of 100 in the 2015 Open Budget Survey indicates that the government provides limited budget information to the public. The survey findings also conclude that with a public participation score of 10 out of 100, there is substantial room for improving opportunities for public participation in the national budget process.

The *Permanent Program of Tax Culture*, created by Guatemala's Tax Administration Department in 2005, aims to promote civic values and foster a sustainable tax culture in Guatemala through education and awareness-raising regarding taxes and their importance to economic development and social progress. The program works closely with the ministries of education, finance, and municipalities; the National Association of Municipalities; Instituto de Fomento Municipal; the German Development Co-operation (GIZ), Proyecto Educativo Pantaleón; International Plan; Centro Educativo Benito Juárez; Colegio Naleb'; and Share Guatemala.

Classroom-Based Budget-Literacy Initiatives
Curriculum

To foster a strong tax culture at various levels of the educational system, the Tax Administration Department partnered with the Ministry of Education to incorporate fiscal issues into the basic national curriculum for primary and secondary education. Fiscal education is introduced in primary school in the *citizenship formation* course and in secondary school in the *social sciences and citizenship formation* course.[57]

Learning Outcomes

The primary-level *citizenship formation* course aims to strengthen social participation and promote a democratic and peaceful culture. From first through sixth grades, students develop values such as solidarity and respect for the community and are motivated to participate in activities promoting the common good at home and school.

At the secondary-school level, the objective of the *social sciences and citizenship formation* course is to equip students with a better understanding of social context and a sense of their responsibility toward their communities. Teachers are encouraged to discuss the implications of effective resource utilization with students.

Content

The *citizenship formation* course focuses on citizenship, nation building, and the importance of education. A *citizenship building* module and a *citizen project*,

International Practices to Promote Budget Literacy • http://dx.doi.org/10.1596/978-1-4648-1071-8

part of the *social sciences and citizenship formation* course, include lessons on the structure, division of power, and social responsibility of the government; the role of taxation; and the adverse impact of tax evasion on public-service delivery. Students are encouraged to ask their parents about the types of taxes they pay.

Pedagogical Approach and Materials

The *Permanent Program of Tax Culture* has been particularly active in promoting tax culture as a subject in the basic national curriculum. For each of the six levels of primary education, there is a set of "Cooperation Is Progress" guidance notes which includes methodological suggestions for classroom activities and learning. The notes introduce budget-literacy concepts through *Simon Tax* a cartoon character created to represent a responsible and entrepreneurial citizen who dreams of a better Guatemala. The program has also developed online games and distributed multiple board games to help students and their families learn about tax culture and budget concepts.

For the first three years of secondary school, the Tax Administration Department prepared guidelines for teachers as part of developing the curriculum for budget literacy. The guidelines include group exercises, cases studies, and tools to teach citizenship and tax-related cultural values in the classroom. These guidelines, which are aligned with the national curriculum, propose monthly activities to help students develop social competencies.

Finally, to achieve even broader educational coverage, the program launched the "100 in Tax Culture" initiative, implemented in partnership with state and municipal governments and local educational authorities. The initiative targets private and public schools in urban and rural areas, with the objective of teaching children and youth values associated with active citizenship. Implementation of this initiative includes distribution of educational materials for all educational levels to raise awareness of fiscal education among school directors and teachers and continued monitoring and evaluation of the program's implementation.

Out-of-Classroom Budget-Literacy Initiatives

To expand awareness of tax issues, the *Permanent Program of Tax Culture* has invested in media such as press publications, radio advertisements, and television broadcasts, including tax dramas based on the story of Simon Tax.

The *Strength Lies in Numbers Annual Festival* uses musical events, talent shows, plays, and information stands to educate citizens about the social significance of taxes. Several activities are geared toward children, such as puppets to teach about tax and citizenship issues and spending a day at work with the Superintendent of the Tax Administration Department and five officials.

Moreover, universities and research centers have participated in festival events by convening forums such as "The Role of the Press in Citizenship Training," "Citizenship and National Identity," "The Role of Taxation in Municipal Strengthening," and "Taxation Psychology."

Lesson Learned

The *100 in Tax Culture* initiative is a useful example of the ripple effect that school budget-literacy programs can generate by expanding their influence to state officials, municipalities, school directors, and teachers—in short, by broadening their outreach to include the adult population.

D1.13 Hong Kong SAR, China

Economy: Hong Kong SAR, China
Level: National
Implementer: Education Bureau

Context

In Hong Kong SAR, China, the Education Bureau oversees the school system, in which years 1–6 of primary education are followed by another six years of secondary education (S1–6). The purpose of including budget literacy in the national school curriculum in Hong Kong SAR, China is for citizens to acquire an understanding of the government's fiscal constraints as well as the economic and social implications of public financial management over the short and medium term.

The *general studies* curriculum encourages students in primary-school years 4–6 to reflect on the balance between the rights and responsibilities of being a resident of Hong Kong SAR, China (CDC 2011). At the junior secondary-level (secondary 1–3), the *resource management* module of the enriched curriculum called "Technology Education Key Learning Area" (secondary 1–3) introduces budgeting and addresses topics such as managing personal and family resources (Curriculum Development Institute 2013). Introductory elements to budgeting can also be found under the business, accounting, and financial studies umbrella (secondary 4–6) which cover topics such as business financial statements, purposes of budgeting, usefulness and limitations of budgetary control, and the causes of budgeting variance and corresponding remedial actions (CDC and HKEAA 2014a).

Classroom-Based Budget-Literacy Initiatives

Specific budget-literacy content is mostly covered in the *life and society* curriculum[58] (secondary 1–3), including a core module on the public financing of Hong Kong SAR, China, and the *economics* curriculum[59] (secondary 4–6), which includes a section on fiscal policy.

Curriculum

For the most part, all students are exposed to elements of budget literacy at the junior secondary level. Aspects of budget literacy are included as essential learning elements in the *life and society* curriculum (secondary 1–3) (CDC 2010), which was developed in 2010 by the Curriculum Development Council as part of the *personal, social, and humanities education* key learning area. Schools choosing not to adopt the entire *life and society* (S1–3) curriculum are expected to incorporate the learning elements into their school-based, junior-secondary *personal, social, and humanities education* curriculum.

At the senior-secondary level, budget literacy is included in the *economics* curriculum, updated in January 2014 by the Curriculum Development Council and the Examinations and Assessment Authority in Hong Kong SAR,

China (CDC and HKEAA 2014b). According to a 2013–14 survey about subjects taught at the senior-secondary level, 95 percent of schools offer *economics* as an elective. The *economics* curriculum introduces budgets at a macro level, focusing on the state's economic policies.

Learning Outcomes

The desired learning outcomes for the *life and society curriculum*[60] are for students to acquire a preliminary understanding of the principles of the financial management by the government, the right of citizens to enjoy public services and their responsibility for paying taxes; and the characteristics of taxes in Hong Kong SAR, China (CDC 2010). The elements of budget literacy in this curriculum fit its objectives of fostering values and attitudes such as equality, promoting the common good, mutuality, and human rights and responsibilities, with a view toward educating critical, caring, concerned, and responsible citizens.

The *economics* curriculum[61] seeks to improve the economic literacy of students so they can understand and apply fundamental economic concepts to explain real-world situations, particularly with regard to the economy of Hong Kong SAR, China (CDC and HKEAA 2014b). The curriculum equips students with the knowledge and skills they need to participate in discussions about economic issues and decision making and to contribute to the well-being of the local community, the nation, and the world through active and responsible citizenship.

Content

Four lessons in the *life and society* curriculum are dedicated to the economic and social consequences of the public finances of Hong Kong SAR, China. Learning points encompass major items of government revenue and spending, the government policy agenda, income redistribution, the fostering of long-term economic development through public finance, and a comparison of tax rates in Hong Kong SAR, China with those of developed countries. Students are encouraged to reflect on issues such as the influence of public opinion on public spending, the extent of expenditures made for welfare benefits, and possible ways for the government to finance housing and medical expenditures for the elderly.

As part of the ten core compulsory topics[62] in the *economics* curriculum, the penultimate topic on *macroeconomic problems and policies* covers business cycles, inflation and deflation, unemployment, and fiscal and monetary policy. The section on fiscal policy focuses on public finances and describes taxation principles, tax classifications, and the effects of fiscal policies.

Pedagogical Approach

The *economics* curriculum recommends synchronizing aspects of budget literacy with course content that offers authentic learning opportunities, such as the government's announcement of the annual budget in February. Suggested activities for students include the preparation of a display board exhibiting the salient features of Hong Kong SAR, China's budget, and for comparison, a similar display board for the draft central and local budgets presented by the Ministry of Finance of the Central People's Government in March for comparison (CDC and HKEAA 2014b). The curriculum recommends combining teacher instruction with other methods, including "teaching as enquiry," when students compile the information or "teaching as co-construction," which provides students with the opportunity to engage in collaborative problem solving of economic issues, such as the narrow tax base in Hong Kong SAR, China.

Materials
Teaching materials for the *life and society* curriculum include textbook exercises for students and a variety of learning and teaching resources developed by the Education Bureau and local tertiary institutions to promote the teaching and learning of this subject. Among other aspects, the materials introduce how public finances affect the daily lives of citizens, including health care, social welfare services, profits, and income taxes. The government's main sources of income and expenditures, and the priorities and specificities of Hong Kong SAR, China's taxation system are explored using international comparisons.

Sample teaching materials for the 2014 *life and society* curriculum include worksheets with exercises on government expenditures, public revenue and spending trends, and the characteristics of Hong Kong SAR, China's taxes. In addition, a website dedicated to Hong Kong SAR, China's budget presents the finance secretary's budget speech along with explanatory documents, budget visualizations, and educational videos in Chinese (with English subtitles).

Lessons Learned
- Stressing the specificities of the country's tax system and providing international comparisons to help students understand the budgetary choices made by the government could prove useful.
- Students can be introduced to public finances before the last three years of secondary education, forming a basis for a more in-depth study of economics during the last three years of secondary education.

D1.14 India

Country: India
Level: National
Implementers: National Council of Educational Research and Training; Model Youth Parliament

Context

The 2015 Open Budget Survey finds that with a score of 46 out of 100 on budget transparency, the government of India provides the public with limited budget information. It also confirms that there is substantial room to improve India's score of 19 out of 100 for public participation in the budget process.[63] The National Council of Educational Research and Training defines the national curriculum. The motivation to include budget literacy in the curriculum stems from a desire to improve knowledge among youth about the ways that government can affect the economy, and thereby the lives of citizens. Subject curricula for lower grades contribute toward building a knowledge base for a more detailed inquiry during the final year of secondary school.

The *social sciences* curricula for seventh and eighth grades focus on the functions and responsibilities of political actors (NCERT 2006). The seventh grade curriculum includes a unit on *state government* that introduces students to the legislative, executive, and administrative aspects of state government. Students benefit from acquiring knowledge about the nature of the state government's decision making and gain insight into the politics underlying the provision of services and distribution of resources. A unit on the *economic presence of the government*, part of the *social sciences* curriculum for eighth grade, describes the rationale as well as the means of government involvement in developmental activities, especially in infrastructure and social sectors.

Classroom-Based Budget-Literacy Initiatives
Curriculum
The *economics* curriculum for eleventh and twelfth grades dates back to 2008 and stretches over four semesters. Its approach to teaching budget literacy is anchored within an economic framework, which reviews public budgets in substantial depth.[64]

Learning Outcomes
Content related to budget literacy in the *economics* curriculum helps students understand the government's approaches to regulating national economic issues, such as formulating fiscal policies, and the impact of government actions on citizens.

Content
As part of the sequence on *introductory macroeconomics*, the *government budget and the economy* unit explains how receipts and expenditures are classified, the

meaning and implications of surplus and deficit budgets, and outcomes related to downsizing the role of government. Graphic representations of the impact of tax policies on aggregate expenditures and equations explaining the concept of the *tax multiplier* are used. The unit introduces complex concepts such as *built-in/automatic stabilizers* and *Ricardian equivalence*. Students learn how to critically analyze suggested fiscal policies, evaluate their impact, and understand the rationale behind them.

Pedagogical Approach

Guidelines for the *economics* curriculum suggest that teachers use media and technology in the classroom when appropriate and acquaint students with the particulars of the national budget by asking them to watch the annual budget announcement and to participate in subsequent group discussions to analyze the impact of the budget on different sectors of the economy (Srinivasan n.d.:112).

Out-of-Classroom Budget-Literacy Initiatives
Model Youth (MY) Parliament

Model Youth (MY) Parliament is a civic engagement platform established to allow youth to engage with governance and public-policy processes with the aim of strengthening participatory democracy. In 2015, *MY Parliament* collaborated with multiple partners[65] at an event arranged at the Indian Institute of Management in Lucknow, engaging 120 participants (ages 18–26) in the national budget process. The pilot was conducted to:

- Enhance the representation of the views and interests of youth in the budgetary process;
- Provide youth with a platform to raise and debate matters of national importance, and pass important legislation; and
- Contribute toward building an informed and responsible citizenry and fostering young leaders[66]

Pedagogical Approach

MY Parliament has used an experiential learning approach to convey knowledge about public budgets and budget processes. The MY Parliament team organized a policy workshop that provided instruction on parliamentary procedures and budget analysis as well as online training programs about the national budget process. The team held an orientation session and workshop at Amity University in Lucknow to acquaint participants with budget-literacy concepts and terminology as well as its implications for fiscal policy. Finally, the team organized a one-day simulation of the lower house of the Indian parliament (*Lok Sabha*), which included discussion on a variety of clauses from the 2015 budget and the passage of the final budget.

Materials

The MY Parliament team prepared a *budget preparatory kit* that included relevant articles, editorials, and other relevant items as well as a series of detailed and nuanced perspectives on the budget. The team also used other materials, such as the government-issued *Budget Primer 2015–16*,[67] the *Economic Survey of India*,[68] and books assigned as part of the National Council of Educational Research and Training's syllabi for the eleventh and twelfth grades.[69]

Outcomes

Several public policy experts expressed a great deal of appreciation for the quality of the debate and the arguments presented by participants during the budget simulation. Key observations from the simulation exercise were presented to members of Parliament and subsequently debated during its budget session in April and May 2015.

Lessons Learned

Curriculum

- The assessment samples for the Indian curriculum are good examples of the level of detailed knowledge about specific concepts that final-year secondary students are expected to have. At the same time, it would be useful to explore assessment methods that also test the students' ability to think on their feet and critically evaluate budgetary policies.

MY Parliament

- The use of new technologies such as *Google Hangouts*[70] and webinars is useful in scaling up training programs about budget literacy and works well in combination with face-to-face interactions.
- Based on their role in the capacity building and preparation of useful pedagogical materials, civil society organizations are well placed to assume the role of intermediaries between government and relevant constituencies, such as young people.
- *MY Parliament* links knowledge of budgetary issues with leadership and public-policy training, making the project more attractive to young people. In fact, this link resulted in additional requests to work on long-term projects related to governance and public policy issues.
- *MY Parliament* is a good example of a broad-based coalition effort that can contribute to making participatory-budgeting processes for youth successful by drawing on different kinds of expertise from policy experts, educators, and civil society.

D1.15 Ireland

Country: Ireland
Level: National
Implementers: Educators as Advised by the National Council for Curriculum and Assessment; the Professional Development Service for Teachers

Context

The International Monetary Fund's 2013 Fiscal Transparency Assessment for Ireland attests to the high quality of its fiscal transparency and reporting. The Maastricht Treaty reporting requirements obliged the government to begin producing fiscal statistics that cover the general government, capture some accrual flows, and are classified according to the European System of Accounts. The pace of transparency-related reforms quickened in the wake of the 2008 crisis with the passage of the new Fiscal Responsibility Law and the establishment of the Irish Fiscal Advisory Council, among other measures (O'Connor 2011).

The Irish education system is made up of primary, secondary, and senior levels of schooling as well as further education.[71] The Department of Education and Skills has overall responsibility for education and training. The National Council for Curriculum and Assessment (NCCA) advises the Minister for Education and Skills on curricula and assessments from early childhood to the end of the secondary level and engages with learners, teachers, practitioners, parents, and others to support innovation in schools and other educational settings. The Professional Development Service for Teachers (PDST) is a generic, integrated and cross-sectoral support service that was established by the Department of Education and Skills in 2010. It offers professional learning opportunities to teachers and school leaders in a range of pedagogical, curricular, and educational areas.

Budget literacy is featured substantively in Ireland's secondary-school curriculum, though students are exposed to related concepts such as democracy and the distribution of scarce resources even earlier in the *social, personal, and health education* curriculum for fifth and sixth grades, and acquire basic numeric skills by studying mathematics in primary school.

Classroom-Based Budget-Literacy Initiatives
Curriculum

During lower-secondary school (ages 12–15—a three-year cycle), students develop an understanding of budget literacy through the optional subject of *business studies*. As of 2013, 56.5 percent of secondary-level students chose to study the subject (NCCA 2013). In addition, the *mathematics* syllabus teaches students how to interpret graphic summaries of data and apply basic arithmetic skills (NCCA 2015a).

During the upper-secondary level of school (ages 15–18—a two-year cycle), *business* and *economics* courses (Government of Ireland 1996; NCCA 2014a) provide students with opportunities to learn more about public budgets

(NCCA 2014a), and the *mathematics* curriculum (NCCA 2014b) introduces more complex financial literacy concepts. As of 2013, because *economics* was not a mandatory subject, only about 9 percent of students opted to study it at that stage of their education.[72]

Based on the NCCA's consultations with a range of stakeholders, including teachers, school leaders, parents, students, educational partners, and other members of the general public new specifications were developed for *business studies and economics* courses in May 2015.

Learning Outcomes

Based on the premise that it is becoming increasingly difficult to make political and economic choices without a basic level of economic knowledge, the lower-secondary-school *business studies* course aims to contribute to the economic literacy of students, enabling them to make informed contributions to the democratic process (NCCA 2013). The 2015 specifications for the subject are intended for youth to be able to differentiate between different sources of government revenues and expenditures; examine the purpose of taxes from a financial, social, legal, and ethical perspective; explain the relevance of economic indicators such as inflation, employment rates, interest rates, economic growth, national income, and national debt for individuals and the economy; use their knowledge and information from a range of media sources to discuss current economic issues and present an informed view; and evaluate the benefits and costs of a government economic policy and assess who enjoys the benefits and who bears the costs (NCCA 2015b).

In addition to other learning outcomes, the upper-secondary-level *business* course aims for students to develop a critical understanding of the overall environment in which business functions, including the impact of the economy on business, taking into account the general state of the economy, inflation, interest rates, taxes, and grants; the impact of business on the economy at the local and national levels in light of issues related to employment, tax revenues, and the environment; and the interaction between business and the wider economy (Government of Ireland 1996).

The *economics* curriculum intends for students to develop an interest in everyday economics, including fiscal issues, which would contribute to their citizenship education and to critically apply economic principles (NCCA n.d.).

Content

The *business studies* syllabus is balanced between the individual/household area and a purely commercial context. Recently revised draft specifications for the *business studies* syllabus specify three interconnected strands on *personal finance, enterprise,* and *our economy.* The strand on *our economy* closely examines the supply and demand of goods and services; the role of the government in managing the economy; and economic issues such as trade, employment, and Ireland's membership in the EU, with a more detailed focus on the role and functions of government, knowledge of public budgets, and economic policy implications (NCCA 2015b).

Building on its concern to remit understanding of the environment in which business operates in Ireland and in the wider world, the upper-secondary business syllabus is divided into three modules: *people in business, enterprise,* and *the environment.* The *business and the economy* section in the latter introduces public budgets in the context of describing the government's role in encouraging and regulating business and articulating the government's role as an employer.

The *economics* course relays a range of concepts related to money and banking, international trade, economic growth, and economic policies and development. Its *government and the economy* module outlines the government's economic role and introduces students to government finances; sources of income for central and local governments; the size, composition and influence of government expenditures; and the economic implications of budget deficits and surpluses. The draft "Background Paper and Brief for the Review of Leaving Certificate Economics" (NCCA 2014a) refers to Ireland's National Strategy on Education for Sustainable Development 2014–20 and suggests that the revised *economics* syllabus emphasize *economics for sustainable development* and examine both how economic activity is shaped by social processes and the social impact of economic activity and policy in a postrecession context (NCCA n.d.).

Pedagogical Approach

Because the design of the *business studies* syllabus is based on an integrated approach that connects different sections, teachers can choose among them to begin teaching the course and can adopt various teaching strategies. Educators teaching this subject endeavour to integrate core skills across subject areas, such as *business studies* and *mathematics* or *business studies* and *home economics*; and key skills, such as communication, working with others, and managing information. Teaching techniques to engage students include puzzles, word searches, and quizzes on economic awareness and frameworks, government finances, and taxes. Those teaching *business studies* also seem to rely on other methods and activities, such as encouraging students to compile scrapbooks on specific topics and to conduct research (NCCA 2015b).

The draft "Background Paper and Brief for the Review of Leaving Certificate Economics" advocates for an inquiry-based approach (NCCA 2014a). Intended to bring an economic problem to the foreground, this approach enables students to apply key economic models and principles to explore the issue and requires them to use inquiry to analyze the problem, make evaluations, and draw conclusions.

Some government and private institutions organize competitions for teachers and students, such as the Students Enterprise Awards organized by the city and county enterprise boards. These competitions encourage students to apply their skills in an authentic context.[73]

Box D.1 Sample Examination Questions

Business Studies (Junior Certificate)

1a. Which government department prepares the national budget?

1b. Every year the Irish government spends large sums of money on education. Give two examples of government spending on education.

2a. At present, the Troika from the European Central Bank (ECB), European Commission (EC), and the International Monetary Fund (IMF) regularly visit Ireland to monitor our financial position, our bank bailout and our budget deficit. Explain the term "budget deficit."

2b. Suggest two ways Ireland could reduce this deficit.

Business (Leaving Certificate)

1. Outline how the Irish government's policy of increased taxes and decreased public expenditure is affecting business.

2. The government increased taxes on petrol and diesel in its 2011 budget. (1) Outline one reason for this increase in taxes. (2) Describe two effects of this increase in taxes.

Economics (Leaving Certificate)

1. The Irish government introduced the household charge (property tax) of €100 per household in its 2012 budget.

   (a) State two advantages of this charge/tax for the exchequer.

   (b) Is this a progressive tax or a regressive tax? Explain your answer.

2. "Most eurozone countries with large deficits are using VAT to generate revenue." (Irish Tax Institute, The Irish Times, November 2011)

   (a) Explain, using examples, the difference between direct taxes and indirect taxes.

   (b) Discuss the economic advantages and disadvantages for the government of increasing VAT rates instead of income tax rates in its most recent budget.

   (c) Outline how imposing a tax on sugary foods (for example, fizzy drinks) could benefit the Irish economy.

Sources: Junior Certificate Examination 2013 Business Studies—Ordinary Level, State Examinations Commission, Exam Material Archive: https://www.examinations.ie/tmp/1473652579_9678641.pdf; Junior Certificate Examination 2013 Business Studies—Higher Level—Paper I, State Examinations Commission, Exam Material Archive. https://www.examinations.ie/tmp/1473652488_5107082.pdf; Leaving Certificate Examination 2012. Business—Higher Level. State Examinations Commission, State Examinations Commission, Exam Material Archive: https://www.examinations.ie/tmp/1473653420_4472710.pdf; Leaving Certificate Examination, 2011, Business—Ordinary Level, State Examinations Commission. State Examinations Commission. Exam Material Archive. https://www.examinations.ie/tmp/1473653653_8107188.pdf; Leaving Certificate Examination, 2012. Economics—Higher Level. State Examinations Commission. State Examinations Commission. Exam Material Archive: https://www.examinations.ie/tmp/1473654096_3457953.pdf.

Materials

Textbooks are the primary mode of instruction, but relevant resources are also provided by teacher associations, government agencies, and other organizations. Online resources available for educators include the website of the Professional Development Services for Teachers, which features PowerPoint® presentations on budget taxation and government finances; quizzes on government economic policies, and hand-outs on taxes for the *economics* course. Examination questions from prior years are available for *business* and *economics* courses.

Assessment

The majority of questions in the sample assessments for these subjects (see box D.1) are descriptive in nature, testing the students' understanding and knowledge of basic budget concepts. However, draft specifications for the *business studies* course propose that their application of such knowledge should also be assessed through: (1) a research project and digital presentation on an entrepreneurial opportunity, a current economic trend, development, or change due to a current financial challenge for a consumer or a business; and (2) an assignment in written, digital, audio, or visual form that asks students to record their reflections, observations, and analyses about at least four business-related issues. Examination questions for the *economics* course also test the students' ability to apply these concepts and make and validate arguments with reference to fiscal policy tools.

Lessons Learned

Ireland's approach to teaching budget literacy in the broader context of the business environment is useful when introducing this aspect in courses oriented toward entrepreneurship education but as indicated, not all students at the junior- or senior- post-primary levels access these opportunities.

D1.16 Illustrative Budget Literary Practices in Japan

Country: Japan
Level: National, Provincial, and Local
Implementers: Ministry of Education, Culture, Sports, Science and Technology; Ministry of Finance; National Tax Agency; Board of Audit; Cabinet Secretariat; Japan Broadcasting Corporation; Tax Education Promotion Councils

Context

One of the key drivers to introduce budget literacy to students in Japan is to strengthen tax education. The importance of teaching about taxes at all educational levels is evident in the "Outline of 2011 Tax Reform,"[74] endorsed by the Cabinet of Japan in December 2010, which espoused further improvement of tax education at all levels of schooling, raising awareness of educators who are in charge of tax education and increasing coordination among relevant ministries and associations. In addition, the government ministries' National Tax Education Promotion Council[75] was established in 2011 with the mandate to develop basic policies on tax education; coordinate with relevant ministries, agencies, and private associations; and collaborate with prefectural- and municipal-level Tax Education Promotion Councils[76] and educators across the country. Each year, the national council organizes the Tax Education Symposium to discuss policies and approaches to enhance tax education and to raise awareness of the issue among teachers and college or university professors.

Classroom-Based Budget-Literacy Initiatives

Tax education and therefore budget literacy are part of the compulsory curricula for primary and junior high school students and the noncompulsory curricula for high school students in Japan.

At the primary-school level (grades 3–4), the Internal Revenue Service curriculum emphasizes the students' awareness of their part in a larger community and the importance of cooperation and observing rules. During fifth and sixth grades, students are endowed with a basic knowledge of taxes, including their relevance to daily life, the constitutional obligation of every citizen to pay taxes, and how the obligation to pay taxes is shared.

For junior high school students, budget literacy is embedded in the *civics* component of the *social studies* curriculum,[77] which aims to strengthen the students' understanding of the purpose of democracy and to develop their perceptions of contemporary society. The *civics* component comprises four sections, including *our lives and economy*, which is further divided into two subsections: (1) *function of market and economy* and (2) *life of citizens and the roles of government*. Curriculum guidelines for the second subsection identify seven learning objectives or areas, including two that are directly related to budget-literacy: the role of public financing in securing and distributing financial resources and the purpose and role of taxes.

1. **The role of public financing in securing and distributing financial resources.** This area addresses how, given the broad range of demands regarding public expenditures, national and local government revenues should be secured and distributed effectively and equitably. Students are able to reflect on the characteristics of contemporary society and are encouraged to deliberate on how they, as future taxpayers, should resolve issues around social security and the securing of financial revenues in an aging society with fewer children.
2. **The purpose and role of taxes.** This area introduces the basics of the taxation system and its characteristics. It highlights the students' civic responsibilities as taxpayers and deepens their knowledge of and interest in how taxes are used.

High school students (ages 16–18) are introduced to budget-literacy concepts through the compulsory subject of *civics* and the elective, specialized subject of *commerce*.

The key areas of study in the *civics* curriculum are *contemporary society, ethics,* and *politics and the economy*. High school students can opt to study either *contemporary society* or *ethics* as well as *politics and the economy*.[78] Tax education is featured in the *contemporary society* and *politics and the economy* areas. Overall, the *contemporary society* course helps students develop respect for human life and the skills and attitudes necessary to become citizens who are able to understand, analyze, and appraise the fundamental issues of contemporary society. The course is divided into three key sections: (1) *the society in which we live,* (2) *contemporary society and how human beings should behave,* and (3) *coexisting in society*. These sections are further divided into subsections, two of which cover concepts relevant to budget literacy. The subsection on the *purpose of democratic government and political participation* impresses upon students the significance of political participation, and apprises them of their rights and obligations to engage in the political processes of a democratic, sovereign nation. The subsection on *how modern economic society and economic activities operate* is designed to help students explore the subject of *public finances* in more depth. It describes the government's vital role in the provision of public services in a market economy and the need for taxes; citizens' obligation to pay taxes; and the importance of taxpayers' assuming an active interest in how their taxes are spent. It also refers to the objectives, benefits, and challenges of the social security system and encourages students to think about the consequences of demographic aging on public finances.

The *politics and economy* course is geared toward strengthening the students' understanding and ability to make fair judgments about issues regarding politics, the economy, and international relations and to develop the capacities and attitudes needed to become reasonable public citizens. The course has three main sections on *various issues in contemporary society, contemporary politics,* and *the contemporary economy,* the last of which incorporates subsections on *domestic and international markets* and *mechanisms and characteristics of contemporary economy*. Budget-literacy content is included in the latter; it enhances students' understanding of how the national economy operates at the micro- and macro levels and describes the role of the modern government in the provision of services and implementation of fiscal policy to improve national welfare by adjusting resource distribution, redistributing income and assets, and stabilizing the economy. The subsection includes a discussion of the importance of appropriate fiscal administration to ensure effective distribution of limited fiscal resources, improvement of national welfare, and management of public finances by national and local governments according to their roles and responsibilities. The obligation of citizens to pay taxes and take an interest in how tax revenues are used is emphasized.

For high schools that offer specialization in this area, students have the option of enrolling in the elective course on *commerce*.[79] There are 20 sections in this course, including one on the *business economy*, which draws on five subsections to help students understand economic concepts and mechanisms and develop the ability to think proactively about economic phenomena. The *economic policy* subsection provides an overview of fiscal policy as a primary type of economic policy. By using actual examples of Japan's fiscal policies, it describes the functions and challenges of national government and local government finances in stabilizing the economy.

Because the Ministry of Education, Culture, Sports, Science and Technology's (MEXT) curriculum guidelines and commentaries are not specific, the development of annual teaching plans and unit-based teaching plans concerning budgets, taxes, and the like is left to the discretion of every school. At many schools, in addition to classroom teaching, school-wide lessons about taxes are organized during school hours, and staff members of local tax offices are invited as lecturers. These classes, which are designed to develop the students' interest in taxes, budgets, and public finances, offer budget quizzes and create avenues for students to learn about issues such as the amount of tax revenues being used for their school.

Textbooks are the primary teaching material in schools. Developed by textbook publishers, the education board, and others, they are based on the detailed curriculum guidelines and commentaries issued for each subject, and they are evaluated by the MEXT. Currently, tax education is included in textbooks for all levels of schooling in accordance with each subject's guidelines and written comments submitted by the National Institute for Educational Policy Research. In some cases, the National Institute for Educational Policy Research,[80] educational centers, and prefectural- and municipal-level boards of education share supplementary materials and professional support through expert lecturers. In April 2015, the National Tax Education Promotion Council released a collection of tax education cases.[81] Other examples of budget-literacy materials produced by ministries and agencies are as follows.

Ministry of Finance
The Ministry of Finance's *Think about the Finance of Japan* web page[82] is aimed at helping junior high and high school students acquire knowledge of national and local government finances based on themes and amounts. Students watch

videos about Japan's fiscal conditions and participate in interactive media, including online quizzes and simulation games about fiscal reform.

Another web page, *Finance Land*[83] is oriented toward younger, primary-level students. It presents a story about two children who, with their parents, recently moved to "Happy Town." By interacting with Happy Town's long-time animal residents, youngsters learn what taxes are, why they are important, and how they are used. A section on taxes and finance[84] is designed to improve the children's understanding of taxes and finance by addressing how decisions about taxes are made; the history of the taxation system in Japan; the current state and future outlook of the nation's finances; and the role of the Ministry of Finance.

National Tax Agency

The National Tax Agency's *Studying Tax for Kids* web page[85] features a range of tax resources and supplementary teaching and learning materials. Different versions of an overview of taxes and supplementary tax-education materials cater to different grade levels. Students can access games and quizzes about taxes as well as video libraries, including several animated programs about tax.[86]

Cabinet Secretariat, Cabinet Public Relations Office

The website of the Office of Prime Minister for Kids[87] is intended to foster interest and understanding among youth, particularly primary-level students, of the role of the Prime Minister's Office and the Cabinet of Japan. A section on budget and taxes describes how the national budget is planned; how taxes are collected from citizens; how government bonds are issued to supplement temporary tax-revenue shortages; and the implications of Japan's declining birth rate and aging population on social security.

Board of Audit of Japan

A website designed for primary-level students introduces the role of the Board of Audit and using actual examples, describes its functions. Children can take online quizzes to confirm their understanding of the topic. If they have questions regarding the contents of the website, they can contact the board by phone or mail.[88]

Nippon Hoso Kyokai (NHK) (Japan Broadcasting Corporation) for School

A television program called "10-minute-box"[89] has a number of episodes devoted to public finances and taxes. The ninth volume introduces the role of national and local governments, provides a breakdown of a variety of public expenditures and how they are used, and presents future challenges relating to public finances. Volume 10 emphasizes the obligation of citizens to pay taxes and describes different types of taxes (for example, income or corporate taxes). The last segment of the program features examples of taxes from around the globe and explores future challenges related to taxes.

In addition to national ministries and agencies, prefecture- and local-level ministries and agencies have taken initiatives to promote budget literacy at all levels of schooling, primarily in the form of tax education. For example, tax quizzes on the Tokyo Metropolitan Government's Bureau of Taxation website cater to primary- and advanced-level students.[90] Primary-school students answer questions such as: "Choose one of the following options for which taxes are used: convenience stores, department stores, and the fire department." Advanced-level questions intended for junior high school students include: "Which taxes are specifically determined by an ordinance of the Tokyo Metropolitan Government?" The website of Toyama Prefecture Tax Education Promotion Council, *Hello! Let's Study Tax*[91] presents expenditures and revenues at the national, prefectural, and municipal levels. For Wakayama Prefecture, the Tax Education Promotion Council's website, *Our Life and Taxes*[92] introduces *Kinokuni-Mori-Zukuri Zei*—a tax unique to the prefecture—along with the explanation of its purpose and actual use in different areas within the prefecture.

Out-of-Classroom Budget-Literacy Initiatives

A number of activities and pedagogical approaches are being used across various ministries and agencies to convey concepts related to public finance and taxation, including the following:

- The Ministry of Finance's website, *Finance Land*,[93] includes a game called "Finance Roulette"[94] that allows children to learn about the basics of taxes by playing a game of roulette.
- Efforts by the National Tax Association include:
  - Study tours and tax-education classes organized by the Tax Space Ueno facility within the Ueno local tax office in Tokyo.[95] According to its website, as of September 2011, over 10,000 people had visited the facility since its opening in June 2003. In fiscal year 2014, students from 34 junior high schools and six high schools visited the facility.
  - National-level essay contests about taxes for junior high school[96] and high school students.[97] Students are encouraged to write about tax-related topics, such as what they learned about taxes from their daily lives, school, television, newspapers, or other sources. There were 615,230 essays submitted from 7,422 junior high schools in 2014. Winners were recognized with a range of awards, including the Prime Minister Award, the Minister for Internal Affairs and Communications Award, the Minister of Finance Award, the Minister of Education, Culture, Sports, Science and Technology Award, and the National Tax Agency Commissioner Award, among others, and were presented with certificates and trophies. High school students from 1,547 high schools submitted 193,393 essays, and from these 12 winners were awarded the National Tax Agency Commissioner Award and also presented with award certificates and trophies.
  - Awards programs for schools, local boards of education, and other relevant private associations that deserve special credit for promoting tax education

for students. In 2014, one junior high school was awarded the National Tax Agency Commissioner Award and six schools, including two certified tax accountant's associations, two junior high schools, one primary school, and one high school, were selected to receive the Head of the Tokyo Regional Taxation Bureau Award.

- The Toyama Prefecture's Tax Education Promotion Council organizes a poster competition and essay competition on taxes that targets students in junior high and high school. Winning posters are featured on the council's *Hello! Let's Study Tax*[98] website.

- Organized by the Kyoto Prefecture Tax Education Promotion Council and district-level tax education promotion councils in Kyoto, the *Hello Tax Quiz 2013*[99] is aimed at sixth-grade students attending primary schools in Kyoto Prefecture, with prizes being awarded to students with perfect scores.

Lessons Learned

- Continued support to schools by the National Tax Agency for tax education, such as dispatching lecturers and holding tax education classes, would be difficult to sustain without help from other organizations, such as certified tax accountant's associations and corporation associations.

- Although classroom time spent on tax education in high school is limited, various efforts to improve the quality of such classroom education—for example by inviting guest lecturers to enhance topic technicalities—is evident.

D1.17 Luxembourg

Country: Luxembourg
Level: National
Implementer: Ministry of National Education, Childhood, and Youth

Context

The curriculum for primary and secondary schools in Luxembourg has been developed at the national level. While its contents do not appear to be linked to initiatives such as the participatory-budgeting process organized for residents of Luxembourg City since 2013,[100] the rationale for including budget literacy in Luxembourg's school curriculum is to enable students to acquire the skills necessary for understanding their society from an economic and financial point of view.

The eighth year of school is an orientation year that exposes 15-year-old students to the basics of economics to raise their awareness and interest in the subject and to help them consider their upcoming secondary-school specialization for the next three years—for example, whether they would be interested in sections D (*economic and mathematical sciences*) or G (*human and social sciences*). The eighth year economics module introduces substance on key economic agents, such as households, companies, the state, and foreign actors, as well as basic monetary matters. The government budget and essential functions of the state are explained. The *economics* curriculum for the eleventh year (the final year of high school) explores budget literacy in more detail.

Classroom-Based Budget-Literacy Initiatives
Curriculum

During the 2013–14 academic year, 1,839 students were enrolled in the last year of secondary school (Grand-Duché De Luxembourg 2014a). In recent years, more than 40 percent of students have chosen either section D (*economic sciences and mathematics*) or section G (*social sciences*) (Sorlut 2014).

Budgets are discussed in the most recent curriculum for academic year 2014–15[101] within the broad framework of building economic knowledge among students. The *economics* curriculum dedicates four chapters to *microeconomics* before moving on to *macroeconomics* and addressing the state's economic and social roles. Lessons such as "Microeconomics: The Theory of the Consumer," which describes preference curves and budget constraints, establish a useful foundation for understanding budget constraints at the macro level.

Learning Outcomes

Expected learning outcomes include a sound knowledge of the economic terminology and concepts presented in the curriculum, and the development of analytical, oral, and written expression skills, reflected in examples of the assessments for *economics*: the final examination includes a written and an oral test and features at least one exercise requiring a written commentary and an interpretation of results. There is at least one question on *microeconomics* and one on *macroeconomics*. The *macroeconomics* test includes at least two questions on a previously unread text, several statistical tables, and/or several graphs related to the topic. Reasoning is deemed more important than mathematical skills for this subject and, therefore, calculations are not required.

Content

The curriculum presents the national state budget in a chapter entitled "The State: Economic and Social Role." The first section begins with a discussion on the role of the state and whether it should adopt an active or passive approach to managing the economy. The second section on the state budget begins with an explanation of the budget process and then examines state income and expenditures. With regard to income, the program details the state's various sources of financing and differentiates between various types of taxes. It also discusses how to establish an optimal tax rate, including a presentation of the Laffer curve, according to which, beyond a certain point, an increase in taxes results in less revenue. State expenditures are also presented and categorized, leading the way toward defining *budget surpluses, deficits*, and *equilibrium* and toward an overview of how state debt can be financed.

The curriculum proceeds to explain the objectives of the government's economic policies and the emerging challenge of balancing a range of objectives, including employment, price levels and growth, balanced public finances, as well as a good business environment, social justice, and environmental protection.

Further, the lesson plans detail possible fiscal policy mechanisms as a tool for social and economic policies. Cyclical, expansionary, restrictive, structural, social, environmental, and budget policies; the EU framework; and Nicholas Kaldor's magical square, which sums up tensions between the four objectives of growth, employment, stable prices and favorable trade balance, are presented. Lastly, students learn about Keynesian policy and the Keynesian multiplier before turning to monetary policy in the following chapter.[102]

The curriculum gives limited attention to civic consciousness. Instead, it is primarily focused on the students acquiring knowledge of political economy concepts and mechanisms.

Pedagogical Approach

Employed teaching methods rely on traditional methods—that is, a textbook-based approach. As mentioned, because students are required to acquire analytical skills, some of the materials provided include graphic representations and statistics.

Lessons Learned

- Because an increasing number of municipalities, such as Luxembourg City, conduct participatory-budgeting initiatives, there is room to combine classroom teaching and curricular content with real-life budgeting experiments.

- Although various curricula mention the budget process and actors involved in the formal approval of the annual budget, there is scope to include a stronger focus on discussing the political character of budgets rather than presenting the state as a monolith when teaching about its actions and influences in the economic sphere.
- The curriculum does not present students with an understanding of how they themselves can influence the budget or voice their preferences. Going forward, adding this element to school programs could be useful to create a personal link to the subject and to reinforce the students' interest in this area.

D1.18 Namibia

Country: Namibia
Level: National
Implementer: Ministry of Education

Context

According to the 2015 Open Budget Survey, Namibia's score of 46 out of 100 for budget transparency indicates that the government provides the public with limited budget information, and its score of 15 out of 100 for public participation during the budget cycle suggests there are few opportunities for the public to engage in the budget process.[103] In order to encourage public understanding of the national budget, the Ministry of Finance published the *Citizen's Guide to the Budget*.[104]

National-level education in Namibia, which is overseen by the Ministry of Education, incorporates a substantial focus on financial literacy. For example, in 2012, the Ministry of Finance launched the Financial Literacy Initiative in collaboration with Deutsche Gesellschaft für Internationale Zusammenarbeit (GIZ). A series of financial-literacy publications illustrating topics such as budgeting, saving, and spending were produced.[105] There is, however, only a limited emphasis on budget literacy: students are not introduced to state budgets until the eleventh and twelfth grades.

Classroom-Based Budget-Literacy Initiatives

There is no standalone budget-literacy curriculum, but references to personal, business, and state budgets are included in a range of subjects, including *business studies, economics, entrepreneurship, life skills, home economics,* and *mathematics*. It is therefore plausible that teaching youth about budgets in various subjects and from different perspectives, beginning on a personal and business level and then moving on to explore the issue from an economic-policy standpoint, reinforces budget literacy.

Curriculum

The *entrepreneurship* curriculum for the junior secondary phase (grades 8–10), updated in 2012, is supposed to be taught during six class periods in a seven-day cycle (8 × 40 minute periods per day). The curricula for *life skills and home economics* for the junior-secondary phase, updated in 2007, include a broad range of key topics. The *business studies, life skills, mathematics,* and *economics* curricula for eleventh and twelfth grades were implemented in 2010.

Learning Outcomes

Learning outcomes for these subjects include "self-discipline, diligence, and a sense of responsibility to encourage worthy citizenship" (*entrepreneurship*);[106] to demonstrate an understanding of the government's economic policies (*economics*);

to develop a sound knowledge of taxes (*life skills*), and to build practical, hands-on budgeting skills (*business studies, life skills, home economics,* and *mathematics*).

Content

Overall, the approach to budgets in Namibia is multipronged, and budgets are generally presented as a subset element or category of a larger topic. In this way, from a curricular perspective, budgets are assigned an instrumental rather than intrinsic value. The only subject that makes mention of the state budget is *economics*. Through its focus on taxes, the *life skills* curriculum only presents the *income* side of the national budget; it does not explore the aspect of *expenses*. Other relevant subjects—*business studies, home economics,* and *mathematics*—approach budgets from a personal or business perspective.

The *entrepreneurship* curriculum (grades 8–10) covers key topics, including entrepreneurial traits and culture; scanning the environment for business opportunities; and successfully managing a small- to medium-size business. Beginning in eighth grade, students are introduced to budgets as the last topic in a series of lessons about developing and managing a family or business budget. Budget literacy is linked to other cross-curricular issues as well, such as *information and communications technology* and *population studies* (Republic of Namibia 2008).

In the *life skills* curriculum (grades 8–10), students learn about finances, including unemployment, budgets, and basic financial records. Students are expected to learn how to develop and implement personal budgets and acquire sufficient knowledge to attest to the importance of maintaining financial records (Republic of Namibia 2006).

The *home economics* curriculum (grades 8–10) includes several broad topics, including food and nutrition, consumerism, resource management, family studies, housing, and clothing. It addresses the topic of budgets in the context of resource management in tenth grade (Republic of Namibia 2007).

In the *economics* curriculum (11–12), the sixth theme is the *role of government in an economy*. It describes the government's role as a producer and employer, shaper of economic policies, and controller of business activity. In the second subset, the *government's role as a shaper of economic policies*, students learn to define government economic policy and discuss its aims and why they should be achieved, notably full employment, prevention of inflation, economic growth, redistribution of income, and stabilization of balance of payments. Students are also taught about fiscal and monetary policies. They learn to describe the different types of taxes and discuss how taxes are used by the government to influence business activities as well as the role of the budget (Republic of Namibia 2009a).

In the *life skills* curriculum (grades 11–12), students approach the topic of finances, specifically taxes. The objective is for students to learn about different types of taxes. By the end of eleventh grade, students are expected to have acquired basic competencies, including the ability to research different payable taxes in Namibia, such as income or sales tax; discuss the reasons for paying taxes; and engage in debates about the responsibilities of taxpayers (Republic of Namibia 2005).

In the *mathematics* curriculum (grades 11–12), students are expected to conduct calculations with money and understand issues regarding personal and household finances, including using data to solve tax- and budget-related problems (Republic of Namibia 2009b).

In the *business studies* curriculum (grades 11–12), students approach budgets from a business perspective and learn to explain *the nature and usefulness of budgets* as well as key accounting concepts, such as profit-and-loss accounts, balance sheets, and cash flow forecasts (Republic of Namibia 2010).

Pedagogical Approach
Overall, the traditional textbook approach appears to be most common, particularly for *business studies, economics,* and *mathematics.* For the *entrepreneurship, home economics,* and *life skills* syllabi, suggestions for teachers include building, extending, and challenging learners' prior knowledge and experiences and encouraging cooperative and collaborative learning. For the *life skills* curriculum, suggested activities include group work, such as research, case studies, and projects; performing art tasks, such as role-play, mime, and dance; creative tasks, such as designing posters and drawing pictures; cultural expression tasks, such as debates, role-play, and songs; and written tasks, such as essays, case studies, and articles.

Lessons Learned
- The Namibian case suggests that, even if budgets are explored in-depth in one subject (for example, in *economics*), it is still useful to complement this approach with additional references to budgets in a variety of other subjects. This strengthens the acquisition of budget literacy and provides students with a fuller perspective.
- Because of the existing entry points to further strengthen budget-literacy elements, additional research could consider a cost-benefit analysis of modifying the curricula to include more in-depth explorations of public budget issues. In particular, there seems to be a window of opportunity to move on to an analysis of public budgets following the stage when students learn about personal and business budgets.

D1.19 New Zealand

Country: New Zealand
Level: National
Implementer: Ministry of Education; New Zealand Treasury

Context

The Government of New Zealand's budget transparency score of 88 out of 100 in the 2015 Open Budget Survey attests to the fact that the public has access to extensive budget information, and its score of 65 out of 100 on public participation confirms that the public has adequate opportunities to engage in the budget process.[107]

Education in New Zealand is overseen by the Ministry of Education. The motivation for including budget-literacy elements in the school curriculum is to achieve the objective of educating young citizens regarding their participation in and contributions to society, notably through the taxes that they will pay in the future. Students are taught about public budgets during the secondary level of education as part of the *social sciences* learning area, which builds on knowledge and skills developed at the lower levels. For instance, requirements for years 2–10 of *social sciences* intend for students to acquire an understanding of their social, cultural, and economic roles, rights, and responsibilities.

Classroom-Based Budget-Literacy Initiatives
Curriculum

Last updated in 2007,[108] the achievement objectives for the *social sciences* learning area (years 2–10) integrate concepts from conceptual strands that include *identity, culture, and organization; place and the environment; continuity and change,* and the *economic world.* This establishes the foundation for the separate social science disciplines offered in senior secondary school. During years 11–13, students are able to specialize in one or more of these, depending on the choices offered by the schools. Achievement objectives are provided for *social studies, economics, geography,* and *history,* but the range of possible social science disciplines that schools can offer is much broader, including, as examples, *classical studies, media studies, sociology, psychology,* and *legal studies.*

For years 2 through 10, the *economic world* module facilitates learning about the way in which people participate in economic activities and about the consumption, production, and distribution of goods and services. Students also develop an understanding of their role in the economy and of how economic decisions affect individuals and communities. As part of the curriculum for level 4 (years 7–8) and level 5 (years 9–10), a unit on *tax education and citizenship* facilitates understanding of budgets by linking it to tax education.

At the senior secondary level (years 11–13) students acquire more detailed knowledge of public budgets as part of the *economics* course for levels 6–8. This subject is part of the student assessment for New Zealand's senior-secondary-school qualification: the National Certificate of Educational Achievement.[109]

Learning Outcomes

The rationale for budget-literacy elements that are taught as part of the *social sciences* curriculum (years 7 through 10) is to introduce taxes what they are used for, how citizens are involved in this process, and how they can benefit from tax payments. Learning outcomes for students include a solid understanding of their country's taxation system and its purpose. For the *economics* curriculum (years 11–13), desired learning outcomes include helping students acquire skills to understand government policies and public finances, recognize the different perspectives and values individuals and groups bring to economic decision-making, and participate effectively in public life.

Content

The *social sciences* curriculum for years 7 through 10 (levels 4 and 5) facilitates an understanding of budgets by linking knowledge of public budgets with tax education and focusing on the key competencies of *participating and contributing* and *managing self*, both of which have strong links to citizenship. It introduces level 4 students to basic facts about taxes and their impact, how decisions are made about public finances, and differing opinions of various constituencies regarding tax spending. It then moves on to become more student-centered for level 5 students, exploring questions such as: How do taxes relate to me? How do decisions regarding taxes affect young people? How can young people influence tax policy?[110]

The senior-secondary *economics* curriculum teaches students about key micro-economic and macroeconomic concepts and examines issues that serve as useful stepping-stones for a critical understanding of budgetary policies. In addition to other topics, it compares the impact of government policies on various groups in society, the types of government interventions to correct market failures, and the influence of values on economic choices.

Pedagogical Approaches

Rooted in the social inquiry approach,[111] pedagogical methods used by the *social sciences* curriculum (years 4–5) to teach students about public budgets and taxes are highly interactive and, to a great extent, rely on student participation. Examples of relevant activities include:

- **Outdoor mapping exercise.** Students are taken for a walk in their local community and are asked to identify features paid for by the government or local council.
- **Direct interaction with experts.** Speakers from the local council are invited to speak to students or the school principal or treasurer provides feedback on the students' estimations of school expenses and financing mechanisms and respond to questions about the school's income and expenditure patterns.
- **Role-play.** Students engage in role-playing scenarios that include community discussions about local funding issues and parliamentary or cabinet discussions about financial support for specific activities, such as disaster management after the 2010–11 Christchurch earthquakes.

- **Survey design.** Students are asked to design surveys to find out how people in the school and community feel about taxes and to conduct perception-based interviews with adults about taxes and tax use by the government, followed by class discussions and cross-comparisons.
- **Scenario analysis.** Students engage in discussions on, for example, fairness based on various scenarios of people paying or not paying taxes.[112]

The enquiry approach is also recommended for the *economics* curriculum. Teachers are encouraged to establish an inclusive learning environment for students and adopt pedagogical practices that foster participation; reward initiative; encourage innovation, inquiry, and curiosity; respect diversity; build positive and respectful relationships; and promote equity and cooperative learning. Teachers are also advised to adopt pedagogical methods such as: making connections to students' lives, aligning experiences to important outcomes, building and sustaining learning communities, and designing experiences that interest students.[113]

Materials
Several online teaching resources are available to educators to help engage students around public budgets and taxes. For the *social sciences* curriculum, these include cartoons,[114] introductory videos,[115] interactive tools, school budget charts,[116] and the *Tax Education and Citizenship Survey*.[117] While they are not directly related to budget literacy, a range of resources is available for the *economics* syllabus, including teaching and learning guides, assessment specifications, and exemplars of students' work.[118]

Out-of-Classroom Budget-Literacy Initiatives
New Zealand's Treasury Department has made several efforts to engage with young people on fiscal issues.

High School Challenge
Since 2012, the Treasury Department has cosponsored an annual challenge with the Victoria University of Wellington where high school students from around the country present solutions to challenging policy issues, such as how to address New Zealand's long-term fiscal priorities and increase productivity. High school students work in teams and submit essays, and finalist teams are invited to present their proposed solutions to the Minister of Finance.

The Treasury Department has also organized an annual essay competition for university students since 2013. Students from all disciplines are invited to submit essays on one of a number of assigned topics designed to test economic analysis and broader social, distributional, and environmental impacts. Finalists are invited to the Treasury Department to present their analyses, and the winner of the competition receives a $ 2,500 scholarship toward their university fees for the following year.

Policy Workshops

Occasionally, the Treasury Department convenes workshops with young people to seek their inputs on specific policy projects. Such workshops serve to provide experiential learning experiences for youth as well as opportunities to engage in policy debates that they might not otherwise have. So far, the workshops, cosponsored by the McGuinness Institute, have addressed issues such as long-term fiscal pressures, the Treasury Department's Living Standards Framework, and regional governance. Twenty-seven students who had participated in the December 2012 LongTermNZ workshop prepared the "2012 Youth Statement on New Zealand's Long-Term Fiscal Position 2012–2052,"[119] which they presented to Treasury officials. This statement prioritized fiscal policy areas such as reducing costs, increasing tax revenues and savings, building human capital, improving productivity, and improving social cohesion as the means to attain the vision for New Zealand in 2052 (Krieble and O'Dwyer-Cunliffe 2013).

Visits and Lectures

Because Treasury Department staff members are available to share their insights with final year high school economics classes, schools across New Zealand have availed themselves of this opportunity by planning visits to the Treasury Department. Treasury Department analysts from the Macroeconomic Policy Team have been invited as guest lectures for *economics* classes at the Victoria University of Wellington. Moreover, following the publication of the *2013 Statement on the Long-Term Fiscal Position*,[120] the Treasury Department ran feedback sessions at universities around New Zealand in conjunction with the New Zealand Union of Student Associations.

Lessons Learned

- Rather than beginning with an analysis of budgets, which may be difficult to relate to, New Zealand's curriculum uses *taxes* as an entry point to broach the topic of *public budgets*. This creates for students a tangible link to their environment by highlighting how taxes directly affect them.
- Emphasizing the rationale for taxes at an early stage may be a win-win situation for government and citizens: citizens develop the necessary skills to influence tax spending, should they wish to do so, and the government secures responsible tax-paying behavior from its citizenry.

D1.20 Peru

Country: Peru
Level: National
Implementers: National Tax Administration Office; Ministry of Education; General Comptroller's Office

Context

Peru's 2015 Open Budget Index score of 75 out of 100 indicates that the government of Peru provides the public with substantial budget information. However its score of 40 out of 100 on public participation in the budget process means that it is challenging for citizens to engage with the government and hold it accountable for its management of the public's money.[121]

Education in Peru is under the jurisdiction of the Ministry of Education, which is in charge of formulating, implementing, and supervising the national educational policy. According to the Constitution of Peru, education is compulsory and free in public schools at the preschool, primary, and secondary levels. SUNAT (Superintendencia Nacional de Administración Tributaria)—Peru's national tax administration office—has the strategic objective of promoting fiscal and customs consciousness among citizens at the national level. In 2006, SUNAT and the Ministry of Education signed an Inter-Institutional Co-operation Agreement to include tax awareness content in the curricular programs of the Department of Initial Education, the Department of Primary Education, and the Department of Secondary Education.

Classroom-Based Budget-Literacy Initiatives

Curriculum

As a consequence of the Inter-Institutional Co-operation Agreement between SUNAT and the Ministry of Education, by 2009, tax culture subjects became compulsory for all students from preschool through the secondary level of education. That same year, a course was designed to ensure quality teaching of tax matters that followed the new national curricular design. Training workshops were launched in 2010, and a virtual course has been designed and implemented since 2012 to help teachers construct concepts based on their prior knowledge. A web portal has also been created to make relevant materials accessible to all primary and secondary school teachers and students.[122]

The *social life* course for primary school grades 1, 2, 5, and 6 focuses on personal development and citizenship. The *history, geography, and economics* course for grades 1–5 of secondary school includes an introduction to economics. Although neither subject includes topics directly related to budget literacy, some topics, such as *participation in public life* and *responsible use of economic resources*, represent building blocks for the teaching of budget literacy.[123]

Learning Outcomes

The *social life* course aims to foster ethical behavior and strong social identity among students, to motivate them to participate in public issues promoting the common good and to act responsibly regarding the utilization of economic resources. The *history, geography, and economics* course for grades 1–5 includes content to teach youth how to use economic resources responsibly.

Content
While the *social life* class focuses on aspects of civics, the *history, geography, and economics* course seeks to build the students' capacity for understanding the economic and financial system, to help them gain consciousness about how citizens are part of an economic system, and to teach them how to manage resources responsibly.

Pedagogical Approach and Materials
To complement the rather sparse budget-literacy elements in the curriculum, SUNAT's *Tax Culture Program* developed teaching materials for educators that complemented classroom activities, including a magazine with cartoon characters introducing budget-literacy concepts such as citizen rights, public services and goods, the role and purpose of taxes, and the importance of payment receipts and customs. The Ministry of Education has also created a series of pedagogical materials entitled "Learning Routes" to support teachers implementing the curriculum in primary and secondary schools. Among these, some modules present budget-literacy concepts that explain the national budget, the role of taxes to provide basic services and pursue the common good, and the link between taxes and public expenditures. As part of the *Tax Culture Program*, trainings, lectures, and workshops have been organized for educators across the country.

Out-of-Classroom Budget-Literacy Initiatives
SUNAT also organizes out-of-school activities to promote fiscal education among young people ages 5–12, including setting up booths for youth in parks, plazas, playgrounds, and other public places to distribute pedagogical materials on tax and fiscal issues and organize games and contests for children. For example, a board game called *Building Our Country* tests children's knowledge of citizenship and tax issues. Occasionally, such activities are organized in schools at the request of principals.

Other activities that are particularly popular among children are theatrical presentations that address citizenship values related to tax and fiscal issues. One pedagogical element that is particularly engaging to children is *Ayni*, a penguin mascot who, with human friends *Mateo* and *Clarita*, participates in learning activities. So far, more than 170,000 children have engaged in these types of activities.

Payment Receipt Raffle
SUNAT also runs a *School Payment Receipt Raffle* through which educational institutions can win prizes of up to US$ 300,000.[124] In 2014, nearly 9,000 schools across the country participated in this initiative, an increase of 70 percent since 2013. This is useful to emphasize the importance of payment receipts and

discourage informal economic activity to teachers, students, and their parents. A similar initiative—called *School Certifications*—encourages fifth-year secondary school students around the country to demand payment receipts when making a purchase or requesting a service.

Youth Auditors

The *Youth Auditors* program, established by the General Comptroller's Office and the Ministry of Education in 2010, is aimed at promoting values of social auditing among youth. The program has trained more than 200,000 secondary-school students across the country. These students have conducted more than 3,700 social audits for their schools and other agencies, and their efforts have helped to improve education and public infrastructure.

Lessons Learned

- Beyond participatory budgeting at the school level, Peru's experience high-lights that other forms of involvement, such as social audits at the school level, may also be envisaged to engage students in the monitoring of public finances.
- The use of mascots and fictive characters highlights the added value of person-alizing tax and budgetary education.

D1.21 Philippines

Country: Philippines
Level: National
Implementers: Department of Education; Philippines Center for Civic Education and Democracy

Context

Findings of the 2015 Open Budget Survey indicate that the government of the Philippines provides the public with substantial budget information, demonstrated by its transparency score of 64 out of 100. Moreover, with an Open Budget Survey score of 67 out of 100 on public participation and as one of the eight founding Open Government Partnership countries, efforts in the Philippines have to date clearly prioritized the strengthening of citizen participation in the budgetary process as well. National and local government agencies have been mandated by the government to publish major information on budgets, finance, and performance indicators online (OGP 2014b). Moreover, several government institutions, cities, municipalities, and civil society organizations have been engaged in developing the national budget by forging Budget Partnership Agreements, by which more than US$ 195 million worth of projects identified through a grassroots participatory-budgeting process were incorporated into the 2013 national budget; they are still being implemented today. Nevertheless, participation in the budget process is a fairly new phenomenon in the Philippines, and citizens have a limited familiarity with public budgets.

Measures to specifically incorporate budget-literacy education into the syllabus are yet to be implemented. The national curriculum is overseen by the Department of Education. Its focus has been on strengthening financial literacy, money management skills, and entrepreneurship rather than budget literacy. At the same time, there are subjects that introduce budget-literacy elements, including *social studies* at the lower-secondary level, *economics and contemporary issues* at the junior high school level, and *applied economics* and *Philippine politics and governance* at the senior high school level.[125]

Classroom-Based Budget-Literacy Initiatives

The Philippine school system used to consist of six years of elementary school and four years of secondary school, but it is transitioning toward a K–12 curriculum. The first cohort of high school students who have studied the K–12 curriculum will graduate in March 2018.

Curriculum

As part of its commitment to achieving the goals of the Education for All program, the government is implementing K–12 educational reform, which involves decongesting and enhancing the basic educational curriculum to allow students to master basic competencies, and lengthening the basic educational cycle to cover the K–12 syllabus. Education based on the K–12 curriculum will enable students to acquire certificates of competency and national certifications issued by the Technical Skills Development Authority.

Rather than explicitly focusing on budget-literacy education, the curriculum seeks to build political awareness among youth and adopts a multipronged approach that refers to public budgets in various subjects.

Learning Outcomes

At the lower-secondary level, the new *social studies* curriculum is intended for students to acquire a deep understanding and appreciation of contemporary issues and challenges associated with the economy, the environment, and politics in addition to human rights and civic responsibility in the Philippines, in Asia, and around the world. It seeks to develop skills such as critical thinking, logical reasoning, creativity, research, and communication among students and to encourage values of responsibility, productivity, environmental consciousness, and having a global vision.

The junior high school *economics* course expects students to be familiar with key economic concepts as well as the operations of the domestic economy. It is based on the hypothesis that knowledge of the market economy is important to enable youth to fruitfully participate in discussions regarding economic issues. The *contemporary issues* course is intended to increase students' awareness of graft and corruption and their impact on public trust and civic participation, as well as avenues for participating in public processes.

The subject of *applied economics* aims to equip senior high school students with competencies to identify basic economic problems, explain how applied economics can be used to solve economic problems, and identify and explain various socioeconomic factors that affect business and industry.[126] Students enrolled in the senior-level *Philippine politics and governance* course are expected to acquire knowledge regarding political engagement and youth empowerment, assess existing programs with these areas of focus, and draft research proposals to improve such programs.

Content

The K–12 curriculum's *social studies* program incorporates key details related to civics education that are useful in establishing a context for budget-literacy education. In second grade, students learn about the qualities of good governance and the importance of public service to meet the needs of the community. In third grade, they are introduced to the economy, the governance system of the provinces, and civic rights and responsibilities. During fourth grade, the focus shifts to the structure and framework of the government of the Philippines, including the three branches of government, the separation of powers, and provisions for checks and balances. The curriculum also accommodates specialized topics, such as disaster preparedness, human rights, and the environment.

At the junior high school level, the *macroeconomics* module in the *economics* course describes the purpose of fiscal policy, the government's spending priorities, national tax policies, priority assistance development funds, privatization of government-owned and -controlled corporations, and conditional cash transfers, followed by an introduction to monetary policy, savings, and entrepreneurship.[127] The *contemporary issues* course will be offered to students beginning in 2017.

At the senior high school level, the *accountancy, business, and management* strand includes an *applied economics* course focused on applying economic principles to contemporary economic issues for Filipino entrepreneurs, such as commodity prices, minimum wages, rents, and taxes. The main output of the course is the socioeconomic impact study of a specific business venture. Course elements relevant to budget literacy include basic economic problems and the socioeconomic development of the Philippines in the 21st century; the impact of taxes from an entrepreneurship perspective; and a socioeconomic impact study on government tax revenues, poverty alleviation, and basic services.

The *humanities and social sciences* strand offers a course on *Philippine politics and governance*. This introduces students to the basic concepts and vital elements of politics and governance from a historical-institutional perspective and high-lights important features of the political structures and institutions, processes, and relationships that have developed over time. The curriculum also covers topics such as decentralization and local governance, elections and political par-ties, civil society and social movements, and citizenship in practice.[128]

Pedagogical Approaches

Overall, the new K–12 curriculum is oriented toward enhancing the learning experience of students through its emphasis on critical thinking rather than memorization (Franco-Velasco 2012). Moreover, the Department of Education has stressed the need to contextualize the curriculum based on local needs and contexts. Teaching methods for the *Philippine politics and governance* course involve encouraging the active participation and direct engagement of students with political representatives. Activities include sending formal correspondence to legislators to advocate for specific policy issues; appraising the impact of the performance of the Congress on socio-economic development in the Philippines; conducting interviews with local public officials about community programs; and evaluating the performance of local government units.

Out-of-Classroom Budget-Literacy Initiatives
Civic Education Training Seminar

The Philippines Center for Civic Education and Democracy (PCCED) has developed a civics education training seminar to enhance teacher competence in the subject and a teaching manual that recommends adding a sequence on *economic citizenship* to the existing junior high school *economics* curriculum. The module is geared toward strengthening students' consciousness regarding their civic responsibility to pay taxes correctly, avoiding tax evasion and double accounting in business, reporting on corrupt practices, promoting greater trans-parency and accountability for persons responsible for financial transactions, and encouraging independent auditing of budget spending.

Project Citizen

PCCED recommends that the Department of Education pilot a program that would allow students to participate in the public local budgeting process. In addition, in 2013–14, the PCCED implemented "Project Citizen" in ten areas (National Capital Region, Batangas, Baguio, Sorsogon, Bohol, Bacolod, Davao, Kalinga, Pampanga, and Butuan City). Intended to increase democratic participation, political efficacy, and civic engagement among students at the high school level, PCCED has drawn on this program to systematically train teacher-moderators to embed education about democracy into the classroom and to provide a venue for students to participate in community problem solving and apply what they have learned in the *citizenship* course to real life. Project Citizen also creates avenues for students to engage with the local legislators and authorities to whom they present their policy proposals. In some instances, local authorities respond positively and adopt the policies or fund the suggested projects. In this way, Project Citizen emerged as an important mechanism for youth participation in the budget process.

Lessons Learned

- Incorporating a participatory/experiential learning component to existing syllabi which is focused on the basics of public budgets could serve to strengthen students' knowledge in this area.
- Exploring the possibility of incorporating budget-literacy elements in additional subjects, such as science and mathematics, could also be useful.
- Suggested activities in the Philippine *politics and governance* subject contribute to forming active citizens who are aware of how they can interact with public officials. The inclusion of direct contact with political representatives lends credibility to the program and lays the foundation for participation of youth in the public sphere, including engagement in issues related to budget literacy.
- Based on feedback from the PCCED, a deficit of teacher training poses a major challenge to efforts at incorporating budget literacy into the school curriculum.

D1.22 Poland

Country: Poland
Level: National
Implementers: Ministry of National Education

Context

The 2015 Open Budget Survey[129] finds that with a score of 64 percent on transparency, Poland's government provides the public with substantial budget information. On the other hand, Poland's score of 44 percent on public participation indicates that the public has limited opportunities to engage in the budget process, and that there is scope to establish credible and effective mechanisms (such as public hearings, surveys, and focus groups) for capturing a range of public perspectives on budget matters.

Budget literacy education is not featured in Poland's core curriculum for preschool or general education. However, a compulsory *history and society* course taught during stage 2 of primary school (grades 4–6) provides students with a basic knowledge of the state and the modern world. Over the course of three years, 130 hours are devoted to teaching this subject. During stage 1 of primary school (grades 1–3), integrated education consists of *civics*, *Polish language*, *mathematics*, *nature*, and *technical* classes. The compulsory focus on *mathematics* education equips students with basic knowledge of money calculations, coins, bank notes, debt, and the necessity of paying off mortgages.

Classroom-Based Budget-Literacy Initiatives
Curriculum

Based on the new core curriculum introduced by the Ministry of National Education in 2008, budget-literacy content is incorporated into two compulsory subjects during secondary school—*civics*, which is taught in lower- and upper-secondary schools and *basics of entrepreneurship*, which is taught in upper-secondary school.

In the *civics* curriculum for the lower-secondary level, students discuss sociological issues related to the functioning of the group, learn about the modern political system, and become familiar with the Polish constitution. They acquire knowledge regarding the functions of local government and the importance of ethics in public life. Over a three-year period, 65 hours are devoted to civics education. At the upper-secondary level (ages 16–20), the *civics* curriculum is more interdisciplinary. It is taught for 30 hours over a three-year period and includes *sociology*, *politics*, and *law and international relations* units, a limited portion of which include budget-literacy elements.

The *basics of entrepreneurship* course introduces entrepreneurial concepts in the context of work, the economy, and contemporary issues. At least 60 teaching hours are allocated to entrepreneurship over the course of three years.

Learning Outcomes

For lower-secondary-level students (ages 13–16), the overarching objectives of the *civics* curriculum are to encourage involvement in civic activities and develop the attitudes and values of responsible and civic-minded citizens. Specific learning outcomes regarding knowledge of public budgets include: an understanding of decision-making processes at the municipal level, particularly those related to budget-related decisions; the allocation and utilization of EU funding; important sources of state revenue and expenditure priorities; and the main types of taxes in Poland.

The *civics* course at the upper-secondary level is also geared toward fostering a sense of responsibility for society and the state; promoting patriotism and responsibility for the common good, acquiring skills to understand and apply the provisions of law; and build self-esteem and encourage participation in civic life. Budget-literacy learning outcomes include knowledge of the tasks and responsibilities of local government at the provincial and municipal levels; the municipal budget process and sources of revenue and major expenditure items for local governments; the procedure for adopting the EU budget and key sources of budget revenue and expenditure priorities at the national level; and general rules for use of EU funds by citizens, businesses, and other organizations in Poland.

The broad learning objectives of secondary-level *entrepreneurship* education is to prepare young people to participate in economic life by developing an entrepreneurial attitude, understanding what steps are needed to become an entrepreneur, and learning how entrepreneurship is relevant to the broader workings of the macro-economy. With regard to public budgets, students are expected to be familiar with the policy instruments governments use to influence the economy and phenomena related to economic recession and growth.

Content

In the lower-secondary *civics* curriculum, because budget literacy is referred to in the broader context of orienting students with the levels and functions of government in Poland, topics such as citizen participation in public life; the functions of provincial and municipal governments; Poland's membership in the EU; and the role of households, financial institutions, and the government in Poland's economy are introduced.

Aspects of the upper-secondary-level *civics* budget-literacy related curriculum focus on local governments in Poland, European integration, and Poland's role in the EU. The basic *entrepreneurship* curriculum introduces a broad range of topics, such as work and entrepreneurship, the market economy, households, and financial institutions. Content associated with understanding public budgets are concentrated in modules on *the national economy, ethics in economic life, European integration* (including the EU budget), and *issues of the contemporary world* (including globalization).

Pedagogical Approaches

As part of the *civics* curriculum at the lower and upper-secondary levels, students are encouraged to work on solving selected problems relating to their environment and the wider community and to participate in student council activities. Pedagogical methods to teach civics, including budget-literacy concepts, include problem solving, case studies, debate, discussion, role-play, brainstorming, and working in pairs and groups.

Various teaching strategies have been used to clarify budget literacy and other concepts for the *entrepreneurship* course, including simulations, projects, problem solving, preparing conceptual maps and business plans, engaging in discussions, group work and workshops, and addressing case study questions.

Out-of-Classroom Budget-Literacy Initiatives

- Poland's Ministry of Finance has launched an educational program for lower-secondary students that aims to raise awareness among students regarding taxes and state funding of basic activities, such as education and road safety. This program is also intended to support teachers imparting budget-literacy concepts by producing educational materials that are engaging and appealing.
- The Warsaw Centre for Socio-Educational Innovation and Training has prepared lesson plans on participatory budgeting for primary and lower- and upper-secondary schools as a learning activity related to the implementation of the public budget.
- The Youth Entrepreneurship Foundation (*Fundacja Młodzieżowej Przedsiębiorczości*) is a part of Junior Achievement Worldwide[130] and Civil Development Forum.[131] It has prepared and disseminated educational materials such as publications and lesson plans on economic education, including budget literacy.
- In 2013, the Association Civil Initiatives Development Centre launched the *School Participation Project*. Students from 10 schools (five from Rybnik and five from Kielce) developed project proposals that were subject to student voting. Projects receiving the most student votes were implemented for a total amount of 20,000 Polish Zloty (approximately US$ 5,000).

Lessons Learned

- Collaboration among schools, local partners, nongovernmental organizations, and government agencies is essential for establishing a support network that provides budget-literacy education through existing curricula.
- Student engagement in participatory budgeting is substantially reliant on the degree of openness a school administration has toward such initiatives.

D1.23 Singapore

Country: Singapore
Level: National
Implementers: Ministry of Education; Ministry of Finance

Context

Singapore's Ministry of Finance utilizes its website and the online *Reach* portal to solicit citizens' views regarding the upcoming annual budget. Still, there is room to improve public participation in the budget process by extending the timeframe for public budget consultations; releasing the prebudget statement at least one month prior to the executive budget proposal; disseminating a citizens' budget; and providing access to disaggregated information on the prior performance of respective policies and programs (Shaddick and Wee 2014).

Singapore's educational system is overseen by the Ministry of Education and is ranked among the best in the world. The ministry manages the development and administration of state schools and fulfills an advisory and supervisory role with regard to private schools. Budget-literacy concepts are introduced through the primary level syllabi for *character and citizenship* and *social studies* and examined in further depth in secondary-level *economics* and *social studies* curricula.

Classroom-Based Budget-Literacy Initiatives
Curriculum

Ratified by the 2003 Compulsory Education Act, primary education begins at the age of seven. There is a four-year *foundation stage* (primary 1–4) and a two-year *orientation stage* (primary 5–6). At the end of primary 6, all students are assessed on their academic progress through a primary school leaving examination.

Students usually enroll in secondary school at the age of 13 years and attend for four to five years. Based on the results of the primary school leaving examination, students are placed in secondary education tracks or streams: *special, express, normal (academic),* or *normal (technical)*. *Special* and *express* are four-year courses leading up to the Singapore-Cambridge General Certificate of Education ordinary-level ("O") examination before going on to a two-year advanced level (A-level) education (Ministry of Education, Singapore 2015).

Learning Outcomes

Among other overarching learning outcomes, the *character and citizenship* curriculum aims for students to emerge as informed and responsible citizens who have a strong sense of national identity and commitment to nation-building; are capable of reflecting on and responding to community, national, and global issues; and are able to contribute to the progress of their community and nation.

Social studies education seeks to develop the students' sense of civic consciousness and related competencies. With regard to budget literacy, the upper-secondary module called "Managing Our Financial Resources" aims for students to acquire a sufficient level of financial and economic literacy so that they can examine how financial resources are managed, allocated, and consumed at the personal and national levels; assess the consequences of the mismanagement of financial resources; and develop an awareness of the need to responsibly manage financial resources. It also intends for students to hone their skills at gathering and organizing information, using sources and data to make observations and interpretations, considering different viewpoints to make informed judgments, and clearly communicating their ideas and findings through various tools and modes of presentation. Finally, this module encourages youth to develop values such as being considerate to others and exercising thrift and prudence in the management of financial resources.

Expected learning outcomes for the *economics* curriculum for GCE O-level students includes their being able to draw conclusions from economic information and critically evaluate economic data, distinguish between evidence and opinion, make reasoned judgments and communicate them in an accurate and logical manner, and evaluate the social and environmental implications of particular courses of economic action. The GCE advanced-level curriculum for *economics* focuses on enhancing the students' ability to select and apply economic concepts and principles to explain and analyze contemporary events at the micro- and macro levels; recognize unstated assumptions; and evaluate alternative theoretical explanations and perspectives of economic problems, issues, and policy decisions.

Content

The *character and citizenship* curriculum elaborates on concepts and values such as active citizenship, economic and financial literacy, taking care of public property, and understanding government constraints. Within this syllabus, the *nation* and *world* modules introduce concepts that are most relevant to budget-literacy education.

In primary school, the *nation* module teaches students about their national identity and the value of civic responsibility. In secondary school, this module elaborates on the students' role in Singapore's economic defense and on skills and values such as responsible decision making, consideration of issues from the national perspective, and a commitment toward Singapore's well-being. The *world* module (primary 5–6) creates awareness among students about current issues that countries in the region are contending with, and familiarizes secondary-level students with regional trends and their impact on Singapore as well as with the importance of assuming civic responsibility to remain informed about global issues.

The *social studies* syllabus for primary-school students is based on three clusters of study: "Discovering Self and Immediate Environment," "Understanding Singapore in the Past and Present," and "Appreciating the World and the Region We Live In." As part of the instruction for the second cluster, the curriculum focuses on social living and quality decision-making and inculcates students in the importance of social responsibility and their role as active and concerned citizens.

At the upper-secondary level, a module called "Managing Our Financial Resources" acquaints students with basic financial-literacy concepts such as the use of a budget as a decision-making tool; personal budgets, savings, and expenses; and managing personal finances to promote self-reliance. It then highlights the role of government expenditures and the development of Singapore through the national budget. Students are familiarized with the relevance of the national budget to their lives and the role of citizens in contributing to the management of Singapore's financial resources.

Within the GCE O-level *economics* curriculum, a module called the "Role of Government in the Economy" explains and analyzes the use of fiscal, monetary, and supply-side policies; discusses potential conflicts among government goals; and describes the types of taxes, such as direct, indirect, progressive, regressive, and proportional taxes, as well as their impacts.

As part of the GCE A-level curriculum (high levels 1 and 2), budget-literacy content in the *macroeconomics* module examines the effects of fiscal policy on the economy, including the multiplier process; the effectiveness of fiscal policy in achieving macroeconomic aims; potential conflicts among government objectives; and the links between different macroeconomic problems and their interrelatedness.

Pedagogical Approaches and Materials

For both primary- and secondary-school students, the teaching of the *character and citizenship* curriculum is process-based and focused on the *why* and *how* rather than on the *what*. It relies on a range of pedagogical approaches (see box D.2) and draws on instructional strategies such as role-play, dialogue, cooperative learning, thinking routines, group work, and reflection.

Box D.2 Pedagogical Approaches for the Character and Citizenship Curriculum

- The *story-telling* approach involves telling, both fictional and true stories to facilitate the internalization of values.
- The *consideration* approach builds on empathy and enables students to empathize with the perspectives of other people to develop a balanced view of a situation.
- The *experiential learning* approach enables students to acquire experiences and platforms that enable them to reflect on values, concepts, and ideas and to internalize the values through the application of skills and knowledge learned in real-world situations.
- The *cognitive development* approach encourages students to respond to real or hypothetical moral dilemmas and to focus on societal and universal perspectives.
- The *modified values clarification* approach enables students to think about and clarify their values by examining their personal feelings and behavior patterns using rational thinking, empathy, and emotional awareness.

Source: Ministry of Education, Singapore 2014.

Overall, the *social studies* syllabus adopts an inquiry-based pedagogical approach. Driven by the questions of teachers and students, it creates and capitalizes on students' curiosity to make the learning experience authentic and meaningful. It is based on four fundamental elements: question-driven learning, double movement of reflection, and reliance on evidence and knowledge construction (see box D.3).

The *social studies* syllabus for primary-school students refers to teaching approaches such as creating posters, jingles, stories, show-and tell, role-play, and information and communications technology presentations. The secondary-school syllabus highlights methods such as sharing stimulus materials to trigger interest among students and encouraging them to question their assumptions and beliefs about specific issues; asking them to gather information through sources such as books, journal articles, websites, and films; and assigning fieldwork that lets students make observations about authentic scenarios or to conduct interviews and surveys with community members.

Finally, the economics unit of the Curriculum Planning and Development Division of the Ministry of Education has been closely partnering with the Ministry of Finance to promote budget literacy among students by reaching out to secondary schools (students ages 13–16) and junior colleges (students ages 17–18) before and after the release of the budget proposal and implementing the following measures:

- **Budget quiz.** Prior to the release of the annual budget in January, the Ministry of Finance launches an online budget quiz, where students compete to win

---

Box D.3 Pedagogical Approaches for the *Social Studies* Curriculum

Question-driven learning allows teachers to develop the students' interest, assess their learning, and challenge them to push the boundaries of their thinking and explore alternative perspectives. Appropriate questions for this approach are open-ended; deliberately thought-provoking, counter-intuitive, and/or controversial, and require students to draw on their content knowledge and personal experiences.

Iterative double movement of reflection relies on a constant revisitation of an existing hypothesis that leads to the creation of certain beliefs or theses—that is, the point where our experiences and new evidence cause us to no longer question our hypothesis. This is particularly useful to deepen understanding of specific concepts or issues.

Teaching methods that encourage *reliance on evidence* help students distinguish fact from opinion, evaluate the reliability and usefulness of information, draw conclusions based on evidence, and judge whether or not conclusions drawn by others are supported by evidence.

Knowledge construction takes into account the students' prior knowledge and assumptions. It promotes learning opportunities that help students become aware of how they see things and reconstruct their existing knowledge in light of new knowledge.

Source: Ministry of Education, Singapore 2013.

---

prizes for themselves and for their schools. It is a fun and interactive learning opportunity for students to understand the national budget process; some of Singapore's economic, social, and tax policies; and budgetary measures. The budget quiz consists of a series of weekly mini-quizzes that lead to a final quiz in which youth with perfect scores are able to participate.

While the budget quiz is open to all citizens, the Ministry of Finance actively reaches out to local schools to encourage student participation. Secondary schools, junior colleges, and centralized institutes with the highest number of students with perfect scores on the budget quiz are awarded the Singapore Budget Challenge trophy.

- **Preparing for the budget.** To support the efforts of the Ministry of Finance, the *economics* unit of the Ministry of Education created a set of lesson ideas called "Preparing for the Budget," which are used by teachers to engage students prior to the release of the annual budget at the end of February.

  Teachers are encouraged to allow secondary-school students to explore the Ministry of Finance website's section on the budget, which introduces the government budget, its purpose, agencies involved in its preparation, the budget process, and avenues for citizens to participate in the budget cycle.

- **Learning about the budget.** Following the release of the budget in early March, the *economics* unit follows up with "Learning about Budget 2015"—a just-in-time resource package to help teachers guide their students toward a deeper understanding of the annual budget from a range of perspectives and to spark classroom discussions on various fiscal measures. The package includes two sets of lesson ideas and a summary of the budget debate round-up speech.

  Lesson 1—"Building Our Future and Strengthening Social Security"— focuses on highlights of the budget proposal and their impact on various segments of the population and Singapore's economy. Students are asked to discuss in groups and present findings of their analyses on the effects the budget would have from the perspectives of the government, the private sector, and households.

  Lesson 2—"Enhancing Productivity"—emphasizes the impact of proposed budget measures on Singapore's innovation and productivity. Secondary-school students are encouraged to engage in debates and to learn about the implications of the budget proposal for firms in Singapore. As part of this discussion, students assume the roles of various owners of firms in order to understand the budget's impact on their productivity. The package also includes the "Budget-in-Brief"[132] and the transcript of the complete "Budget Speech,"[133] which provides additional information about the budget.

Assessment

The overall assessment of *character and citizenship* education is a student-centric and whole-school approach based on self-assessments, peer assessments, and teachers' views of student performance. Strategies include reflection, journal writing, peer-to-peer questioning, collaborative learning and questioning, and observations by teachers. Tools being used include checklists, rubrics, journals, behavioral indicators, and report cards.

Assessment approaches for the primary-level *social studies* curriculum include comprehension, application, analysis, synthesis, and evaluation of subject knowledge; skills for planning, processing, and communicating information; and values such as awareness of personal and collective responsibility, integrity in access, and the ethical use of information. Quizzes, interviews, activity books, simple map reading, and reflections are among the assessment formats used.

The secondary-level curriculum draws on formative and summative modes of assessment. Activities for the former include: pair/group discussions, analysis of budget sources and activities and peer checking of data and information during group activities. Activities for the latter rely on "performance tasks," which involve students gathering information through field-based learning, processing the information gathered, creating a product, and communicating their findings in a variety of presentation formats to provide further information on the budget.

The GCE O-level curriculum for *economics* utilizes multiple choice questions as well as structured questions that require students to interpret and analyze unseen data relevant to real economic situations. The assessment format for the GCE A-level syllabus (high level 1) includes essay questions and case study questions. The latter include *data response type* questions based on quantitative data and *higher-order type* questions that require candidates to apply economic principles when analyzing, synthesizing, evaluating, or solving economic problems.

Lesson Learned

In addition to the Ministry of Education, other stakeholders, such as the Ministry of Finance, can also engage youth in fun and interesting activities for learning about public budgets.

D1.24 South Africa

Country: South Africa
Level: National
Implementer: Ministry of Basic Education

Context

With a score of 86 percent on transparency, South Africa is among the top performers of the 2015 Open Budget Index, following New Zealand and Sweden, and the public has adequate opportunities to engage in the budget process based on its score of 65 out of 100 on public participation in the budget process.[134] Developing budget literacy in South Africa appears to be part of a pragmatic approach to equip students with valuable skills in several areas of their lives. Thus, an understanding of budgets is introduced through curricula for *economic and management sciences, mathematical literacy*, and *economics*.

As per the South African Schools Act of 1996, education is compulsory for children ages 7–15 (grades 1–9). The focus on budget literacy is split between the primary- and secondary-levels of education. At the primary level, students in grade 7 are taught financial literacy in the *economic and management sciences* class, which includes an introduction to personal and business budgets. This introduction is then taken further in the eighth grade curriculum, which explores the national budget. Budget-literacy elements are explored in greater depth at the secondary level as part of the instruction for *mathematical literacy* and *economics*.

Classroom-Based Budget-Literacy Initiatives

Education is compulsory from the first through ninth grades. Students who achieve the exit qualification, that is, the National Senior Certificate, are offered at least seven subjects, including two official South African languages, *mathematics* or *mathematical literacy* (the approximate ratio of students who study these subjects is 60 to 40 percent), *life orientation*, and three elective subjects.

Adopted at the national level, the *economics and management sciences* syllabus is taught in the seventh, eighth, and ninth grades, and curricula for *mathematical literacy* and *economics* are taught in the tenth, eleventh, and twelfth grades.

Curriculum

The most recent versions of the *economics and management sciences, mathematical literacy,* and *economics* curricula date back to 2011. The *economic and management sciences* curriculum broaches the topic of budget literacy in that it specifically explores government income and expenditures. The *mathematical literacy* course adopts a numeracy-based approach, and the *economics* course highlights how the public sector fits within the broader economic context as well as its link with fiscal policy.

The *economics and management sciences* curriculum for the eighth grade dedicates two weeks for students to explore the national budget (two hours per week) as part of the first of three main topics covered by the course—*the economy, financial literacy*, and *entrepreneurship* (Republic of South Africa 2011a). Before this, in seventh grade, two hours per week are devoted to the study of financial literacy over a two-week period, including an introduction to the concepts of income; expenditures; and types of budgets, such as personal and business budgets.

Students are progressively introduced to budget-literacy concepts through the *mathematical literacy* curriculum in the tenth, eleventh, and twelfth grades. The syllabus content covers personal and business finances as well as budget issues related to broader social and political concerns. Therefore, budget-literacy aspects of the curriculum gradually become less familiar and more removed from the students' direct experiences and hence more complex and demanding. The suggested time allocation for budget-literacy topics is two to three weeks for each grade (Republic of South Africa 2011c).

Over a two-week period, the tenth-grade *economics* syllabus teaches students about the public sector, including indirect taxes, subsidies, and welfare. It examines these concepts over a three-week period in further detail during the twelfth grade (four hours per week) and encourages evaluation of the public sector's role in the economy with special reference to its socioeconomic responsibility in the South African context (Republic of South Africa 2011b).

Learning Outcomes

The *economic and management sciences* class aims to equip students with real-life skills for personal and community development and to promote the notion of sustainable economic growth. It emphasizes economic, entrepreneurship, financial, and managerial skills to prepare students to make meaningful and informed financial decisions (Republic of South Africa 2011a:8).

The *mathematical literacy* curriculum seeks to provide youth with opportunities to analyze problems and devise the mathematical means to solve them. It is geared toward helping students develop the ability to use and apply technology, interpret information, make decisions based on reasoning, manage resources, and solve problems (Republic of South Africa 2011c).

The expected learning outcomes of the *economics* course include students being able to use resources efficiently in order to satisfy the competing needs and wants of individuals and society; apply principles underlying basic economic processes and practices; understand human-rights concerns; reflect on the wealth-creation process; engage in poverty alleviation efforts; analyze and assess the impact of local and global institutions on the South African economy; and explain and forecast the consequences of economic events or predict likely future outcomes (Republic of South Africa 2011b).

Content

The *economic and management sciences* curriculum for eighth grade consolidates key concepts related to personal, business, and national budgets. It begins with a description of the respective levels of government and their roles in terms of the use of resources and services by households and businesses. The course also introduces the national budget and examines issues such as government revenue, including direct and indirect taxes; government expenditures on services such as education, health, housing, social grants, transport, and security; and the national budget's influence on growth and the redressal of economic inequalities (Republic of South Africa 2011a:16). This learning builds on the seventh-grade curriculum, which reviews personal budgets, including household budgets, income, expenditures, and the importance of saving, as well as business budgets: why and how businesses should budget.

Overall, the *mathematics literacy* syllabus for students in the tenth, eleventh, and twelfth grades is made up of two parts: *basic skills*, including patterns, relationships, and representations; and *application*, including finance and data handling. It adopts a progressive approach that deals exclusively with personal and household banking in the tenth grade and then gradually expands to include workplace and business finance in the eleventh grade, and national and global finance and more complex financial scenarios in twelfth grade. Youth are exposed to financial contexts, such as income-and-expenditure statements, budgets, and taxes. They are expected to work with complex money values, including those expressed in the thousands, hundreds of thousands, millions, and billions, such as municipality, provincial, and national budgets (Republic of South Africa 2011c).

The twelfth-grade *economics* module describes the composition, objectives, and functions of the public sector; government budgets; fiscal policies; issues of public-sector provisioning; reasons for public-sector failure; and the influence of national macroeconomic policy on taxes, socioeconomic rights, education, health, the environment, social security, and compensation for human-rights abuses (Republic of South Africa 2011b:33).

Pedagogical Approach
As part of the pedagogical approach for the *economic and management sciences* curriculum, learners are presented with real-life situations through case studies provided by newspaper articles, magazine articles, and television or radio programs. Students are expected to draw on their own experiences and those of their peers of their peers, and prior learning to interpret, analyze, and solve problems.

The *mathematical literacy* syllabus emphasizes the use of authentic real-life contexts that relate to the workplace and the wider social, political, and global environments. For instance, each year when the national budget speech is read by Parliament, students and teachers are encouraged to take part in a tutorial that includes tasks such as discussing the impact of the government's budget on fostering entrepreneurship and the educational sector. These class discussions provide youth with opportunities to think critically about the importance of budget literacy in schools and reflect on topics such as the impact of socioeconomic issues on the South African economy. Students are also encouraged to develop and practice decision-making and communication skills and use integrated content to solve problems.

Because the *economics* curriculum covers valuable skills such as responsibility, accountability, problem solving, analysis, interpretation, and decision making, which prepare students to participate in a complex economic society, teachers are encouraged to take such skills into account when planning teaching, learning, and assessment activities.

Materials

Suggested materials for the *economics* curriculum include textbooks, newspapers, the budget speech, cartoons on the government, taxes, prices and production of goods and services, and resources from Statistics South Africa,[135] the South African Reserve Bank's *Quarterly Bulletin*,[136] the *South Africa Yearbook*,[137] brochures prepared by the South African Revenue Service[138] and legislation related to the economy. Recommended resources for *mathematical literacy* include textbooks, a booklet called "Basic Skills for Mathematical Literacy," (Republic of South Africa 2009) the *Pocket Guide to the National Budget*[139] and the *People's Guide to the National Budget*.[140] Students are also expected to work with a calculator.

Assessment

For the *economic and management sciences* course, preferred forms of assessment include projects, class and controlled tests, data responses, examinations, oral presentations, case studies, assignments, and posters. Both short-answer and paragraph-style questions are used to test the students' knowledge.

Criteria for the design of *mathematical literacy* assessment tasks are that they must be based on authentic real-life contexts and use real data, require learners to select and use appropriate mathematical content in order to explore contexts, and expect students to take into account possible nonmathematical considerations that could have a bearing on the desired outcome to a problem. Examples include: in the tenth grade, working with a value-added tax in the context of shop purchases; payment receipts; and utility bills, such as water, electricity, and telephone; in the eleventh grade, doing calculations related to unemployment insurance fund payments; and in twelfth grade, analyzing income and expenditures for large organizations, such as municipal, provincial, and national governments, by comparing income, expenditures, and profit values over a two-year period or by contrasting projected and actual incomes, expenditures, and profit/loss values. Informal means of assessing *mathematical literacy* knowledge include observations, discussions, practical demonstrations, learner-teacher conferences, and informal classroom interactions.

Assessment methods being used for the *economics* course include research assignments and projects; written and oral presentations; and reports based on survey evidence, analysis, or investigation.

Lessons Learned

• Even though the South African approach illustrates how budget-literacy education can span across various curricula, because such curricula are usually studied by students in the commercial stream, it is likely that most science students are not budget-literate.

- It is difficult to cohesively externalize the social benefits of budget-literacy education unless there are opportunities for youth to engage in local budget processes and therefore be able to appreciate the importance of public budgets and of being socially responsible citizens.
- In addition to the current horizontal approach by which budget literacy is introduced through three curricula, sustained vertical progression of such knowledge from the seventh through twelfth grades should also be encouraged so that students can acquire in-depth technical knowledge of public budgets and an understanding of the importance of budget literacy in their personal lives, businesses, and the government.

D1.25 United Kingdom

Country: United Kingdom
Level: National, Subnational, and Local
Implementers: Department of Education; Oxford, Cambridge and RSA; Her Majesty's Revenue and Customs; Citizenship Foundation

Context

The 2015 Open Budget Survey finds that with a score of 75 out of 100 on transparency, the government of the United Kingdom provides the public with substantial budget information but limited opportunities to engage in the budget process given its score of 58 out of 100 on public participation. During the mid-1990s in the United Kingdom, there were mounting concerns regarding the decline of social capital and community participation and doubts about whether or not the national curriculum requirements were leading to the development of well-educated, well-rounded individuals capable of contributing to economic and public life. Citizenship was therefore introduced as a subject of the national curriculum based on a statutory order passed by Parliament in 1999. Aspects of budget literacy regarding how economic decisions are made, including where public money comes from and the collection and allocation of public monies, were included in the content to help strengthen the students' knowledge and understanding of politics, the law, and the economy (KeyCoNet 2012).

A 2010 review of children's participation in decision making in the United Kingdom revealed that despite the steady increase in student voice and democracy initiatives in schools and youth forums after the ratification of the 2004 Children Act, youth involvement in setting budgets is limited (Davey 2010). This may be due in part to a lack of familiarity with the management of public resources, and it attests to the need for efforts to strengthen budget literacy. Efforts in the United Kingdom, such as the Youth Budget Program, are based on the conviction that a minimum level of economic literacy is required to understand the interaction between individual decisions and macroeconomic repercussions in addition to the policy choices that the governments of Europe continue to contend with as they withdraw from the post-World War II welfare state "cradle-to-grave" consensus (Bower 2015).

In the United Kingdom, basic elements of budget literacy are introduced to students through the *personal, social, and humanities education* curriculum in primary school. This knowledge, combined with basic mathematical reasoning skills derived from the *mathematics* curriculum (key stages 1–2) establishes the foundation for deeper study of budget literacy in the secondary-school curriculum.

Classroom-Based Budget-Literacy Initiatives
Learning Outcomes

Personal, social, and humanities education is part of a whole-school approach for developing the qualities and attributes students need to thrive as individuals, family members, and members of society. Under section 78 of the Education Act 2002 and the Academies Act 2010, such a curriculum must promote the spiritual, moral, cultural, mental, and physical development of students and society; and it must prepare students for the opportunities, responsibilities, and experiences of adult life. The secondary-level (key stages 3 and 4) *personal, social, and humanities education* curriculum is pertinent to budget literacy in that it aims at improving the students' understanding of the economic and business environment as well as their rights and responsibilities as active citizens and participants in the local and national economy.

Geared toward students ages 11–16 years, the secondary-school (key stages 3 and 4) *citizenship* curriculum seeks to ensure that students develop knowledge and a sound understanding of how the United Kingdom is governed, its political system, and how citizens actively participate in its democratic system of government. Students are also given the skills needed to think critically and debate political questions, manage their money on a day-to-day basis, and plan for future financial needs. The 2012 General Certificate of Secondary Education's *citizenship studies* curriculum aims for students to gain the confidence and conviction to participate in decision-making processes and play active roles as effective citizens in public life.

As of 2012, budget-literacy learning outcomes for the General Certificate of Secondary Education for *economics* expect students to:

- Understand the perspectives of a range of different stakeholders in relation to economic activity;
- Consider the moral issues that arise as a result of the impact of economic activity on the environment and economic development; and
- Recognize that their economic knowledge, understanding, and skills helps them understand current events and provides a basis for their roles as citizens and for the possible further study of economics (OCR 2012b).

As per the 2014 specifications, the aims and learning outcomes of *A-level economics* (OCR 2014), include encouraging students to understand the wider economic and social environment; use an enquiring, critical, and thoughtful approach to the study of economics; and develop analytical and quantitative skills, together with qualities and attitudes that will equip them for the challenges, opportunities, and responsibilities of adult and working life.

Content

Personal, Social, and Humanities Education. Students are expected to grasp key concepts that underpin personal and economic well-being and financial capability—that is, *career, capability, risk,* and *economic understanding.* As part of the latter, students learn about the structure and function of different businesses across the public, private, and voluntary sectors, and how some of these could be relevant to their future lives and careers, how employment trends and opportunities are influenced by economic forces, and the important role of personal finance and how it is affected by changes in the economic environment (Department for Education 2011).

Citizenship. In September 2009, the new key stage 4 program of the *citizenship* study became mandatory for all students in year 10. The *citizenship* curriculum for secondary school (key stages 3 and 4) addresses topics such as how public money is raised and spent, income and expenditures, credit and debt, insurance, savings, pensions, and financial products and services (Department for Education 2013. Its emphasis on personal budgeting and financial services contrasts with the earlier 2007 *citizenship* curriculum's more intensive focus on budget literacy by introducing where public money comes from, who decides how it is spent, and how economic decisions are made about collection and allocation of public monies.

The 2012 General Certificate of Secondary Education's *citizenship studies* curriculum has four modules: (1) *rights and responsibilities—getting started as an active citizen;* (2) *identity, democracy, and justice—understanding our role as citizens;* (3) *rights and responsibilities—extending our knowledge and understanding;* and (4) *identity, democracy, and justice—leading the way as an active citizen.* The first module apprises students of their rights and responsibilities at school, at college, and in the wider community; as citizens within the economy and welfare systems; and as global citizens. Budget literacy content in this module covers differences between direct and indirect national taxes and council tax as well as the main areas of expenditure for national and local governments. It seeks to inform the students' understanding of the government's role in helping to manage the economy and in the planning and regulation of public services. Students are taught how to evaluate and discuss a variety of opinions on how much responsibility the state and individuals should take in the provision of income protection, health, and education (OCR 2012a).

Economics. The content for the General Certificate of Secondary Education's *economics* curriculum for secondary-school students (ages 16–18 years) and the General Certificate of Education Advanced Level (A-level) *economics* is highly relevant to budget literacy, but *economics* is only studied by a very small proportion of 16-year-olds, usually those attending private schools.

Broadly, the General Certificate of Secondary Education's *economics* curriculum comprises three units on *how the market works; how the economy works;* and the *U.K. economy and globalization.* In addition to introducing the economic objectives of a government, the section on how the economy works also addresses how the government raises and spends money and government policies that affect the macroeconomy.

The A-level *economics* course incorporates in-depth budget-literacy content. But even though it is relatively more popular than the General Certificate of Secondary Education's *economics* course, it remains one of several elective subjects that students can choose. It includes three key components: *microeconomics, macroeconomics,* and *themes in economics.*

The *macroeconomics* component aims at strengthening students' comprehension of the possible impact of macroeconomic policies and issues that a government faces in managing the macroeconomy and enables them to argue for and evaluate the effectiveness of different policy approaches. Concentrated in the fiscal policy area of macroeconomics, the curriculum's budget literacy content addresses issues such as the main sources of tax revenues and government expenditures in the U.K. economy; progressive, proportional, and regressive taxation; budget surpluses and deficits; and improvement of macroeconomic performance through discretionary fiscal policy.

Pedagogical Approach and Materials

Personal, Social, and Humanities Education. The Citizenship Foundation, through its *Paying for It* economic awareness program for youth ages 14–18, has produced budget-literacy resources such as lesson plans that introduce how the economy functions, including the role of business and financial services and the importance of playing an active part in democratic processes. For example, the *government and economy* module provides an overview of the economic challenges faced by the government. It addresses six main areas of public spending—welfare, health, education, employment, public protection, and the environment—each of which is explored in more detail in the other "Paying for It" lesson plans.

The *Paying for It* module on *government and economy* uses a range of activities to convey budget-literacy concepts. For instance, students are asked to:

- Use the interactive tool "How Will You Be Paying for It?"[141] to illustrate how much of the income tax paid by citizens is spent on various public services.
- Assume the roles of government ministers and formulate arguments about why their departments should receive a larger share of the upcoming budget and as a result, which departments should receive less funding.

The United Kingdom's tax authority, Her Majesty's Revenue and Customs (HMRC), has produced *Tax Facts*, a comprehensive pack of materials designed to provide an introduction to the tax system for student ages 14–17. In addition to resources for teachers that include detailed lesson plans and guidance, HMRC produced four short, animated videos to inform students about some of the key tax issues they are likely to contend with as they begin their working lives. In addition to HMRC's YouTube channel,[142] the animated videos are available on DVD and can be ordered by e-mail.[143] Teachers' resources are published on the Times Educational Supplement website.[144]

Resources that enhance budget literacy constitute only a small part of the extensive resource base available for strengthening financial literacy in the *citizenship* curriculum (key stages 3 and 4). Organizations such as the Association for Citizenship Teaching, Teachit Citizenship, Citized, Citizenship Foundation, Personal Finance Education Group, the Bank of England, and Parliament–Education Service have produced or compiled lesson plans, fact sheets, activities, presentations, interactive games, and case studies.[145] Activities to teach budget literacy include the following:

- **Government spending.** Students consider the stories of eight characters and decide whether their situations make them worthy of increased government expenditures. They discuss the differences between wants and needs.[146]
- **Expenses of members of Parliament.** Students discuss the types of expenses claimed by members of Parliament, compare differing viewpoints about such expenses, and explain their own views on the issue.[147]
- **Reporting on tax avoidance.** Using details on the HMRC website of convictions for tax evasion, students are asked to review stories of people who avoided paying taxes and to write a piece of reporting that describes one of the cases.[148]
- **Calculating the cost of chocolate.** Using information from the Internet on value-added tax rates (general sales tax), students are asked to make a list of five countries with the highest rates and five with the lowest to determine the actual cost of a chocolate bar costing 60 pence minus sales tax in each of these countries.[149]

Resource options to teach the General Certificate of Secondary Education's *economics* curriculum include the Heinemann textbook, the Treasury Department's website, and "The Rich List," published annually by the *Sunday Times*. Some pedagogical approaches for students to grasp budget-literacy concepts are:

- Explaining the economic effects of changes in both direct and indirect taxes and introducing arguments for and against each type of tax.
- Writing an essay about whether or not to fund extra health spending with an income tax or value-added tax.
- Having students take a quiz about the richest business people, musicians, pop stars, and sports professionals. Discuss and debate: Why are these people so well-rewarded? Should redistribution of wealth take place (OCR 2012b)?

Among the key resources for the AS- and A-level *economics* curriculum is the *AS and A Level Delivery Guide. H040/H460 Theme: Macroeconomics. Application of Policy instruments.*[150] It refers to additional resources such as:

- A lecture by Robert Chote, Head of The Office of Budget Responsibility— "Introduction to Fiscal Policy;"[151]
- A BBC video and news article to distinguish between budget deficit and government debt;[152] and
- The International Monetary Fund video on the difference between gross and net debt.[153]

The AS- and A-level *economics* curriculum makes use of several approaches and activities to teach students about the budget. For instance:

- **Laffer curve.** Using variables (tax rate and tax revenue) provided to them, students are asked to draw what they think the relationship is between the two variables. They are asked to explain why they have chosen that relationship to ascertain whether their responses correspond with Arthur Laffer's curve and the idea of an optimum tax rate.
- **Difference between deficits and debt.** Students are given various scenarios, such as a rise in unemployment and a consequent fall in income tax receipts, and have to decide whether or not it would affect the cyclical or structural deficit.
- **Once upon a time.** Students write a short children's story that explains to a primary school student the difference between budget deficits and government debt as well as the causes of the United Kingdom's current fiscal problems.
- **Fiscal rules.** In small groups, students represent various firms, organizations, and households, and consider how they would be affected by the fiscal rules.
- **Flat tax.** Students are asked to read various articles on the flat tax and write an evaluation paragraph in response to the question: Should Britain introduce a flat rate for income tax?
- **Distinguishing between current and capital government expenditures and progressive, proportional, and regressive taxation.** Students are asked to design images and use them to represent various types of expenditures and taxes.

Out-of-Classroom Budget-Literacy Initiatives
Chance to be Chancellor/Youth Budget Initiative

Founded in 2007 by the Citizenship Foundation, the *Chance to be Chancellor Program* is the United Kingdom's largest economic literacy initiative. Young people develop informed opinions about how the economy is managed and how government tax, fiscal, and spending policies affect their lives. Using accredited resources produced by the Personal Finance Education Group and an online budgeting tool, students from across the United Kingdom, ages 14–18, develop their own alternative budgets based on three tax areas—work, consumer, and business—and seven spending areas—employment, health, education, welfare, public protection, environment, and government and the economy. The *Chance to be Chancellor* online tool is used to compile the views of young people about the budget contributing to the Youth Budget report. The results are collated and published in a report, see "Youth Budget—Chance to be Chancellor Evaluation 2012–13" (Citizenship Foundation 2013), which is launched at an event prior to the actual budget announcement to provide a platform for young people to express their opinions. The *Chance to be Chancellor Program* includes a competition that invites participants to make a case for their budget in a 90-second video. Winning schools and students are given the opportunity to present their ideas to the Chancellor of the Exchequer and HM Treasury at the House of Commons.

International Practices to Promote Budget Literacy • http://dx.doi.org/10.1596/978-1-4648-1071-8

During the 2012–13 academic year, 4,343 teachers and least 89,549 students were involved in the *Youth Budget* and *Chance to be Chancellor* activities. In terms of outcomes, 88 percent of teachers rated the content and range of issues covered by the lesson plans as *good* or *very good*; 92 percent of teachers rated the effectiveness of lesson plans to raise students' economic awareness as *good* or *very good*. Between 2010 and 2013 the *Chance to be Chancellor* competition has been highly rated on indicators regarding "effectiveness in promoting young people's opinions on the budget" and "a unique/interesting way to learn about the economy" (Citizenship Foundation 2013). Despite its success, the program encountered difficulties with financing and was discontinued.

Lessons Learned

Curriculum

- For education to express its potential to sustain and develop democratic processes, the current focus of financial literacy for individuals will need to be extended to the roles and responsibilities of financial institutions and governments (Davies 2015).

Chance to be Chancellor/Youth Budget Initiative

- It may be possible to make teacher trainings to introduce budget-literacy content across various curricula more accessible if such trainings or workshops were directly marketed to school networks and if a webinar version of such trainings were to be developed (Citizenship Foundation 2013).
- Guidance on differentiating budget-literacy materials that can cater to varying student abilities would be useful in order to tailor content to student needs (Citizenship Foundation 2013).
- Lesson plans that address budget literacy would be more engaging for students if they included additional online starter activities; if they added local, national, and global economics into the mix; and if they involved cross-cutting themes most relevant to young people (Citizenship Foundation 2013).

D1.26 United States

Country: United States
Level: National, Subnational, and Local
Implementers: Teachers College Columbia University; National Council for the Social Studies; Council for Economic Education; iCivics; City of Boston–Department of Youth Engagement and Employment

Context

Findings of the 2015 Open Budget Survey indicate that based on its score of 81 out of 100 on transparency, the government of the United States provides the public with extensive budget information and adequate opportunities for public participation in the budget process as demonstrated by its score of 69 out of 100 on public participation. The *civics and government* curriculum in the United States is geared toward meeting one of the goals of the 1994 Educate America Act that "students demonstrate competency over challenging subject matter including … civics and government … so that they may be prepared for responsible citizenship, further learning, and productive employment …." Moreover, the Standards in Economics, including those for budget literacy, are intended to prepare students for entering a complex global economy so they can fully and effectively participate as better-informed workers, consumers, and producers, savers, and investors, and citizens. As one of the top performing countries on the 2015 Open Budget Index, the United States provides moderate opportunities for public participation in the budget process.[154]

A "News IQ" test administered by the Pew Research Center for the People and the Press in 2007 found that only 15 percent of respondents ages 18–29 (the youngest group in the survey) qualified as what it called *most informed*. In terms of civic participation, young people ages 18–24 were the most underrepresented voters in the 2008 presidential election.[155] In addition, limited economic literacy among high school students indicates that they are not wholly equipped to make effective contributions to economic debates and processes. A 2010 baseline study conducted by Teachers College Columbia University found that current economics education about the federal budget and fiscal policy is virtually nonexistent in U.S. high schools. In 2007, over 2,000 high school students averaged a grade of 53 out of a possible 100 on a survey quiz on basic economic concepts administered by the Council for Economic Education (Columbia University 2010).

Classroom-Based Budget-Literacy Initiatives
Curriculum

At the elementary school level, students are introduced to the concept of the national government and the roles and responsibilities of its three branches based on the K4 Content Standards for the *civics and government* curriculum. This introduction provides an initial basis for understanding the national government and how it goes about fulfilling its responsibilities. That understanding, when it is extended and deepened, enables citizens to evaluate the actions of the government, including its economic functions, and therefore to participate more effectively in public processes. As per the K4 content standards for the *civics and government* curriculum, students should be able explain how state government services are paid for, such as with sales taxes, taxes on individual and business income, fees for using parks and toll roads, and licensing fees, as well as how local government services are paid for, such as with property, sales, and other taxes or with money from the state or national government (Center for Civic Education 2014b). Students explore budget-literacy concepts in more detail during upper-secondary school as part of the *economics* curriculum.

Civics and Government. According to the National Curriculum Standards for Social Studies, which was revised in 2010, students in fifth through eighth grades are expected to explain why taxes are necessary to pay for the government and to identify provisions of the United States Constitution that authorize the national government to collect taxes, the important responsibilities of state and local governments, and major sources of tax revenue and their uses.

Learning outcomes for students in grades 9–12 include the ability to explain the history of taxation in the United States and why taxes are necessary to pay for the government, provisions of the United States Constitution that authorize the national government to collect taxes, and underlying tensions between citizens' desire for government services and benefits and their unwillingness to pay for them through taxes. They should be able to identify the main priorities for government expenditures and the main responsibilities of their state and local governments. Students should be able to evaluate the equity of various kinds of taxes and main revenue sources for state and local governments (Center for Civic Education 2014a).

Economics. The National Curriculum Standards for Social Studies provide the following guidance on production, distribution and consumption:
"Young learners explore economic decision-making and consider the wider consequences of those decisions on groups, communities, the nation, and beyond. In the middle grades, learners expand their knowledge of economic concepts and principles, and use economic reasoning processes to address issues related to fundamental economic questions. High school students develop economic perspectives and deeper understanding of key economic concepts and processes through systematic study of a range of economic and sociopolitical systems."[156]

For students introduced to the section called "Role of Government and Market Failure," budget-literacy learning outcomes for relevant grade levels are as follows:

- Governments provide certain kinds of goods and services in a market economy, and they pay for the goods and services they use or provide by taxing or borrowing (grade 4).
- Most state and local government revenues come from sales taxes, grants from the federal government, personal income taxes, and property taxes, and the

bulk of state and local government revenue is spent on education, public welfare, road construction and repair, and public safety (grade 8).
- Different tax structures affect consumers and producers differently (grade 12).

Twelfth-grade students being taught *fiscal and monetary policy* are expected to be familiar with the following:

- Fiscal policies are decisions to change spending and taxation levels by the federal government and are adopted to influence national levels of output, employment, and prices.
- In the short run, increasing federal spending and/or reducing taxes can promote more employment and output, but these polices also put upward pressure on price levels and interest rates.
- The federal government's annual budget is balanced when its revenues from taxes (and other sources) equal its expenditures (Council for Economic Education 2010).

Content

Civics and Government. Detailed voluntary national standards for *civics and government* have been developed by the Center for Civic Education, the contents of which address budget-literacy concepts in some detail for students in grades 5–8 and 9–12 (Center for Civic Education 2014a).

Content standards for *civics and government*, which are intended to help schools develop competent and responsible citizens who possess reasoned commitments to the fundamental values and principles of American constitutional democracy, are organized into five key areas:

1. Civic life, politics, and government;
2. Foundations of the U.S. political system;
3. How the government established by the Constitution embodies the purposes, values, and principles of democracy;
4. The relationship of the United States to other nations and the world;
5. The role of the citizen in the U.S. democracy.

For grades 5–8 and 9–12, a section called "How Does the Government Established by the Constitution Embody the Purposes, Values, and Principles of American Democracy?" addresses budget-literacy concepts in the context of explaining the roles and responsibilities of national, state, and local governments.

The nonprofit organization iCivics produced a *civics* curriculum intended as a supplemental resource for teachers. It is grouped by topic into several modules that are aligned with state and Common Core standards. Of these, the *government and the market* module[157] introduces taxation and government spending. It is expected to equip students with sufficient knowledge to describe the impact of taxes, analyze a pay stub and federal spending data, and identify reasons for people's differing views about government spending.

International Practices to Promote Budget Literacy • http://dx.doi.org/10.1596/978-1-4648-1071-8

Economics. Revised in 2010, the voluntary national content standards in *economics* are designed to teach school children about basic economics and the economy. Budget-literacy concepts are introduced in some depth in the twelfth grade, less extensively in the fourth and eighth grades (Council for Economic Education 2010). A range of key economic concepts are discussed, including scarcity, decision making, allocation, incentives, trade, specialization, markets and prices, the role of prices, competition and market structure, institutions, money and inflation, interest rates, income, entrepreneurship, economic growth, the role of government during market failure, government failure, economic fluctuations, unemployment and inflation, and fiscal and monetary policy. Budget-literacy concepts are more prominently featured in the core standards on the role of government and market failure and fiscal and monetary policy.

Finally, Teachers College, Columbia University has introduced the *Understanding Fiscal Responsibility* curriculum for five subject areas: economics, civics, U.S. history, world history, and mathematics. It uses a cross-disciplinary, nonpartisan, and inquiry-based approach to address public-policy dilemmas regarding the federal budget. Five lessons per subject area are included, which are thematically linked but that do not need to be taught in any particular sequence or as a unit. Topics addressed include *the history of social security, taxation and the national debt,* and *demographic shifts and the federal budget.*

Pedagogical Approach and Materials

Largely based on a cross-curricular approach to impart budget-literacy concepts to students, a broad range of relevant teaching materials are available (see appendices B and C) including lesson plans, activity sheets and materials, interactive games, interactive data, cartoons, webinars, and media materials. Examples of teaching approaches that utilize these resources are presented in table D.3.

Table D.3 Approaches to Teaching Budget Literacy

Lesson	Approach
Taxation and the national debt[a]	Two cartoons are used as a trigger for discussing arguments in favor of taxes and against too many of them. Students share with each another their cartoons, interpretations, and responses to the trigger questions.
	Students do a "five-minute write" answering the question: "What responsibility does the federal government have to ensure the elderly have a secure and stable standard of living?" When students have finished writing, they divide into small groups and are asked to share their writings with one another.
Historic events and the federal budget[b]	Based on the periods they are assigned, students research changes in the budgetary process from 1789 to the present day and create brief PowerPoint® presentations to share their research with the class.

table continues next page

Table D.3 Approaches to Teaching Budget Literacy *(continued)*

Lesson	Approach
History of social security[c]	Students carefully review an excerpt from *The 1936 Government Pamphlet on Social Security* and, pretending it is 1936, explain the Social Security program to a somewhat confused aunt or uncle.
Europe's debt crisis[d]	Students are assigned articles to read on views against and in favor of austerity. Students should be prepared to restate the writer's key points and, based on what they now know about the debt crisis, identify at least three important questions that the writer does not address or that would challenge the writer's point of view. Volunteers are selected to summarize each writer's point. Once a consensus is reached, students identify questions they feel remain unanswered.
What do you get for your $1,818,600,000,000?[e]	Using Microsoft Excel® and data from the Bureau of Economic Analysis website on federal government spending, students compare amounts spent on various sectors and programs over a range of years.
"Why cities provide tax breaks even when they are strapped for cash"[f]	Students explore the websites of three different cities and determine what incentives are being offered and what problems they are trying to solve. Students are asked to determine if the benefits gained from the incentives offset the costs incurred.
Taxation[g]	Students are asked to analyze a sample paycheck stub and answer questions about the types of taxes that are deducted from the check, gross and net pay amounts, and other matters. They are asked to calculate sales tax and compare the effect of different tax rates on the total price paid.
The mathematics behind taxes[h]	Students take a quiz about earning income and paying a tax. Through this activity, they generate data for a table, for a graph, and to build equations that represent relationships between quantities. Students scale and label axes as they create graphs of relationships between income and tax. Tables and graphs of data are then used by the students to construct equations representing relationships between income, tax, and average tax ratio.
Write a letter to your congressperson[i]	Students write letters to their congressperson about something they would prioritize regarding federal spending and/or revenue and what impact their decision would have on them and/or on their community.

a. http://teachufr.org/admin/taxation-and-the-national-debt/.
b. file:///C:/Users/WB371127/AppData/Local/Microsoft/Windows/Temporary Internet Files/Content.Outlook/150MMP53/History of the Federal Budget.
c. http://teachufr.org/admin/the-history-of-social-security-2/.
d. http://teachufr.org/admin/europe%E2%80%99s-debt-crisis/.
e. http://www.econedlink.org/lessons/index.php?lid=319&type=educator.
f. http://www.econedlink.org/teacher-lesson/273/.
g. http://www.sharemylesson.com/teaching-resource/taxation-50037265/.
h. http://www.sharemylesson.com/teaching-resource/the-mathematics-behind-taxes-50037684/.
i. https://www.nationalpriorities.org/budget-basics/educator-toolkit/peoples-guide-federal-budget/write-letter-your-congressperson/.

Out-of-Classroom Budget-Literacy Initiatives

Youth Lead the Change Participatory Budgeting Initiative

In 2014, the City of Boston initiated *Youth Lead the Change*, the nation's first participatory-budgeting process focused exclusively on youth.[158] Its goals were civics education and engagement and the inclusion of youth voices that are typically marginalized in the city's capital planning process. Its objectives were teaching youth about the city budgeting process; helping to ensure that the capital plan reflects the priorities, interests, and energy of Boston youth; and empowering youth to participate in government processes.

The City of Boston led and funded the project, and $ 1 million was written into the 2014 fiscal year capital budget for *Youth Lead the Change*, with the actual spending to be determined through the *Youth Lead the Change* process. However, because the money was allocated in the capital budget, only capital projects were eligible, which meant that projects being proposed through the participatory-budgeting process had to be for physical infrastructure or technology, be located on city-owned property, cost no less than $ 25,000, and last at least five years. The participatory-budgeting process had several key stages: establishing a steering committee to create a rulebook for the process, which included 30 youth-serving organizations, holding idea assemblies to generate ideas in a variety of neighborhoods throughout Boston, engaging a core group of young people as "change agents" to turn those ideas into specific proposals, and holding a vote to determine which proposals would be funded through the one-million-dollar youth budget.

An initial set of 473 proposals generated by the idea assemblies was divided into six categories, and committees of change agents were tasked with turning them into concrete proposals. They engaged in a dialogue with city officials who determined whether or not the ideas were capital-eligible and provided cost estimates for the individual proposals. Ultimately, change agents prepared a set of 14 proposals that were included on the ballot; each voter could vote for up to four of them. The voting process resulted in the funding of seven projects, including an upgrade to the Franklin Park playground and picnic area, art walls in Boston, Chromebooks® for three high schools, a feasibility study for a skating park, and security cameras for the Dr. Loesch Family Park.

The steering committee developed the *Youth Lead the Change Participatory Budgeting Rulebook*, which introduced participatory budgeting and the objectives for engaging with Boston youth. The "Participatory Budgeting Project" developed tools and guide materials for participants and provided trainings for participants, facilitators, and outreach volunteers (Participedia 2015).

In terms of the effects on participants, an evaluation study prepared by Harvard University notes that the types of competencies that children and youth developed during this process included heightened awareness about public needs across Boston, governmental processes, and broader issues related to youth. The program also helped improve civics education and skills such as leadership, teamwork, networking, communications, and professionalism (Grillos 2014).

Lessons Learned
- Since the overarching focus of relevant textbook content suggests that matters related to the federal budget, federal debt, and budget deficit are out of the hands of everyday citizens, it would be helpful to explore aspects of the budget-literacy curriculum that can be geared toward what citizens can do to bring about change in the budgeting process.
- Budget-literacy materials and lessons can be more accessible and usable if they are: aligned with existing curricula and standards, particularly given the competing demands on scarce time; flexible—that is, they can stand on their own

or be taught as part of a unit; and relevant—that is, they can be connected to current events with a blog or other tool that keeps the curriculum fresh.

• Although online training for teachers is useful, in-person contact is ideal because teachers are the most likely to take up the topic if they have experienced the curriculum directly.

D1.27 Uruguay

Country: Uruguay
Level: National
Implementers: General Tax Directorate of the Ministry of Economy and Finance; the Ministry of Education and Culture

Context

Uruguay's Ministry of Education and Culture has jurisdiction over coordinating national education policies, including the Framework for Basic Education. At the primary school level, education is compulsory and free for all children ages 6–14. For lower-secondary school, the first phase lasts for two years and involves instruction in the fundamentals of subjects such as history, languages, mathematics, and sciences. During the upper-level of secondary school, students choose between several subject streams, all of which conclude with a certificate awarded for completion of both cycles of general secondary education and which entitle them to enter university.

School education is complemented by the *Tax Education Program* of the Ministry of Economy and Finance's General Tax Directorate (DGI), which aims to strengthen fiscal consciousness by promoting civic attitudes such as solidarity, justice, equality, and responsibility and encouraging public participation in public and community life. DGI's main tax education partners are the National Administration for Public Education (ANEP), the Council for Basic and Primary Education, the Council for Secondary Education, the Plan Ceibal initiative, the Ministry of Education and Culture, and the Film and Audiovisual Institute of Uruguay (Instituto del Cine y del Uruguay).

Classroom-Based Budget-Literacy Initiatives
Curriculum

Revised in 2008, the framework for basic education introduces *civics* instruction during primary and secondary school and aims to build knowledge of government responsibilities and citizenship. The Tax Education Program completes the picture by familiarizing students with fiscal topics.

Learning Outcomes

The desired learning outcome of the primary-level *social knowledge* curriculum is for students to develop the capability to relate their personal lives with social responsibility and the pursuit of justice. The secondary-level *civics and social education* course aims to generate young people's interest in public issues and apprise them of the government's role and functions as well as their civic rights and responsibilities.

Content

The *social knowledge* course is divided into three core topics: *history, geography,* and *building citizenship.* As part of the latter, sections on *ethics and law* provide instruction on the structure and functions of government and public participation in a democratic context during the third and sixth grades.

Content for the *civics and social* education course consists of modules on *human society, state and government, participation,* and *human rights.* Approximately 20–25 class hours are devoted to each topic. The *state and government* module focuses on political organization, and the unit on *participation* highlights public participation and citizenship.

Pedagogical Approach

The educational framework suggests the use of different strategies that involve all forms of learning, such as individual and group-learning exercises. It also highlights the importance of progressively building on the students' existing knowledge, employing learning strategies that are familiar to them, and encouraging their active participation.

Materials

Prior to the launch of the *Tax Education Program,* the Council on Primary Education and the General Tax Directorate developed learning materials, including a handbook on participatory and responsible citizenship for sixth-grade primary-school students and a guidance note for teachers. These resources are intended to facilitate classroom instruction about budget-literacy issues, civil rights and responsibilities, the role of the state, and the relationship of the state with its citizens. The main topics covered in the student handbook are human rights, society, the state and taxes, and national culture. As part of the latter, the handbook introduces national and tax culture, the history of taxes, the national budget, main taxes, and the functions of the tax collection agency. It also contains learning resources such as poems, stories, games, songs, riddles, and ideas for group activities. Between 2005 and 2008, these handbooks were distributed to more than 45,000 sixth-grade students.

After the *Tax Education Program* was launched in 2007, DGI, working in collaboration with teachers, developed a range of teaching materials (comics and text books) that could be used in schools across the country. In addition, the DGI organizes workshops for teachers and other educators and facilitates agreements for jointly developed syllabi for primary and secondary education. The DGI has collaborated with El Abrojo—a local nongovernmental organization—to prepare budget literacy learning materials. The materials include a book of stories that are divided into ten chapters introducing students to scenarios of public and social life to help them learn values such as solidarity, responsibility, justice, rights and duties, the common good, public participation, the socioeconomic role of taxes, and the national budget. Between 2007 and 2011, this book was distributed to more than 78,000 third-grade secondary-school students, in tandem with a teacher's guide.

Out-of-Classroom Budget-Literacy Initiatives

Tax Education Portal

The *Tax Education Portal* is a one-stop shop for tax-education learning materials and resources for primary and secondary-school students, although educational content is also offered for the general public. Educational games as well as technical information regarding taxation are featured on the tax portal.

A range of games can be downloaded from the portal or played online. For example, one of the video games on the portal—"+*Ciudadano*" (+Citizen)—helps students in the fifth and sixth grades develop citizenship skills. With the help of Iván—a cartoon character, children learn about public-sector topics, including rights and responsibilities, society, the state, and tax culture. Another video game on the portal—¡*Clink!*—is intended for third-grade secondary-school students. It challenges them to help resolve the phenomenon of a natural disaster that has affected their city by assuming responsibility for collecting and allocating resources for the city's rehabilitation.

Presented in a user-friendly format, technical information on taxation covers the relevance of tax, such as data charts to explain the role of tax in society, Uruguay's tax system, and the relevance of tax receipts); DGI's tax collection efforts, such as interactive graphs to explore aggregate tax collected during the fiscal year and sources of tax revenues); and tax evasion, such as interactive graphs that analyze tax evasion trends in Uruguay compared with other Latin American countries.

Video Games Contest

In partnership with the Council for Basic and Primary Education, the Council for Secondary Education and the Plan Ceibal,[159] DGI has developed digital tax education content for the *Ceibal* platform.[160] The first product was an interactive book generated by primary school teachers. In 2011, the DGI launched the +*Ciudadano* application, which invites children to improve their city while they learn about taxes. Along with the fictional character Iván, children visit and improve their own neighborhood, gradually completing various levels by focusing on topics such as rights and obligations, society, and state and tax culture.

DGI and Ceibal have also collaborated to launch a contest for secondary-school students to submit proposals for the development of a video game about the positive elements of citizenship that would be of interest to other youth. Suggested topics for the video game proposals included a sense of community, contributions to the common good, civic responsibilities, solidarity, the national budget, taxation based on need, and combating tax evasion.

Lesson Learned

The video games contest launched in Uruguay introduced an interesting dynamic because its goal was for young people to develop resources for other young people. Teaching others about a topic is often a useful way to guarantee in-depth understanding of an issue, which makes this approach worth highlighting. It can further consolidate the students' knowledge of fiscal issues, and it can facilitate the development of resources that would be of interest to youth because they were developed by their peers.

Notes

1. Australia's educational system is decentralized, with policy largely determined by the ministers of education in the six states and two territories rather than by the Federal Department of Education. However, over the last decade, Australia has been moving toward a national curriculum and assessment system that will provide a common framework for the states and territories. In 2008, Australia began developing the comprehensive National Assessment Programme and the national "Foundation to Year 10" curriculum for states and territories. However, Australia, does not currently have an official curriculum. The ministers of education for each state and territory as well as the federal minister have not approved most of the curriculum. The National Assessment Programme is centered around literacy and numeracy tests (collectively known as NAPLAN) administered annually to students in grades 3, 5, 7, and 9; additional national sample assessments in science, civics and citizenship, and information and communication technology literacy are administered every three years. Now that both the national curriculum and the assessment program have been developed, Australia is working to ensure that the two systems are aligned to create common educational standards for all students.

2. The Northern Territory uses the South Australian curriculum for senior secondary studies (SCSA 2014a, 2014b).

3. Other areas explored as part of the preliminary course, which focuses on microeconomic issues, are: (1) introductory economics, (2) consumers and business, (3) markets (4) labor markets, (5) financial markets, and (6) government in the economy.

4. See https://www.sace.sa.edu.au/web/economics.

5. Based on data from Statistics Austria: The Information Manager (database): http://www.statistik.at/web_de/statistiken/bildung_und_kultur/formales_bildungswesen/schulen_schulbesuch/index.html.

6. See the Austrian Federal Ministry of Education and Women's Affairs website at https://www.bmbf.gv.at/schulen/unterricht/lp/lp_ahs_oberstufe.html.

7. See the website of the Austrian Federal Ministry of Education and Women's Affairs website at https://www.bmbf.gv.at/schulen/unterricht/lp/lp_neu_ahs_06_11858.pdf.

8. See https://www.wko.at/Content.Node/kampagnen/ufs_en/index.en.html.

9. See http://www.advantageaustria.org/zentral/news/aktuell/UF_Folder_en.pdf.

10. See http://www.advantageaustria.org/zentral/news/aktuell/UF_Folder_en.pdf.

11. See http://www.iv-net.at/b3652.

12. See http://www.eesi-impulszentrum.at/wettbewerbe/.

13. Based on International Budget Partnership's Open Budget Survey 2015—Brazil at http://internationalbudget.org/wp-content/uploads/OBS2015-CS-Brazil-English.pdf.

14. See https://www.nafsa.org/uploadedFiles/Chez_NAFSA/Resource_Library_Assets/Networks/ACE/EDU%20Systems%20Brazil.pdf.

15. See https://www.oecd.org/finance/financial-education/G20_OECD_NSFinancialEducation.pdf.

16. See the Programa Nacional de Educação Fiscal website at http://www.esaf.fazenda.gov.br/assuntos/educacao-fiscal.

17. See Sofinha e sua Turma, Secretary of Federal Budget website at http://www
    .orcamentofederal.gov.br/educacao-orcamentaria/sofinha/Sofinha_Ingles.pdf.

18. See Leaozinho website: http://www.leaozinho.receita.fazenda.gov.br/.

19. See http://www12.senado.leg.br/orcamentofacil.

20. See http://www.plenarinho.gov.br/camara/orcamento.

21. See http://www.cgu.gov.br/portalzinho.

22. This estimate comes from the internal draft report, "Summary of the One for All
    and All for One Program" (March 2015) from the Office of the Comptroller
    General.

23. See *social studies* curriculum guides from the Department of Education and Early
    Childhood Development, Newfoundland and Labrador at http://www.ed.gov.nl.ca
    /edu/k12/curriculum/guides/socialstudies/index.html.

24. See British Columbia Ministry of Education curriculum documents. Government of
    British Columbia at https://www.bced.gov.bc.ca/irp/plo.php.

25. See http://www2.gnb.ca/content/gnb/en/departments/education/k12/content
    /anglophone_sector/curriculum_anglophone.html#4.

26. See "Curriculum Kindergarten to Grade 12" on the Manitoba Education website at
    http://www.edu.gov.mb.ca/k12/cur/index.html.

27. The course comprises five units: (1) fundamental economic concepts; (2) microeco-
    nomic concepts (demand and supply, market structures, labor market, and labor
    unions); (3) macroeconomic concepts (national economic performance and the role
    of government); (4) global economic concepts (trade and global economics); and
    (5) economic issues (distribution of income and standard of living, sustainability,
    technology, and personal finance).

28. See http://www.civix.ca/sbc/teaching-tools/.

29. See Currículum Nacional, Ministerio de Educación at http://www.curriculumnacional.cl.

30. See http://www.thechilepages.com/schools-in-chile-2/the-chilean-education-system/.

31. See http://www.siieduca.cl/index.php.

32. Based on International Budget Partnership's Open Budget Survey 2015—Costa Rica
    at   http://www.internationalbudget.org/opening-budgets/open-budget-initiative
    /open-budget-survey/country-info/?country=cr.

33. Social Studies National Advisor for Primary Education Mr. Jorge Cartin (1–6) has
    stated that the "education program seeks to promote a responsible tax culture from
    early age … a country that does not pay taxes, does not have access to economic
    growth and to public services." Comments provided by Dr. Mario Enrique Alfaro
    Rodriguez (Director of Curriculum Development, Ministry of Public Education) on
    draft case study for Illustrative Budget Literacy Practices in Costa Rica. These com-
    ments were provided by e-mail dated August 24, 2015.

34. See http://www.fiiapp.org/en/noticias/los-ninos-costarricenses-aprenden-la-importancia
    -de-los-impuestos-jugando/.

35. Based on International Budget Partnership's Open Budget Survey 2015—Czech
    Republic at http://internationalbudget.org/wp-content/uploads/OBS2015-CS-Czech
    -Republic-English.pdf.

36. See http://www.dgii.gov.do/et/Paginas/default.aspx.

37. See http://www.ibe.unesco.org/curricula/estonia/er_usfw_2011_eng.pdf.

38. See https://www.hm.ee/en/national-curricula.

39. In 2013, 97,700 out of a total of 589,400 secondary-school students passed their baccalaureate in the *economics and social sciences* branch.

40. See "The French Educational System," Ministère de l'Éducation Nationale at http://www.education.gouv.fr/pid32482/newsroom.html.

41. See http://dessinemoileco.com/lelaboration-du-budget-de-letat/.

42. See http://dessinemoileco.com/lelaboration-du-budget-dune-commune/.

43. See http://www.financespubliques.fr/.

44. See http://statapprendre.education.fr/comptes/etat/comment/def_loi.htm.

45. See http://www.performance-publique.budget.gouv.fr/sites/performance_publique/files/files/flash/cyber-budget/minefi_start.swf.

46. See http://www.performance-publique.budget.gouv.fr/sites/performance_publique/files/files/flash/bd_budget/premiereplanche.html.

47. See http://www.lefigaro.fr/economie/objectif-budget.php.

48. See http://www.iledefrance.fr/sites/default/files/mariane/RAPCP14-670RAP.pdf.

49. Based on International Budget Partnership's Open Budget Survey 2015—Germany at http://www.internationalbudget.org/opening-budgets/open-budget-initiative/open-budget-survey/country-info/?country=de.

50. See the Federal Agency for Civic Education (Bundeszentrale für politische Bildung) at http://www.bpb.de/nachschlagen/lexika/18224/soziale-marktwirtschaft.

51. Curricular development is an ongoing process. This table serves as a useful snapshot of current practices.

52. See http://www.dekade-thueringen.de/media/public/pdfs/Planspiel_BHH.pdf.

53. See http://www.bertelsmann-stiftung.de/fileadmin/files/BSt/Publikationen/GrauePublikationen/ZD_Schuelerhaushalt_Infobroschuere_2015.pdf and http://www.bertelsmann-stiftung.de/fileadmin/files/BSt/Publikationen/GrauePublikationen/ZD_Schuelerhaushalt_Handbuch_2015.pdf.

54. See http://www.sch%C3%BClerhaushalt.de.

55. See http://www.kijubue.de/.

56. See https://www.facebook.com/misch.mit.mahell.

57. National Curriculum of Guatemala. Ministry of Education. http://cnbguatemala.org/index.php?title=Bienvenidos_al_Curr%C3%ADculum_Nacional_Base.

58. See http://www.edb.gov.hk/attachment/en/curriculum-development/kla/pshe/l&s_curriculum_guide_eng.pdf.

59. See http://www.edb.gov.hk/attachment/en/curriculum-development/kla/pshe/EconC&AGuide_updated_e_20140212.pdf.

60. See http://www.edb.gov.hk/attachment/en/curriculum-development/kla/pshe/l&s_curriculum_guide_eng.pdf.

61. See http://www.edb.gov.hk/attachment/en/curriculum-development/kla/pshe/EconC&AGuide_updated_e_20140212.pdf.

62. Topics are (1) basic economic concepts; (2) firms and production; (3) market and price; (4) competition and market structure; (5) efficiency, equity, and the role of government; (6) measurement of economic performance; (7) national income determination and price level; (8) money and banking; (9) macroeconomic problems and policies; and (10) international trade and finance.

63. Based on International Budget Partnership's Open Budget Survey 2015—India at http://www.internationalbudget.org/opening-budgets/open-budget-initiative/open -budget-survey/country-info/?country=in.

64. There were an estimated 45,085,000 students in senior secondary (grades 11 and 12, ages 16–17 years) in 2013 (Government of India 2014).

65. Partners for the MY Parliament project included think tanks/nongovernmental organizations, such as the Centre for Budget and Governance Accountability; the Takshashila Institution; and PRS Legislative Research.

66. See the Model Youth Parliament website: http://modelyouthparliament.com/budget_session_2015.php.

67. See http://indiabudget.nic.in/ub2015-16/bh/bh1.pdf.

68. See http://indiabudget.nic.in/survey.asp.

69. According to input from the Youth Parliament team, July 2015.

70. *Google Hangouts* is a unified communications service that allows members to initiate and participate in text, voice, or video chats, either one-on-one or in a group. "Hangouts" are built into Google+ and Gmail.

71. Primary education consists of an eight-year cycle: junior infants, senior infants, and first to sixth classes. The junior cycle caters to 12 to 15-year-old students, and the junior certificate is awarded after three years. The senior cycle caters to students ages 15–18. It includes an optional transition year, which follows immediately after the junior cycle. The transition year provides an opportunity for students to experience a wide range of educational inputs, including work experience. During the final two years of senior cycle, students take one of three programs, each leading to a state examination: the traditional Leaving Certificate, the Leaving Certificate Vocational Program or the Leaving Certificate Applied.

72. E-mail input from NCCA staff in March 2015.

73. E-mail input from NCCA staff in March 2015.

74. See "Outline of 2011 Tax Reform," Cabinet Office, Government of Japan at http://www.cao.go.jp/.

75. The Council is comprised of MEXT, the Ministry of Internal Affairs and Communications, and the National Tax Agency.

76. As of May 1994, the tax education promotion councils at the prefectural level exist in all 47 prefectural and city governments; as of March 2011, there are 738 tax education promotion councils at the municipal level.

77. As a compulsory subject in junior high school, *social studies* is allocated 140 hour credits (7,000 minutes or approximately 117 hours) for grade 3 (equivalent to grade 9 in the United States) students, in which 40 hour credits (2,000 minutes or approximately 33.3 hours) are spent on *history* and 100 hour credits (5,000 hours or approximately 83.3 hours) are spent on *civics*.

78. According to MEXT, Contemporary Society classes are held most frequently at the first grade of high schools (equivalent to grade 10), while both Ethics and Politics and Economy classes are commonly held at the second and/or third grade (equivalent to grade 11 and/or 12). See http: //www.mext.go.jp/b_menu/shingi/chukyo/chukyo3 /028/siryo/06081106/002.htm#001.

79. This subject area is only available for students enrolled in high schools offering a specialized course in *commerce*. In that course, students study subjects issues related

to commerce as well as general academic subjects for three years (grades 10–12). Other specialized courses include *agriculture, industry, fishery,* and *nursing*. High school students enrolled in one of these specialized courses are required to take at least 25 units (approximately 729 hours); those specializing in *commerce* can include up to five credits of *foreign language* (English) subjects as part of their required units.

80. The National Institute for Educational Policy Research is a comprehensive policy research body that seeks to contribute its research and findings to promote and formulate educational policy and plans. See http://www.nier.go.jp/03_laboratory/02 _mokuteki.html.

81. See http://www.nta.go.jp/shiraberu/ippanjoho/gakushu/kyozai/jireishu/index.htm.

82. See http://www.zaisei.mof.go.jp/.

83. See http://www.mof.go.jp/kids/index.php.

84. See http://www.mof.go.jp/kids/qanda/top.html.

85. See https://www.nta.go.jp/shiraberu/ippanjoho/gakushu/index.htm.

86. The videos are also available on Youtube: https://www.youtube.com/playlist?list =PL1094ABAF922B5D53.

87. See http://www.kantei.go.jp/jp/kids/index.html.

88. See http://www.jbaudit.go.jp/kids/index.html.

89. See http://www.nhk.or.jp/syakai/10min_koumin/?das_id=D0005120357_00000.

90. See http://www.tax.metro.tokyo.jp/school/quiz/tax_taku.html.

91. See http://www.pref.toyama.jp/sections/1107/sosuikyo/.

92. See http://wakayama-sozeikyoiku.jp/index.html.

93. See http://www.mof.go.jp/kids/index.php.

94. See http://www.mof.go.jp/kids/life/index.html.

95. See https://www.nta.go.jp/tokyo/shiraberu/gakushu/taiken/01.htm.

96. See https://www.nta.go.jp/shiraberu/ippanjoho/gakushu/sakubun/chugaku/h26 /index.htm.

97. See https://www.nta.go.jp/shiraberu/ippanjoho/gakushu/sakubun/koko/h26/index .htm.

98. See http://www.pref.toyama.jp/sections/1107/sosuikyo/.

99. See http://kyoto-sosuiren.com/study/tax_quiz.html.

100. This project takes place through an online discussion forum open to comments from citizens with no age restrictions. Citizens willing to participate need to fill out a registration form, after which they will be given a personal password and granted access. For more information, see Grand-Duché De Luxembourg (2014b).

101. See http://www.men.public.lu/fr/systeme-educatif/organisation-gouvernance /130919-organigramme-systeme-scolaire.pdf.

102. See "Economie Politique. Classe de 1D de l'enseignement secondaire" (Political Economy. 1D Class of Secondary Education), September 2014, Commission Nationale des Programmes en Sciences Economiques et Sociales at https://ssl .education.lu/eSchoolBooks/QuickSearch.aspx?#-1null.

103. Based on International Budget Partnership's Open Budget Survey 2015—Namibia at http://internationalbudget.org/wp-content/uploads/OBS2015-CS-Namibia -English.pdf.

104. See http://www.mof.gov.na/budget-2015-2016.

105. See the Financial Literacy Initiative's 2012–14 strategy at http://www.fli-namibia .org. See "Strategy of the Financial Literacy Initiative 2012–2014," Financial Literacy Initiative Secretariat, Ministry of Finance, Republic of Namibia at http://www.fli -namibia.org.

106. See http://www.ibe.unesco.org/curricula/namibia/sx_ls_bs_2007_eng.pdf.

107. Based on International Budget Partnership's Open Budget Survey 2015—New-Zealand at http://internationalbudget.org/wp-content/uploads/OBS2015-CS- New-Zealand -English.pdf.

108. See the New Zealand Ministry of Education's website, New Zealand Curriculum Online at http://nzcurriculum.tki.org.nz/The-New-Zealand-Curriculum.

109. See "Economics," Version 4 (2013) at the "New Zealand Curriculum Guides— Senior Secondary" web page of the Ministry of Education at http://seniorsecondary .tki.org.nz/Social-sciences/Economics.

110. See "Tax Education and Citizenship," Levels 4 and 5 at the "Social Sciences Online" web page of the Ministry of Education at http://taxcitizenship.tki.org.nz/.

111. See http://taxcitizenship.tki.org.nz/Level-4-unit/Social-inquiry-overview-Level-4.

112. See the New Zealand Education Portal of the New Zealand Ministry of Education at http://www.taxcitizenship.tki.org.nz/.

113. See "Pedagogy for Economics" at the "New Zealand Curriculum Guides—Senior Secondary" web page of the Ministry of Education at http://seniorsecondary.tki.org .nz/Social-sciences/Economics/Pedagogy.

114. See http://taxcitizenship.tki.org.nz/Resources/Deciding-about-tax.

115. See http://taxcitizenship.tki.org.nz/Level-4-unit/Learning-experience-1-What-is -tax-for/Tax-animation.

116. See http://taxcitizenship.tki.org.nz/Resources/What-s-tax-for.

117. See https://www.surveymonkey.com/s/TaxCitizenship.

118. See the Ministry of Education New Zealand's Economics Subject Resources, New Zealand Curriculum Guides: Senior Secondary 2012 at http://www.nzqa.govt .nz/qualifications-standards/qualifications/ncea/subjects/economics/levels/.

119. See http://longtermnz.org/wp-content/uploads/20130131-Youth-Statement2.pdf.

120. See http://www.treasury.govt.nz/government/longterm/fiscalposition/2013 /affordingourfuture/ltfs-13-aof.pdf.

121. Based on International Budget Partnership's Open Budget Survey 2015—Peru at http://internationalbudget.org/wp-content/uploads/OBS2015-CS-Peru-English.pdf.

122. See www.cultura.sunat.gob.pe.

123. Peru's curriculum for primary and secondary schools can be found at http://recursos .perueduca.pe/rutas/index.php.

124. See http://www.micomprobante.pe/.

125. See the politics and governance curriculum for the humanities and social sciences strand in senior high school at http://www.deped.gov.ph/k-to-12/About/curriculum -guides/Core-SHS.

126. See http://www.deped.gov.ph/sites/default/files/ABM_Applied%20Economics%20 CG_4.pdf.

127. See http://www.deped.gov.ph/sites/default/files/Araling%20Panlipunan%20Grades %20%201-10%2001.17.2014%20edited%20March%2025%202014.pdf.

128. http://www.deped.gov.ph/k-to-12/About/curriculum-guides/Core-SHS.

129. Based on International Budget Partnership's Open Budget Survey 2015—Poland at http://internationalbudget.org/wp-content/uploads/OBS2015-CS-Poland-English .pdf.

130. See http://www.oecd.org/cfe/leed/Rapid-policy-assessment Poland.pdf.

131. See http://4liberty.eu/think-tanks/for-civil-development-forum/.

132. See http://www.singaporebudget.gov.sg/data/budget_2016/download/FY2016 _Budget_in_Brief.pdf.

133. See http://www.singaporebudget.gov.sg/budget_2016/BudgetSpeech.aspx.

134. Based on International Budget Partnership's Open Budget Survey 2015—South Africa at http://internationalbudget.org/wp-content/uploads/OBS2015-CS-South-Africa-English.pdf. The South African government received a score of 65 out of 100 on public participation in the budget process.

135. Statistics South Africa is the national statistical service of South Africa—see http:// www.statssa.gov.za/.

136. Bulletins are vailable at https://www.resbank.co.za/Publications/QuarterlyBulletins /Pages/QuarterlyBulletins-Home.aspx.

137. Published by the Government Communication and Information System, the *South Africa Yearbook* gives a comprehensive account of the government's programs and policies as well as the current state of the South African nation. See http://www.gcis .gov.za/content/resourcecentre/sa-info/yearbook.

138. See http://www.sars.gov.za/Pages/default.aspx.

139. See http://www.treasury.gov.za/documents/nationalbudget/2015/sars/Budget PocketGuide 2015-16.pdf.

140. See http://www.treasury.gov.za/documents/nationalbudget/2015/guides /2015People's Guide-English.pdf.

141. See http://www.payingforit.org.uk/chanceto-be-chancellor/how-will-you-be-paying -forit.

142. See http://bit.ly/1MpfJiM.

143. The e-mail address is hmrc.taxeducation@hmrc.gsi.gov.uk.

144. See http://bit.ly/1fC6iCz.

145. Organizations such as the Association for Citizenship Teaching, Citized, Citizenship Foundation, Hansard Society, and the United Kingdom's Parliament–Education Service have produced or compiled such resources.

146. See http://taxmatters.hmrc.gov.uk/.

147. See http://www.teachitcitizenship.co.uk/index.php?CurrMenu=397&resource =12685.

148. See http://taxmatters.hmrc.gov.uk/.

149. See http://taxmatters.hmrc.gov.uk/.

150. See AS and A Level Delivery Guide. H040/H460 Theme: Macroeconomics, Application of Policy Instruments (March 2015), Oxford Cambridge and RSA Examinations at http://www.ocr.org.uk/Images/206586-application-of-policy -instruments-delivery-guide.pdf.

151. See http://www.bbc.co.uk/news/business-25944653.

152. See http://www.res.org.uk/view/res2011AnnualPublicLecture.html.

153. See https://www.youtube.com/watch?v=LAD1oCHCibI.

154. Based on International Budget Partnership's Open Budget Survey 2015—United States at http://internationalbudget.org/wp-content/uploads/OBS2015-CS-United -States-English.pdf. The 2015 Open Budget Index score for the United States is 81 percent.

155. See "Understanding Fiscal Responsibility. A Curriculum for Teaching about the Federal Budget, National Debt, and Budget Deficit" on the website of Columbia University, Teachers College. http://teachufr.org/about/.

156. "National Curriculum Standards for Social Studies: Chapter 2—The Themes of Social Studies," National Council for the Social Studies, at http://www.socialstudies .org/standards/strands.

157. https://www.icivics.org/curriculum/government-market.

158. See the City of Boston-Department of Youth Engagement and Employment website: http://youth.boston.gov.

159. Plan Ceibal provides low-cost laptops (called XOs), free software, and wireless connections—both inside and outside the classroom.

160. Ceibal is an information technology company.

References

ACARA (Australian Curriculum, Assessment and Reporting Authority). n.d. "F-10 Overview." Senior Secondary Curriculum v8.1. http://www.australiancurriculum.edu .au/curriculum/overview.

———. 2012a. "Draft Shape of the Australian Curriculum: Economics and Business." Australian Curriculum, Assessment and Reporting Authority. http://www.acara.edu .au/verve/_resources/Draft_Shape_Paper_for_consultation_-_Economics_and _Business_file.pdf.

———. 2012b. "The Shape of the Australian Curriculum: Civics and Citizenship." ACARA, Sydney. http://www.acara.edu.au/verve/_resources/Shape_of_the _Australian_Curriculum__Civics_and_Citizenship_251012.pdf.

ASIC (Australian Securities and Investments Commission). 2011. "National Consumer Financial Literacy Framework." http://www.bea.asn.au/cms/files/cms_files/content /Financial_literacy/NationalConsumerFinancialLiteracyFramework_2011.pdf.

Board of Studies NSW. 2009. *Economics: Stage 6 Syllabus*. Sydney, Australia: Board of Studies NSW. http://www.boardofstudies.nsw.edu.au/syllabus_hsc/pdf_doc/economics -st6-syl-from2011.pdf.

Bower, Paul. 2015. "Chance to be Chancellor 2015: Improving Economic Literacy." PowerPoint Presentation.

Budget Allocator. 2014. "Ten Examples of Participatory Budgeting from Around the World." *Budget Allocator* (Blog), September 29. http://www.budgetallocator.com/2014 /09/29/ten-examples-participatory-budgeting-around-world/.

Bürgerhaushalt. 2013. "'Misch mit!'—Der Online-Jugend-Bürgerhaushalt von Marzahn- Hellersdorf." *Bürgerhaushalt*, July 30. http://www.buergerhaushalt.org/de/article /misch-mit-der-online-jugend-buergerhaushalt-von-marzahn-hellersdorf.

CDC. 2010. *Life and Society Curriculum Guide (Secondary 1–3)*. Education Bureau, Government of the Hong Kong Special Administration Region of the People's Republic of China. http://www.edb.gov.hk/attachment/en/curriculum-development/kla/pshe/l&s_curriculum_guide_eng.pdf.

————. 2011. *General Studies for Primary Schools Curriculum Guide (Primary 1–Primary 6)*. Education Bureau, Government of the Hong Kong Special Administration Region of the People's Republic of China. http://www.edb.gov.hk/attachment/en/curriculum-development/kla/general-studies-for-primary/gs_p_guide-eng_300dpi-final%20version.pdf.

CDC and HKEAA (Curriculum Development Council and Hong Kong Examinations and Assessment Authority). 2014a. *Business, Accounting and Financial Studies. Curriculum and Assessment Guide (Secondary 4–6)*. http://334.edb.hkedcity.net/doc/eng/curriculum/BAFS C&A Guide_updated_e.pdf.

————. 2014b. *Economics. Curriculum and Assessment Guide (Secondary 4–6)*. Personal, Social and Humanities Education Key Learning Area, Education Bureau, Government of the Hong Kong Special Administration Region of the People's Republic of China. http://www.edb.gov.hk/attachment/en/curriculum-development/kla/pshe/EconC&AGuide_updated_e_20140212.pdf.

Center for Civic Education. 2014a. "National Standards for Civics and Government. 9–12 Content Standards." Center for Civic Education. http://www.civiced.org/standards?page=912erica#13.

————. 2014b. "National Standards for Civics and Government Learning Outcomes. K–4 Content Standards." Center for Civic Education. http://www.civiced.org/standards?page=k4erica.

Citizenship Foundation. 2013. "Youth Budget—Chance to be Chancellor Evaluation 2012–13." United Kingdom. http://www.youthbudget.org.

Columbia University. 2010. "New Study Finds that High School Students Are Not Taught About the Federal Budget, National Debt or Budget Deficit." Press Release, Teachers College, Columbia University, February 29. http://www.tc.columbia.edu/i/a/document/12949_PRESS_RELEASE_UFR29Feb2010.pdf.

Council for Economic Education. 2010. *Voluntary National Content Standards in Economics*. Council for Economic Education. http://www.councilforeconed.org/wp/wp-content/uploads/2012/03/voluntary-national-content-standards-2010.pdf.

Curriculum Development Institute. 2013. "Technology Education Key Learning Area Curriculum Guide. Supplementary Notes (Secondary 1–3)." Technology Education Section, Education Bureau, Government of the Hong Kong Special Administration Region of the People's Republic of China. http://www.edb.gov.hk/attachment/tc/curriculum-development/kla/technology-edu/whats-new/Supplementary Notes - TEKLA Curriculum Guide Eng.pdf.

Czech Republic. 2011. *The Education System in the Czech Republic. 2011*. Ministry of Education, Youth and Sport of the Czech Republic. http://www.msmt.cz/file/21631/download.

Davey, Ciara. 2010. *Children's Participation in Decision-Making: A Summary Report on Progress Made Up To 2010*. National Children's Bureau. http://www.ncb.org.uk/media/60368/summary_report_jun10.pdf.

Davies P. 2015. "Towards a Framework for Financial Literacy in the Context of Democracy." *Journal of Curriculum Studies* 47 (2): 300–16. doi:10.1080/00220272.2014.934717.

Departments of Education of New Brunswick, Newfoundland and Labrador, Nova Scotia, and Prince Edward. 1999. *Foundation for the Atlantic Canada Social Studies Curriculum*. http://www.ed.gov.nl.ca/edu/k12/curriculum/documents/socialstudies /social.pdf.

Department for Education. 2011. "Personal, Social, Health and Economic Education (PSHEE): Personal Well-Being." Department for Education, United Kingdom. https:// www.education.gov.uk/schools/teachingandlearning/curriculum/secondary /b00198880/pshee/ks3/personal.

———. 2013. "National Curriculum in England: Citizenship Programmes of Study." Statutory Guidance, Department for Education, United Kingdom, September 11. https://www.gov.uk/government/publications/national-curriculum-in-england -citizenship-programmes-of-study.

EACEA (Education, Audiovisual and Culture Executive Agency). 2012. *Entrepreneurship Education at School in Europe. National Strategies, Curricula and Learning Outcomes*. Brussels: EACEA. http://eacea.ec.europa.eu/education/eurydice/documents /thematic_reports/135EN.pdf.

Franco-Velasco, Tanya. 2012. "A Primer on the New K–12 Philippine Education Curriculum." *Smart Parenting*. http://www.smartparenting.com.ph/kids/preschooler /k-12-101-a-primer-on-the-new-philippine-education-curriculum/page/5.

Government of India. 2014. *Educational Statistics at a Glance*. Ministry of Human Resource Development, Bureau of Planning, Monitoring, and Statistics, New Delhi. http://mhrd.gov.in/sites/upload_files/mhrd/files/statistics/EAG2014.pdf.

Government of Ireland. 1996. *Leaving Certificate Business Syllabus*. http://www .curriculumonline.ie/getmedia/fb629c5b-f6e5-4193-ad4c-faf0e3c704c9/SCSEC08 _Business_syllabus_Eng.pdf.

Government of Newfoundland and Labrador. 2004. *Social Studies. Canadian Economy 2203—A Curriculum Guide*. Division of Program Development, Department of Education, Government of Newfoundland and Labrador. http://www.ed.gov.nl.ca /edu/k12/curriculum/guides/economiced/can_econ2203-04.pdf.

Grand-Duché De Luxembourg. 2014a. "Enseignement secondaire Année scolaire 2013/ 2014". Service des Statistiques et Analyses, Le Gouvernement Du Grand-Duché De Luxembourg. http://www.men.public.lu/catalogue-publications/secondaire/statistiques -analyses/statistiques-globales/resultats-scolaires-esg-2013-2014/stat-es-13-14.pdf.

——— 2014b. "Participation des citoyens au budget 2015 de la VDL." (Citizen Participation in the 2015 Budget of the City of Luxembourg), Guichet.lu, November 21. http://www.guichet.public.lu/citoyens/fr/actualites/2014/11/21-budget-vdl /index.html.

Grillos, Tara. 2014. "Youth Lead the Change: The City of Boston's Youth-Focused Participatory Budgeting Process." Pilot Year Evaluation, Harvard University, August. http://scholar.harvard.edu/files/grillos/files/pb_boston_year_1_eval_0.pdf.

KeyCoNet. 2012. "National Curriculum Citizenship." Key Case Note, United Kingdom (2), Key Competence Network on School Education. http://keyconet.eun.org/c /document_library/get_file?uuid=e6b2cc61-47c4-4fa7-900d-405d9830ddb8 &groupId=11028.

Ködelpeter, Thomas. n.d. "Jugendliche und Bürgerhaushalt." Bürgerhaushalt, München. http://www.buergerhaushalt.org/sites/default/files/downloads/Koedelpeter_Jugendliche -und-Buergerhaushalt_0.pdf.

Krieble, Susie, and Finn O'Dwyer-Cunliffe. 2013. "Engaging Youth on New Zealand's Long-Term Fiscal Position." *Policy Quarterly* 9 (4). http://igps.victoria.ac.nz /documents/PQ%20Vol%209%20No%204%202013.pdf.

Ministry of Education, Singapore. 2013. *Secondary Social Studies Normal (Technical) Syllabus*. Curriculum Planning and Development Division, Ministry of Education, Singapore. http://www.ibe.unesco.org/curricula/singapore/si_ls_ss_2013_eng.pdf.

———. 2014. *2014 Character and Citizenship Education (Secondary) Syllabus*. Ministry of Education, Singapore. https://www.moe.gov.sg/education/syllabuses/character -citizenship-education.

———. 2015. *Bringing Out the Best in Every Child. Education in Singapore*. Ministry of Education, Singapore. https://www.moe.gov.sg/docs/default-source/document/about /files/moe-corporate-brochure.pdf.

Ministry of Finance Costa Rica. 2010. "Guía Didáctica de Educación Fiscal—Nivel Primario" (Guidelines for Teaching Fiscal Education in Primary Schools). Ministry of Finance, Costa Rica. http://educa.hacienda.go.cr:8080/costarica_prod/uploads /paginas/guia_docente_primaria.pdf.

NCCA (National Council for Curriculum and Assessment). n.d. "Leaving Certificate: Economics Syllabus." NCCA. http://www.curriculumonline.ie/getmedia/6e2b19a4 -c54b-4a20-ade3-d24896e4e50c/SCSEC12_Economics_syllabus_eng.pdf.

———. 2013. "Background Paper and Brief for the Review of Junior Cycle Business Studies." Draft report for consultation, National Council for Curriculum and Assessment. http://www.juniorcycle.ie/NCCA_JuniorCycle/media/NCCA /Documents/Consultation/Subjects/JC-Business_Studies_BP.pdf.

———. 2014a. "Draft Background Paper and Brief for the Review of Leaving Certificate Economics." National Council for Curriculum and Assessment. http://ncca.ie/en /Curriculum_and_Assessment/Post-Primary_Education/Senior_Cycle/Consultation /Economics-BP_Eng.pdf.

———. 2014b. "Leaving Certificate: Mathematics Syllabus. Foundation, Ordinary and Higher Level." National Council for Curriculum and Assessment. http://www .curriculumonline.ie/getmedia/fd79ce76-9a07-42fb-9dd7-ac6036861816/SCSEC25 _Maths_syllabus_examination_in_2014_eng.pdf.

———. 2015a. "Junior Certificate: Mathematics Syllabus. Foundation, Ordinary and Higher Level." http://www.curriculumonline.ie/getmedia/84da961d-b393-4c05 -be0d-604278c370a8/JCSEC18_Maths_for_examination_in_2015.pdf.

———. 2015b. "Junior Cycle Business Studies: Draft Specification for Consultation." National Council for Curriculum and Assessment. http://www.juniorcycle.ie/NCCA _JuniorCycle/media/NCCA/Curriculum/Business%20Studies/JC-Draft -BusinessStudies-Spec.pdf.

NCEE (National Center on Education and the Economy). 2013. "Australia Overview." Center on International Education Benchmarking. http://www.ncee.org/programs -affiliates/center-on-international-education-benchmarking/top-performing -countries/australia-overview/.

NCERT (National Council of Educational Research and Training). n.d. "Syllabus for Secondary and Higher Secondary Levels." NCERT, New Delhi. http://www.ncert.nic .in/rightside/links/pdf/syllabus/vol2/08HGPES (XI-XII).pdf.

———. 2006. "Syllabus for Classes at the Elementary Level. Social Sciences. Classes VI–VII." NCERT, New Delhi. http://www.ncert.nic.in/rightside/links/syllabus.html.

————. 2007. "Government Budget and the Economy." In *Introductory Macroeconomics*, chapter 5. http://www.ncert.nic.in/NCERTS/textbook/textbook.htm?leec1=4-6.

O'Connor, Nat. 2011. "Ireland's Austerity Woes." *Social Europe*, February 7. http://www.socialeurope.eu/2011/02/irelands-austerity-woes/.

OCR (Oxford, Cambridge and RSA). 2012a. "GCSE Citizenship Studies." J269, J029. OCR. http://www.ocr.org.uk/qualifications/gcse-citizenship-studies-j269-j029-from-2012/.

————. 2012b. "GCSE Economics Specification." J320 Version 1 (April), OCR. http://www.ocr.org.uk/Images/82577-specification.pdf.

————. 2014. "A-Level Specification. Economics." H460 for First Assessment in 2017, OCR.

OGP (Open Government Partnership). 2014a. *Estonia's Action Plan in Participating in the Open Government Partnership 2014–16*. Tallinn: OGP. http://www.opengovpartnership.org/country/estonia/action-plan.

————. 2014b. "Philippines Action Plan." Open Government Partnership. http://www.opengovpartnership.org/country/philippines/action-plan.

OECD (Organisation for Economic Co-operation and Development). 2013. "Building Tax Culture, Compliance and Citizenship: A Global Source Book on Taxpayer Education." Draft for consultation. http://www.oecd.org/ctp/tax-global/sourebook-taxpayer-education.pdf.

————. 2014. *PISA 2012 Results: Students and Money: Financial Literacy Skills for the 21st Century (Volume VI)*. Pisa: OECD Publishing. http://www.oecd.org/pisa/keyfindings/PISA-2012-results-volume-vi.pdf.

Participedia. 2015. "Youth Lead the Change: Boston's Youth-Focused Participatory Budgeting (2014)." Participedia, January 4, updated February 5. http://participedia.net/en/cases/youth-lead-change-boston-s-youth-focused-participatory-budgeting-2014.

RegionalWolfenButtel.De. 2013. "Bertelsmann Stiftung: Der erste deutsche Schülerhaushalt steht." *RegionalWolfenButtel.De*, March 1. http://wolfenbuettelheute.de/bertelsmann-stiftung-der-erste-deutsche-schulerhaushalt-steht/.

Republic of Estonia. 2011a. "Regulation: National Curriculum for Basic Schools." Republic of Estonia, No. 1, Tallinn, Toompea, January 6. http://www.ibe.unesco.org/curricula/estonia/er_befw_2011_eng.pdf.

————. 2011b. "Regulation. National Curriculum for Upper Secondary Schools." Republic of Estonia, No. 2, Tallinn, Toompea, January 6,. http://www.ibe.unesco.org/curricula/estonia/er_usfw_2011_eng.pdf.

Republic of Namibia. 2005. *Life Skills Syllabus, Grades 11–12*. Republic of Namibia: Ministry of Education. http://www.ibe.unesco.org/curricula/namibia/sx_us_lf_2005_eng.pdf.

————. 2006. *Life Skills Syllabus, Grades 8–10*. Republic of Namibia: Ministry of Education. http://www.nied.edu.na/syllabuses2010/JSC%20syllabuses/JSC%20LIFE%20SKILLS%20SYLLABUS%20UPDATED%2025%20JANUARY%202007.pdf.

————. 2007. *Home Economics Syllabus Grades 8–10*. Republic of Namibia: Ministry of Education. http://www.ibe.unesco.org/curricula/namibia/sx_ls_he_2006_eng.pdf.

————. 2008. *Entrepreneurship Syllabus, Grades 8–10*. Republic of Namibia: Ministry of Education. http://www.ibe.unesco.org/curricula/namibia/sx_ls_bs_2007_eng.pdf.

———. 2009a. *Economics Syllabus, Grades 11–12.* Higher Level Syllabus Code 8337, Namibia Senior Secondary Certificate (NSSC), Ministry of Education, Republic of Namibia. http://www.nied.edu.na/publications/Syllabusses/01_NSSCH/NSSCH _Economics-Syllabus_2010.pdf.

———. 2009b. "Mathematics Syllabus, Grades 11–12." Ordinary Level Syllabus Code 4324, NSSC, Ministry of Education, Republic of Namibia.

———. 2010. *Business Studies Syllabus, Grades 11–12.* Ordinary Level Syllabus Code 4346, NSSC. Ministry of Education, Republic of Namibia. http://www.nied.edu.na /syllabuses2010/NSSC%20Folder/NSSC%20O%20Folder/NSSCO%20Business%20 Studies%20Syllabus%2028%20April%202009.pdf.

Republic of South Africa. 2009. *Basic Skills for Mathematical Literacy.* National Department of Basic Education, Republic of South Africa.

———. 2011a. *Curriculum and Assessment Policy Statement. Grades 7–9. Economic and Management Sciences.* Department of Basic Education Republic of South Africa. http://www.education.gov.za/LinkClick.aspx?fileticket=YEgQQlsQNCw%3D&tabid =573&mid=1629.

———. 2011b. *Curriculum and Assessment Policy Statement. Further Education and Training Phase. Grades 10–12.* Department of Basic Education, Republic of South Africa. http://www.education.gov.za/LinkClick.aspx?fileticket=Lv%2B97xKN0eM %3D&tabid=570&mid=1558.

———. 2011c. *Curriculum and Assessment Policy Statement. Grades 10–12. Mathematical Literacy.* Ministry of Basic Education, Republic of South Africa. http://www .education.gov.za/LinkClick.aspx?fileticket=q8%2BSkGy43rw%3D&tabid=570 &mid=1558.

SACE Board of South Australia. 2016. *Mathematics: 2016 Subject Outline—Stage 1.* Government of South Australia. https://www.sace.sa.edu.au/web/mathematics /stage-1/planning-to-teach/subject-outline.

SCSA (School Curriculum and Standards Authority). 2014a. *Economics: ATAR Course. Year 11 Syllabus.* Government of Western Australia. http://wace1516.scsa.wa.edu .au/__data/assets/pdf_file/0013/10057/Economics_Y11_Syllabus_ATAR_PDF.pdf.

———. 2014b. *Economics: ATAR Course. Year 12 Syllabus.* Government of Western Australia. http://wace1516.scsa.wa.edu.au/__data/assets/pdf_file/0007/10060/Economics_Y12 _Syllabus_ATAR_PDF.pdf.

Shaddick, Edwina, and Vivienne Wee. 2014. "Budget Process Needs to Be More Open and Inclusive." Aware.org, January 24, Association of Women for Action and Research. http:// www.aware.org.sg/2014/01/budget-process-needs-to-be-more-open-and-inclusive/.

Sorlut, Pierre. 2014. "Enseigner l'économie est dans l'intérêt du pays" (Teaching Economics is in the Interest of the Country). *Paperjam Business zu Letzebuerg,* July 9. http:// paperjam.lu/questions/enseigner-l-economie-est-dans-l-interet-du-pays.

Srinivasan, M.V. n.d. *Teaching Economics in India, A Teacher's Handbook.* New Delhi: Department of Education in Social Sciences, National Council of Educational Research and Training. http://www.ncert.nic.in/departments/nie/dess/publication /prin_material/Teaching_Economics_in_India.pdf.

TQA (Tasmanian Qualifications Authority). 2010. *Economics.* Office of Tasmanian Assessment, Standards and Certification, Tasmanian Certificate Authority, ECN315111. http://www.tqa.tas.gov.au/4DCGI/_WWW_doc/043469/RND01/ECN315111 _Economics.pdf.

TNI (Transnational Institute). 2006. *Participatory Budgeting in Canada.* TNI.org, February 1. https://www.tni.org/en/archives/act/3969.

VCCA (Victorian Curriculum and Assessment Authority). 2014. *Economics: Victorian Certificate of Education Study Design.* Updated, Victorian Curriculum and Assessment Authority, East Melbourne. http://www.vcaa.vic.edu.au/Documents/vce/economics /EconomicsSD.pdf.

VÚP (Research Institute of Education). 2007a. *The Framework Education Programme for Elementary Education.* VÚP, Prague. http://rvp.cz/informace/wp-content /uploads/2009/09/RVP_ZV_EN_final.pdf.

————. 2007b. *The Framework Education Programme for Secondary General Education.* VÚP, Prague. http://rvp.cz/informace/wp-content/uploads/2009/09/RVP_G-anj.pdf.

Summary of Case Studies on Beyond-School Budget Literacy Initiatives

#	Country	Level	Implementer	Initiative
1	Ecuador	Local	Local Government of Cotacachi	Cotacachi, Ecuador: A Municipality Built on Childhood and Youth
2	Ghana	Local	Plan Ghana and the Integrated Social Development Centre	Perspectives on Youth Budget Advocacy in Ghana
3	Kenya	Local	Plan International	Youth as Drivers of Accountability: Conducting a Youth Social Audit
4	Nicaragua	Local	Network of Municipal Governments, Friends of Children, Municipal Commissions for Children, and Save the Children	An Increase of Local Spending on Children: An Outcome of Budget Participation by Children in Nicaragua
5	Northern Ireland	International	Centre for Children's Rights and Queen's University, Belfast	Conducting a Global Consultation on Public Expenditures with Children
6	South Africa	National	Idasa, Disabled Children's Action Group, Life Hunters, It's Your Move, and the City of Cape Town's Youth Development Programme	Reflections from the Children's Participating in Governance Project: Budget Monitoring Within a Rights-Based Framework
7	Venezuela, RB	Local	Local Government of Caroní	Engaging with Youngsters to Identify Development Priorities
8	Zimbabwe	National, subnational, and local	Save the Children, UNICEF, and National Association of Non-Governmental Organizations	The Impact of Child-Led Groups on Budget Allocations in Zimbabwe

E1.1 Cotacachi, Ecuador: A Municipality Engaging with Children and Youth

Country: Ecuador
Level: Local
Implementer: Local Government of Cotacachi

Context

Since 1996, the municipal administration of the Santa Ana canton of Cotacachi in Ecuador has implemented a policy of civic participation through the Assembly of Cantonal Unity, an independent informal forum composed of 16 elected members. During the second cantonal assembly in 1997, the limited participation of young people was identified as a significant weakness in the development plan, and since 1998, there has been a move to increasingly involve children and youth in local management committees, groups, and work commissions.

Actions (1999–2002)

In February and March 2000, 11 diagnostic workshops were organized through local groups to equip 750 children (in sixth grade or lower) and 644 youth (maximum age 28 years) to participate in the upcoming cantonal congresses. The themes for the diagnosis were survival, such as health, nutrition, housing, and protection; development, including education and recreation; and participation at home and at school, in their communities and cantons. Interactive techniques emphasized recreation and the children's customs, history, culture, and art. Written and oral debates were the primary activities.

- From March to June 2000, delegates elected by their peers participated in congresses in each of the three zones of Cotacachi. In each zone, there was one delegate for children and one for youth. (These congresses were repeated in August 2002.) The children and young people expressed a range of concerns with regard to specific provisions for their age groups, such as recreational facilities, access to information about scholarships, and increasing opportunities for their opinions to be heard, as well as more general community needs, such as improvement of local roads, water quality, electricity, and training for mothers on better nutrition. Young people from urban areas were especially concerned about the quality of services and housing and the passage of laws to protect them.
- Subsequently, plans were specified for which the local government could play a key role. The mayor and the cantonal assembly's board legalized the process by signing the Great Plan of Childhood and Youth (*Gran Acuerdo de la Niñez y Juventud*), which focused on including young people's proposals in the development plan of the canton; setting aside a percentage of the annual municipal budget for these proposals; implementing the projects that were proposed by young people in the First Cantonal Congress; and ensuring that children and youth had continued opportunities to exercise their rights of citizenship.

Results

- **Funding allocated for participatory budgeting.** In 2001, a participatory municipal budget was put in place that protected the sectoral interests of children and youth, and in 2002, a participatory budget of US$ 6,372 was allocated for child and youth participatory budgeting.
- **Realization of funding for youth-related components of public programs.** The local government adopted the role of broker, matching sources of funding to accommodate the recommendations provided by the children and youth. This was done by including the recommended projects in regular sector programs funded through a variety of sources, both national and international. For example, the municipality granted a ten-year contract for the administration of the Yana-yacu eco-tourist complex to the Maquimañachi. This project continues to thrive as a source of income and includes a 3,000-meter swimming pool warmed by a solar heater and run by young people. The solar heating system was funded through a central government program. The funds were channeled to Cotacachi and were based on requests by the youth.
- **Realization of funding for student scholarship program.** In coordination with the Cuban Embassy, a student scholarship program was launched to provide seven young people with the opportunity to study in La Havana.

Educative Implications

Broad collaboration is crucial to provide opportunities for youth to engage in participatory-budgeting processes. The positive outcomes in this case were largely determined by the enthusiasm and active support of the authorities, local institutions, nongovernmental organizations, children and youth, teachers, and citizens.

E1.2 Perspectives on Youth Budget Advocacy in Ghana

Country: Ghana
Level: Local
Implementers: Plan Ghana and the Integrated Social Development Centre

Context

In Ghana, the idea of budgeting at the national level was perceived as very technical and considered to be the sole purview of economists and financial experts. National budget processes were seen to have little to do with youth and children. In 2010, Plan Ghana and the Integrated Social Development Centre sought to enhance youth participation in budget preparation and tracking. Accordingly, they launched a youth budget advocacy project in January 2010.

The project included training young people in budget advocacy, which gave rise to groups such as the Youth Budget Advocacy Group of Awutu-Senya District.

Actions (2010–11)

- The project started with a stakeholders' meeting organized in the Awutu-Senya district to introduce its objectives and to discuss the need to involve youth in budgeting processes. Based on their responses to a questionnaire, ten youth ages 12–30 (five male and five female) were selected for a preliminary "training of trainers."

- A week-long training of trainers workshop was organized to build understanding and capacity for budget advocacy among the selected youth. Participants were introduced to international, regional, and national legal instruments underpinning budgeting for children's rights as well as family budgets, routine budget calculations, the government budget cycle at the local and national levels, and entry points for citizen engagement. Practical field exercises were carried out as part of the training process for building the participants' abilities to conduct research about realization measures for children's rights. There were also engagements with relevant public officials. Participants completed a budget advocacy plan that they intended to implement once they had returned to their districts.

- Upon returning to their districts, the trained participants embarked on community field trips to gather empirical data regarding issues affecting children, such as education, health, water, and social protection, enabling the group to establish a baseline and conduct a situational analysis that could be periodically monitored with regard to the allocations and execution of budgets. It also helped participants make grounded assessments about the adequacy of specific budget allocations and execution of efficient and effective public-service delivery.

- The Integrated Social Development Centre, with the support of Plan Ghana, helped these youth groups organize a validation meeting at which they shared the initial findings of their field survey work with community members and local authorities. At an official gathering hosted by a local chief that convened school children, district assembly officials, parents, and traditional leaders, they also presented an advocacy statement. Using role-play, the youth groups depicted how their district assembly budget could address the basic needs of children. The activity generated a great deal of interest and questions, to which the youth responded with practical examples, using preliminary findings from their field survey.

Results
- **Preparation of materials to support budget training and advocacy activities.** Knowledge products based on the implementation of this project included a training manual and a budget advocacy article published in the journal of *Participatory Learning and Action* (Bani-Afudego and others 2011). Additionally, the Youth Budget Advocacy Group of Awutu-Senya District produced a report on their analysis of the district budget in 2010.
- **Input for national budget.** Some of the youth groups were invited to participate in a civil society forum to provide input for the 2011 budget statement. They strongly supported the continuation of the Youth in Agriculture program, which was approved.
- **Ongoing training of trainers by youth groups.** In addition to continuing to monitor changes in government spending on development projects in their communities, several youths voluntarily conduct workshops on budget advocacy for other groups. By 2011, 70 children and youth (31 female and 39 male) from the central and eastern regions of Ghana had participated in these workshops (Bani-Afudego and others 2011).
- **Continued engagement with local governments.** The youth groups are occasionally consulted by the district assembly on development issues concerning youth and children.

Educative Implication
- In addition to helping the training participants maintain focus on learning, the training-of-trainers approach provides them the opportunity to gain and apply relevant knowledge and boost their confidence through a rights-based and participatory approach to learning before commencing with field interactions.

E1.3 Youth as Drivers of Accountability: Conducting a Youth Social Audit

Country: Kenya
Level: Local
Implementer: Plan International

Context

The demand for accountability in the management of public resources for service delivery has been gaining ground in Kenya over the last few years. According to a report by the Kenya Taxpayers Association (NTA 2009), about KSh 170.2 million (approximately US$ 1.68 million) of constituency development funds was reported missing in 23 constituencies in fiscal year 2006/07 and KSh 500 million in fiscal year 2008/09. Pressure from citizens has therefore increased for the government to account for the use of public finances in public-service delivery.

Since 2009, in line with an increased interest in reducing the waste of public funds, Plan International's governance program organizes youth forums and workshops for government fund managers to share information on the public funds intended for community projects and services. As a result, youth in Kwale, Kilifi, and Nairobi counties have been using social audits to assess the relevance, cost-effectiveness, and quality of schools, health centers, and water services.

Actions

- The participatory social audit process started with compiling publicly accessible information on constituency development funds. Perceived gaps and inconsistencies in the shared information raised questions regarding the implementation of the budget and further justified the need for youth to conduct a social audit.

- Youth were mobilized for the social audit from district youth councils in Kwale and Kilifi and Jipange Youth Organization in Nairobi, which has 32 legally registered youth groups as members. Social audit teams were formed and terms of reference for the social audit were drawn based on shared questions and concerns that could not be clarified without verifying how constituency development funds were being utilized. The teams developed a scorecard methodology to capture their individual and collective criteria for scoring community projects (see table E.1) as well as rules of engagement with the duty bearers at selected project sites.

- The social audit teams reviewed project financial documents and bills of quantities provided by constituency development fund managers and worked with project site committees to schedule site visits. Teams verified projects based on the objectives and standards stipulated in the project documents and engaged in focus group discussions with project committees and beneficiaries during the site visits. (See box E.1, for example, of some of the questions they posed during this process.)

Table E.1 A Simple Project Social Audit Tool

| | Social audit team satisfaction rating | | | |
Project type/name	Highly satisfied	Satisfied	Fairly unsatisfied/ unsure	Not satisfied/ disappointed
Amount allocated				
Community participation in the project resources				
Management of project resources				
Relevance of the project to pressing community needs				
Cost effectiveness and efficiency of resource use				
Project's impact/potential impact on poverty alleviation				
Quality of workmanship				
Number of beneficiaries				
Integrity and competency of the project management team				
Project inputs procurement process				
Promotion of accountability and transparency in project				
Project outcomes/outputs				

Box E.1 Questions Most Frequently Asked by Social Auditors in Interviews and Focus Groups

- How was the project conceived?
- Was the community involved?
- Does the community like the project?
- Who benefitted from the project?
- Did the project provide employment to the local community?
- Does the project provide a proper service to the target population?
- Did the project change the lives of the beneficiaries?
- Did the community get value for the money spent in the project?
- Did the project have any side effects (for example, a school feeding program might increase dependency syndrome)?
- Is there evidence of long-term project impacts (such as poverty reduction or improved standards of living?
- Are there mechanisms for the project to be sustained by the community?

- Teams used key observations, messages, and issues which they had compiled to prepare a report on aspects needing clarifications or improvements, as well as good budget implementation practices that they had observed. Teams organized feedback meetings with stakeholders, beneficiary communities, and young people based on those action plans that had the most detailed descriptions of how public services or facilities would be improved, and the process of negotiating for change and action with constituency development fund teams began.

International Practices to Promote Budget Literacy • http://dx.doi.org/10.1596/978-1-4648-1071-8

Results
- **Increased audit knowledge and skills among youth.** Social audit processes have increased the effectiveness of young people's participation in youth councils by improving their monitoring and advocacy skills and enabling them to become active participants in the process of service delivery. In addition, youth council members are now increasingly perceived as possessing the necessary knowledge and capacity to make contributions to their communities.
- **Improved management of public resources.** Kwale, Kilfi, and Nairobi youth have been using social audits to improve the management of public resources. An example is that of a classroom construction project at Moyeni secondary school in Kwale County. The structure was built in contravention of the specifications. Even though a certificate of completion was issued, the audit found cracks in the floor and poorly fitted windows and doors. Based on the findings of the project site visit, an action plan was implemented that required the contractor to rebuild the classroom.

Educative Implications
- Through continuous self- and group reflection, engaging in the social audit process allows young people to appreciate the value of public resources and the implications of waste and misuse. Youth are progressively socialized toward the virtues of integrity and accountable citizenship.
- While social-audit processes foster youth learning and participation, intra-youth power relations stemming from differences in age, education level, and family socioeconomic circumstances can breed exclusion and have an adverse impact on the learning process.

E1.4 An Increase of Local Spending on Children: An Outcome of Budget Participation by Children in Nicaragua

Country: Nicaragua
Level: Local
Implementers: Network of Municipal Governments Friends of Children, Municipal Commissions for Children; Save the Children

Context

Save the Children started working with local governments in Nicaragua two decades ago. During this time, Save the Children supported the establishment of the Network of Municipal Governments Friends of Children, through which it continues to support local governments. The purpose of the network is to promote the fulfillment of children's rights at the community level by creating spaces such as children's councils and lobbying events that allow children to engage in municipal-level governance processes and by ensuring that children are directly involved in the discussions and approval of projects that directly affect them.[1] As of 2013, 82 percent of the municipalities in Nicaragua were part of this network.

Actions (2006–13)

- Each year in some municipalities, local authorities invited children to a participatory lobbying event, where children present their requests, which are based on gap analyses conducted in their communities.
- In advance of the participatory lobbying event, the network and other organizations organized preparatory assemblies where children learned to develop proposals on how the municipalities should finance specific issues based on their gap analyses. Depending on their age, children drew pictures representing their wishes or wrote about the projects they wanted to see the local government implement. Government officials from some municipalities have also worked with children to develop budgets to estimate the costs associated with their proposals.
- Some months later, the municipal government invited young people to an accountability lobbying event where the municipality presented and discussed projects that had already been implemented or were underway, as well as the expenditures for each project.
- Every year, the Network of Municipal Governments Friends of Children evaluated the commitments of local governments to fulfill children's rights. During a widely attended annual competition ceremony, the local governments with the best annual "child's rights" performances received monetary prizes of US$ 5,000, US$ 4,000, or US$ 3,000 for first, second, and third place, respectively. The funds were then allocated to a project selected by the children of those municipalities.

Results

- **Increase in the amount of municipal investment in children.** The network has contributed to an increase in the annual average of municipal investments in children from 8.5 percent in 2001–04 to 14.5 percent in 2005–08 and to 18.3 percent in 2009–12, directly benefiting thousands of children throughout Nicaragua.
- **Increase in the number of municipalities with children's rights plans.** The number of municipalities that have prepared children's rights plans has increased from seven in 2010 to 60 in 2013, with 43 also having a municipal policy for children, drafted based on proposals submitted by children.
- **Preparation of plans and policies with input from children.** Policies, plans, projects, and budgets have been prepared and approved with input from 15,500 children. Children have directly selected the content of 47 municipal projects, most of which addressed the right to education and recreation and benefitted 363,000 children from 2008 to 2013.
- **Improved adult perception of children's participation.** Generalized results reveal a change in the perception of adults of the capacity of children to participate in governance processes. Mayors and municipal council members have moved from seeing children *in need* to children *with rights*, and are more inclined to listening to the opinions of children and respect their decisions as they relate to projects.

Educative Implications

- Opportunities to share experiences, encouragement, and public recognition could serve as useful incentives for local governments to scale up budget-literacy education through school-based or out-of-school initiatives.
- The participation of children in developing proposals and recommendations from their own point of view is likely to strengthen their proactive role in their municipalities and help define the priorities and strategies for the fulfilment of their rights.

E1.5 Conducting a Global Consultation on Public Expenditures with Children

Country: Northern Ireland
Level: International
Implementer: Centre for Children's Rights, Queen's University, Belfast

Context

Despite the adoption of the United Nations (UN) Convention on the Rights of the Child 25 years ago, the lack of sufficient, efficient, and equitable investment in children is among the greatest barriers to realizing children's rights in many countries. In January 2014, the UN Committee on the Rights of the Child responded by developing the "General Comment on Public Spending to Realize Children's Rights" to provide further guidance to governments and nonstate actors about how to address such gaps so as to realize the rights of all children in a sustainable manner. Toward this end, the Child Rights Connect Working Group on Investment in Children[2] was established to provide input for the UN Human Rights Council meeting "Towards Better Investment in the Rights of the Child," convened in March 2015.

To ensure that children's views are heard and considered in these UN-led processes, a team of children's rights participation experts from the Centre for Children's Rights at Queen's University Belfast were asked to assist in developing methods and research instruments to compile the views and recommendations of children from across the world about this topic.

Actions (2014–15)

- The research team worked with a children's advisory group consisting of five children ages 5–6 (two boys and three girls) and a young person's advisory group of seven young people ages 13–17 (one boy and six girls) in Northern Ireland. The young person's advisory group assisted the research team in identifying key issues to include in the online survey, refining the face-to-face consultation tools, and developing a child-friendly version of the report based on the outcomes of the global consultation. The children's advisory group provided input for the development of consultation tools for engaging with younger children or those with literacy difficulties.
- A guide for face-to-face consultations was prepared and piloted with children ages 10–18 between July and October 2014 (Queen's University Belfast n.d.).[3] A separate consultation guide was developed for younger children ages 4–10.[4] In-person consultations were led by regional and national children's rights organizations, which used the methodology and facilitation guides developed by the research team.
- To ensure participation by as many children as possible, a survey was developed to solicit the views of children and young people ages 10–18. It was made available online in English, French, and Spanish on the Child Rights

Connect website. It was also translated for use in paper-based surveys in the Asia-Pacific region[5] and in Western Europe.

- The research team compiled and analyzed reports by facilitators about face-to-face consultations and survey responses to produce the report, "Towards Better Investment in the Rights of the Child: the Views of Children."

Results

- **Substantive outreach and inputs from children.** A total of 2,693 children from 71 countries, ages 4–19, participated in this global consultation through one of the methods offered, such as face-to-face consultations and online and paper-based surveys. The findings and recommendations of this report demonstrated that children have clear views about how governments should spend money in ways that will realize their rights and that they are able and willing to share their views.
- **Availability of useful evidence for the UN Human Rights Council meeting.** In addition to sources provided by other stakeholders, a report of the survey results was shared with the UN Committee on the Rights of the Child and the Human Rights Council to provide input regarding the advice they give to governments.
- **Adoption of the UN resolution on investment in children.** In March 2015, the UN Human Rights Council adopted a resolution on investment in children: "Towards Better Investment in the Rights of the Child,"[6] which calls on states to make continuous efforts to sustain investments in children at the national and subnational levels, and highlights the importance of the participation of children in budgetary and fiscal processes.

Educative Implication

Guidance prepared for face-to-face consultation with children on budget expenditures is more likely to be effective if it emphasizes the use of pedagogical approaches that rely on familiar contexts for children, and that include efforts to engage children through ice breaking activities, role-play or dramatization, and group discussions or activities.

E1.6 Reflections from the Children's Participating in Governance Project: Budget Monitoring within a Rights-Based Framework

Country: South Africa
Level: National
Implementers: Idasa; Disabled Children's Action Group; Life Hunters; It's Your Move; the City of Cape Town's Youth Development Program

Context

Children growing up in a young democracy have a window of opportunity to advocate for their own rights and engage in governance issues, and their participation in governance ensures that their perspectives, experiences, and priorities inform economic policy and budget allocations, among other things. The process is useful to ensure that policy and budgets are responsive to children's actual needs—not just those perceived by adults, that a society and its economy are shaped by the young people who will one day run it, and that good citizens are nurtured for the future. Keeping in mind this context, in 2004 the Children's Budget Unit of the Institute for Democracy in South Africa (Idasa) initiated the project on Budget Monitoring within a Rights-Based Framework: Children Participating in Governance, with the aim of:

- Creating opportunities for children in South Africa to monitor government budgets;
- Improving children's participation in monitoring of budgets for the realization of rights in a way that ultimately informs policy; and
- Contributing to the alignment of government budgets with the realization of rights.

To implement the project, the Children's Budget Unit selected twenty-five children, ages 12–18, from well-established children's groups the Disabled Children's Action Group, Life Hunters, It's Your Move, and the City of Cape Town's Youth Development Program—to train as peer facilitators.

Actions (2004–06)

- The training introduced topics such as *linking budgets and rights*, including the progressive realization of rights, household budgets, and how government works; *budget analysis as a monitoring tool*, including integrated development plans, organizational budgets, basic budget analysis tools, and personal experiences of rights and empowerment; and *developing a strategic budget advocacy campaign*, including advocacy concepts and strategies, engagement in the budget presentation process in Parliament, preparing responses to the budget, and planning an advocacy campaign.

- The guiding principle behind teaching children about budgets was to build on what children already knew. For example, when adult facilitators wanted children to understand government budgets, they started by reflecting on pocket money or household budgets. Once there was a basic understanding of a concept, the adult facilitators built on this knowledge by changing the context. After children understood household budgets, opportunities were provided for them to visit community projects and interview staff to understand their organizations' budgets.

- Instead of traditional learning methods employed in schools, games were used to impart budget concepts. Children took part in treasure hunts to learn about budget books, did puzzles to understand their constitutional rights, and played the game "Jeopardy" to learn about human-rights instruments. Experiential learning tools included using a cake to demonstrate the levels of government. Instead of talking about *stereotypes as labels*, adult facilitators assigned *labels to individuals* who then had to guess who people were and what power they had in society from the way they interacted with them.

- Supported by Idasa, a group of children participated in an exposure visit to a children's budget project run by Cedec (*Centro de Defesa da Criança e do Adolescente do Ceará*—Ceará Children's and Youth Defense Center) in Fortaleza, Brazil.

Results
- **Replication through peer learning.** The 25 peer facilitators implemented activities with their own constituency groups, reaching approximately 100 children.
- **Lobbying with policy makers.** Children who were given the opportunity to attend the budget speech and the subsequent public question-and-answer session took the opportunity to lobby for accessible transport and employment opportunities for youth with disabilities. They also asked about the implementation plan for fee-free schools, which was discussed in the project workshops. These sessions were televised and nationally broadcast.
- **Release of a budget brief.** After the budget speech, a group of children volunteered to review the budget books and find out what changes were anticipated that might affect children. They then compiled a budget brief, which was released online on the same night that the budget speech was delivered.

Educative Implications
- It is far easier to capture the imagination and attention of youth when learning is made fun. However, sufficient time for reflection should also be built into the program to consolidate the learning.
- Regular breaks and energizing activities increase engagement and participation at training workshops.
- Adult facilitators working with children must critically interrogate their notions of power over children. The more adults let go of their notions of superiority, the more children will actively engage in and guide the initiative. In this project, for example, adult facilitators trained peer facilitators but then acted only as reference points during the trainings led by the youth facilitators, demonstrating their confidence in the children's abilities.

E1.7 Engaging with Youngsters to Identify Development Priorities

Country: República Bolivariana de Venezuela
Level: Local
Implementer: Local government of Caroní

Context

Even though Ciudad Guyana, the capital of the district of Caroní in República Bolivariana de Venezuela, had succeeded in emerging as an outstanding example of planned development by the year 2000, there were still concerns regarding effective service provision and poverty alleviation. Therefore, one of the main objectives of the district's 1998 framework document was to:

> "… improve participatory governance for economic development and to strengthen the participation of children, young people and women in decision-making, in order to consolidate a project for democratic administration of the city, directed at eradicating poverty."

The framework's specific objectives included:

- Finding options for economic development, training, and participation of young people in Ciudad Guyana, and promoting the inclusion of young women in employment, occupations, technology, and local decision making;
- Establishing a municipal council for youth (*Consejo Municipal de Jóvenes*) and a municipal council of boys and girls (*Consejo Municipal de Niños y Niñas*); and
- Formulating a plan of action to implement the proposals developed during the planned urban consultation.

The target population for the urban consultation included young people between ages 7–20 from municipal, state, and national schools as well as colleges run by Faith and Happiness, the civil association that, along with the local government, managed the urban consultation.

Actions (1998–2002)

- After initial commitments were made to the urban consultation process in Ciudad Guyana, an exposure visit to France was organized in 1998 for a delegation of children and youth to provide them with additional experiences of urban consultations. An awareness-raising campaign was launched to inform local citizens about the consultation process. Various media and door-to-door canvassing helped inform local citizens. Meetings with teachers and social organizations from the ten parishes of Ciudad Guyana were organized to familiarize them with the urban consultation process.

- Workshops were organized for children to explain the urban consultation process, and a survey was conducted about the development priorities of over 4,000 school children and adolescents. It focused on five themes: school, home, the community, the neighborhood, and the city. In October 1999, child and youth participants prepared a preliminary plan of action that was based on the survey's findings, in response to which various programs and initiatives were developed. However, in 2000, a change in municipal government meant that many initiatives were discontinued, including the urban consultation process.

- Still, among other reforms, the new municipal government adopted a participatory process to establish a new system of protection for children and adolescents called the Law for the Protection of Children and Adolescents (LOPNA). The team responsible for drawing up the draft bill of the law included representatives who had previously organized the urban consultation in Ciudad Guyana. They were able to use their prior experience to contribute to several provisions included in this law. The protection system for children and adolescents includes the Fund for the Protection of the Child and Adolescent (*Fondo de Protección del Niño y Adolescente*), for which the local government of Caroní has assumed responsibility.

Results
- **Continued engagement of secondary-school students.** An information system has been developed to keep track of developments related to children and young people and working meetings have involved secondary-school students.
- **Provision of basic services for children.** A pilot program—Children of Hope—has responded to the needs of 1,300 children by providing them with food and a roof over their head;
- **Increased opportunities for art education.** In addition to other initiatives funded by the Fund of Protection of the Children, a municipal school of music has been established, which has led to opportunities for nearly 60 adults and adolescents to receive musical training previously unaffordable to them.

Educative Implication
Political will is critical for adopting an agenda focused on children and for involving youth in participatory-budgeting processes.

E1.8 The Impact of Child-Led Groups on Budget Allocations in Zimbabwe

Country: Zimbabwe
Level: National, Subnational, and Local
Implementers: Save the Children; United Nations Children's Fund (UNICEF); National Association of Non-Governmental Organizations (NANGO)

Context

The national budget is crucial in determining a government's commitment to realizing the rights of its children. In 1999, this recognition led to the establishment of the Child-Friendly National Budget Initiative. The effort was spearheaded by nine child-focused organizations working in Zimbabwe, including Save the Children; the United Nations Children's Fund (UNICEF); and the National Association of Non-Governmental Organizations (NANGO), which is in charge of coordinating this initiative. The initiative intends to introduce mechanisms to hold the government accountable for its policies and actions and to find sustainable solutions to the structural causes of poverty. It has therefore involved children from rural and urban areas from all social classes in order to analyze and influence local and national budgets and make them responsive to the needs of children.

Actions (1999–present)

- Save the Children has developed, piloted, and rolled out their model of child-led groups in cities and remote rural areas where youngsters come together to discuss and raise awareness of children's rights, demonstrate to their peers and the communities the importance of involving children, and engage with decision makers on different issues with support from adults. Thirty-four child-led groups have been established in eight of Zimbabwe's 10 provinces with participation from 3,500 girls and 3,012 boys ages 6–18.

- Members of child-led groups are trained on the issue of children's rights and understand how states report to the UN Committee on the Rights of the Child. They have been equipped with knowledge on national legislation related to children, budget literacy, advocacy, project management, life skills, and the importance of talking and listening to others. In 2014, more than 1,500 children were reached through trainings on various aspects of children's rights.

- Group members actively participate in the planning and implementation of the Child-Friendly National Budget Initiative. They have the knowledge and support to analyze and critique the utilization of budget resources and to engage in efforts to raise awareness among policy makers regarding children's rights and the importance of allocating more resources for the realization of these rights.

- They have also facilitated dialogue between members of the child-led groups and a number of government institutions, policy makers, and community leaders. Children have engaged with government officials on budget allocations and spending on different aspects of children's rights. They have also raised concerns about the ineffectiveness of one of the public social assistance programs, the use of corporal punishment in schools, and weak social protection initiatives for children.

Results
- **Increased national-level budget allocations.** Efforts of the Child-Friendly National Budget Initiative contributed to increased budget allocations to key ministries, including the Ministry of Primary and Secondary Education and the Ministry of Health and Child Care.
- **Increased local-level budget allocations.** Two local authorities—Kadoma and Chinhoyi—increased their 2013 budget allocations for education and health in response to shadow budgets and submissions made by the child-led groups. In addition, they set aside budgets to support child participation activities in the districts.
- **Creation of income-generating projects.** Equipped with project management skills, child-led groups contributed to income-generating projects. Funds from these projects were used to assist vulnerable children in their communities to pay school fees. A total of 50 children have benefitted from these projects.

Educative Implications
- Adults should be prepared to listen to children and include them in decision-making activities so that they can develop the confidence to learn and engage meaningfully in budget processes.
- A concerted effort is needed among stakeholders to ensure that children are consulted in decisions that affect them, their views are taken seriously, they learn about their rights, and they take an active role in the development of their community.

For further information about child rights governance, please contact Godwin Kudzotsa, Programmes Advisor (e-mail: godwin.kudzotsa@savethechildren.org).

Notes

1. Save the Children in Nicaragua annual reports are available at https://nicaragua .savethechildren.net/.
2. This group comprises the African Child Policy Forum, Child Rights Coalition Asia, Child Rights Connect, Defense for Children Costa Rica, Eurochild, International Baby Food Action Network, Redlamyc, Plan International, Save the Children, and UNICEF.
3. See http://www.childrightsconnect.org/wp-content/uploads/2014/12/FINAL-Consul tation-Guide-Public-Expenditure.pdf.

4. See http://www.childrightsconnect.org/wp-content/uploads/2014/12/FINAL-Consul tation-Guide-for-Younger-Children-Public-Expenditure1.pdf.

5. See http://www.un.org/depts/DGACM/RegionalGroups.shtml.

6. See http://www.eurochild.org/fileadmin/public/04_News/UN/ROC_towards_better _investment_in_the_rights_of_the_child_-_as_tabled.pdf.

References

Bani-Afudego, Charlotte, George Cobbinah Yorke, and Anastasie Ablavi Koudou. 2011. "Seeing from Our Perspectives: Youth Budget Advocacy in Ghana." Participatory Learning and Action 64, Institute of Development Studies, Plan and I.

National Taxpayer Association (NTA). 2009. "Baseline Scoping Study, Citizen Perceptions of Public Accountability and Potential for Public Action." National Taxpayer Association, Kenya. http://www.nta.or.ke/reports/special/perceptions_final.pdf.

Environmental Benefits Statement

The World Bank Group is committed to reducing its environmental footprint. In support of this commitment, we leverage electronic publishing options and print-on-demand technology, which is located in regional hubs worldwide. Together, these initiatives enable print runs to be lowered and shipping distances decreased, resulting in reduced paper consumption, chemical use, greenhouse gas emissions, and waste.

We follow the recommended standards for paper use set by the Green Press Initiative. The majority of our books are printed on Forest Stewardship Council (FSC)–certified paper, with nearly all containing 50–100 percent recycled content. The recycled fiber in our book paper is either unbleached or bleached using totally chlorine-free (TCF), processed chlorine-free (PCF), or enhanced elemental chlorine-free (EECF) processes.

More information about the Bank's environmental philosophy can be found at http://www.worldbank.org/corporateresponsibility.

green
press
INITIATIVE

www.ingramcontent.com/pod-product-compliance
Lightning Source LLC
Chambersburg PA
CBHW080532220326
41599CB00032B/6287

* 9 7 8 1 4 6 4 8 1 0 7 1 8 *